P9-CTQ-464

ENTANGLED IN IVY

George Castle

Chicago Public Library
Clearing Park Branch
6423 W. 63rd Street
Chicago, Illinois 60638

SPORTS
PUBLISHING
L.L.C.

SportsPublishingLLC.com

ISBN-10: 1-59670-189-7
ISBN-13: 978-1-59670-189-2

© 2007 by George Castle

All rights reserved. Except for use in a review, the reproduction or utilization of this work in any form or by any electronic, mechanical, or other means, now known or hereafter invented, including xerography, photocopying, and recording, and in any information storage and retrieval system, is forbidden without the written permission of the publisher.

Publishers: Peter L. Bannon and Joseph J. Bannon Sr.
Senior managing editor: Susan M. Moyer
Acquisitions editor: Mike Pearson
Editor: Travis W. Moran
Art director: K. Jeffrey Higgerson
Cover design: Joseph Brumleve
Project manager: Kathryn R. Holleman
Photo editor: Erin Linden-Levy

Sports Publishing L.L.C.
804 North Neil Street
Champaign, IL 61820
Phone: 1-877-424-2665
Fax: 217-363-2073
www.SportsPublishingLLC.com

Printed in the United States of America

Library of Congress Cataloging-in-Publication Data

Castle, George.
    Entangled In Ivy / George Castle
        p. cm.
    Includes Index
    ISBN-13: 978-1-59670-189-2 (softcover : alk. paper)
    ISBN-10: 1-59670-189-7 (softcover alk. paper)
    1. Chicago Cubs (Baseball team)--History. I. Title
  GV875.C6C283 2007
    796.357 ' 6640977311--dc22
                        2006102972

R0410768248

CONTENTS

ACKNOWLEDGMENTS

IT'S OBVIOUS to thank scores of players, managers, coaches, front-office executives and scouts working for both the Cubs and a slew of other teams to provide research for *Entangled In Ivy*. They knew it was not a hit-and-run visit of one or two questions when I came calling either in person or via phone. In a number of cases, they knew some tough, painful questions would be forthcoming, and they did not flinch. Their patience in engaging in the lively art of conversation will forever be appreciated.

Access is everything in Major League Baseball, which thankfully still has the most pregame locker-room and on-field time afforded to media in any pro sport. I give particular thanks to former longtime Cubs media relations director Sharon Pannozzo's staff for permitting free rein within the daily Wrigley Field media access rules, and most importantly their cooperation in corralling several top subjects for interviews. Particular thanks go out to Katelyn Thrall, Jason Carr, and intern Edwin Aguilar.

I would be remiss without thanking White Sox media relations chief Bob Beghtol for his continuing unfettered access to U.S. Cellular Field, where a number of interviews were conducted.

In addition, thanks go to a series of sports editors for the *Times of Northwest Indiana*—Dave Campbell, Mike Sansone, Mike Clark, Paul Bowker, and Justin Breen—for allowing me to turn over the furniture at Wrigley Field since the mid-1990s via regular informative features, "inside baseball" stories, and notebooks that inspired much of the material included here.

Appreciation is showered on editors Mike Pearson and Travis Moran as well for believing in the concept of *Entangled In Ivy*, and Moran for bearing with me under tight deadlines.

And, finally, a technologically backward dad couldn't have processed some of the photo on the book's jacket without the assistance of Laura Castle, ace student majoring in interior architecture at Columbia College Chicago. Eventually, I'll learn, kid, but you never had the pleasure of writing a story on a manual Underwood typewriter, either.

PREFACE

THE CHICAGO CUBS are simultaneously an eminent public institution. They're at the center of a fishbowl, as popular as the New York Yankees and Boston Red Sox, perhaps the highest profile of Tribune Company subsidiaries—and a proverbial riddle wrapped inside an enigma.

Only one year away from the 100th anniversary of their last World Series title, the Cubs logically should have been winning pennant after pennant. A romping, stomping dynasty should have been their identity rather than the stereotyped "lovable losers" emblem. What would be more romantic that winning it all in front of 40,000 adoring fans each day, an often national television audience, and a worldwide media throng that would be more than happy to convey the good news to far-flung rooters? What top player doesn't want to take a turn playing in Wrigley Field, its tradition and allure more than balancing out cramped facilities and 51 day games that are enforced by legislative decree?

The payroll has been bumped up to a top-10 status—if not top five—after being artificially held down throughout much of the 1990s. The Cubs have no problem signing premium free agents, who sometimes dismiss other teams' offers in a hurry to jump aboard. With one significant exception, players haven't blackballed the team with no-trade contractual clauses since the bad old Wrigley family ownership days of the 1970s. If the Cubs had an unlimited payroll, they could field an All-Star team annually. But in spite of a whole host of advantages and the mere mathematical probability that they'd win after so many decades of losing, near misses, and stunning collapses, the Cubs sit home come World Series time.

On face value, it doesn't make sense. One year, one time, after all the heartaches, it should have clicked.

"Curses," the wise guys say. "Gotta be the Billy Goat Curse."

But let's debunk that. What magical powers did a Greek saloon owner named William Sianis possess to hex the Cubs forever because his mascot goat was not admitted during the 1945 World Series at Wrigley Field? The mythmakers, no doubt descendants of those who claim Babe Ruth called his shot in the 1932 World Series, have swung into high gear on this one. Ill-informed media and fans latch on to it as gospel, but the storytellers can't even get history straight at times. Another version has Sianis and the goat gaining admittance, but then getting booted in the seventh inning because of the animal's olfactory offense to box-seat patrons. So by this logic, was Sianis a warlock? The devil incarnate? Did only Greek-Americans have a special ability to apply curses? If Sianis was merely the late *Chicago Tribune* columnist David Condon's drinking buddy, what gave him special powers?

In the same manner, couldn't I cast some Kabbalah hex in the Cubs' direction if the team refused to admit my angelic golden retrievers, Polly and Hunter? Worst that could happen is the pooches would shed on fans. They don't bite; they don't bark; they don't stink; they don't mess; they kiss liberally; and Hunter gives his paw at will. They deserve admittance far more than many fans. Polly and Hunter aren't allowed in, yet I have no ability to apply a curse. If I did, a whole bunch of editors, publishers, broadcast program directors, and fellow sports scribes would have been turned into toads long before I'd have been mad at the Cubs.

Failing the supernatural, the stumbling, fumbling, and bumbling must be the day games, the presence of Rush Street, the mid-summer heat, the winds blowing in or out, all kinds of environmental and even sociological factors mixed in the stew. There is merit in some or all of these causes. But, alone, they don't stand the measuring stick.

Must be the "Lovable Losers" image in which the team happily wallows. Put an "X" over that illogic. The players turn over every few years, so only a handful have grown up in the Cubs' environs. Sianis has not possessed them with a losing mentality from the grave, nor have the negatives that preceded them infected their skills. If they came from winning organizations or played in World Series, we're to believe that they lose it all upon arriving in Wrigley Field? Hardly.

Despite the strong celluloid and daily media references of mega-losing, they wash right over the average player when he's trying to toss a 3-and-2 strike, drive in a runner from third with less than two out or making the right read while leading off second on a liner to the left fielder.

Bad luck is also a popular culprit. Broadcaster Jack Brickhouse used to proclaim the Cubs one of the unluckiest franchises in pro sports. Three waves of pitchers whom the Cubs expected to lead them into golden eras of contention have broken down like unfortunate thoroughbreds. There were Dick Drott, Moe Drabowsky, Glen Hobbie, and Bob Anderson in the 1958 to 1961 era. Then a well-paid pack led by Rick Sutcliffe that included Dennis Eckersley, Steve Trout, and Scott Sanderson all came up lame in 1985, leading to the demise of the Dallas Green regime and, subsequently, to the only effective farm system the Cubs have ever possessed. Twenty years later, the repeated breakdowns of Mark Prior and Kerry Wood have been at the core of the Cubs' most recent troubles.

But the misfortune is not the end-all explanation. Every team has injuries, bad bounces, freak plays, and blown umpiring calls. Baseball is a game of failure. The best hitters fail two of every three times at bat. The best pitchers fail to win in probably one-third of their starts. The finest stoppers will cough up games when they need as little as three strikes.

The bottom line is the human factor. Flesh-and-blood decisions have kept the Cubs on the golf course in most Octobers. It's all man-made—whether it's the combination eccentricity and befuddlement of chewing-gum magnate Phil Wrigley, the meddling of Tribune Company executives into baseball matters in which they had no experience, or an under-performing, under-evaluating, and perhaps under-staffed front office of the early 21st Century. Supernatural forces have not traded Lou Brock, Rafael Palmeiro, and Lee Smith; foolishly allowed Greg Maddux to walk after he already had agreed to a five-year contract; and failed to develop Corey Patterson in the manner that the Baltimore Orioles quickly did.

All incarnations of management have wanted to win. It makes no sense that they'd desire to lose, that they'd profit economically or emotionally from constant defeat. Due to personalities, business philosophies, vanity, ignorance, caution, fear, whatever, the successive Cubs stewardships have ignored the tried-and-true methods of winning that stared them in their collective faces. The right blueprints easily could have been adopted. Ownership ability to spend was never an issue. Phil Wrigley was wealthy enough to have owned five teams, having $100 million in gum sales in pre-inflation 1962 dollars. Tribune Company-owned WGN-TV could afford studio color cameras in black-and-white 1957, so Tribune Company-owned Cubs could have paid for Kevin

Brown in 1996 as well. The know-how, the aggressiveness, the will, the open-mindedness—and most importantly, the white-hot passion to win at all costs—have fallen short.

Blaming the Cubs' troubles on unnamed, invisible corporate executives acting in some kind of Vatican-like council, with the smoke billowing up the top of Tribune Tower at decision time is futile. It's like shooting at ghosts. The answers to the riddle wrapped in an enigma could always be found right at Wrigley Field, in the executive offices above the main gate and below the famous red marquee.

—**George Castle**
January 2007

INTRODUCTION

I REMEMBER that enormous bloodshot eye staring at me predator-style, like Moby Dick's cold, calculating orb pierced Gregory Peck's obsessed Captain Ahab as he was lashed to the great white whale and the beast plunged to the depths. Worrying that same fate would befall a landlubber such as me, I usually kept out of the reaching distance of Dave Kingman, owner of that eye. But on one occasion during the hot, nasty summer of 1980, I slipped into the Chicago Cubs' cramped clubhouse in Wrigley's left-field corner to talk to the aloof slugger one on one.

Previously, I was like one of those small Jurassic-era animals who furtively came out at night, lest they be eaten or trampled by the dinosaurs that ruled the daytime. In what was my first season possessing a media credential to Wrigley Field, loads of restrictions were levied by Buck Peden, a former photographer who served as Cubs public relations chief. "You don't cover professional sports [regularly]," Peden reminded me, noting my lowly status of writing sports for the Lerner Newspapers chain, which circulated around the ballpark and all over the North Side.

Barred from the tiny clubhouse, interviews had to be done in and around the dugout. Peden also didn't want me to chomp into owner Bill Wrigley's food bill, so access also was barred to the pregame lunch in the Pink Poodle, the media dining room next to the modest front office. Not that I would have shared the same main course I witnessed broadcaster Vince Lloyd happily consuming—steak tartare, a fancy name for raw hamburger.

Strangely, I was allowed to use the Pink Poodle's kitchen phone to feed a postgame sportscast for WPRZ Radio in Evanston. While I held the tape recorder to the phone's mouthpiece in a jerrybuilt manner to transmit the interviews, media and scouts enjoyed the postgame full-service, full-strength bar. Beer was a chaser.

Under these restrictive circumstances, I slinked around the limited-access areas—that is, when I wasn't sitting in the right-field bleachers with a group of cronies back when the sun-drenched seats weren't a combo high-priced frat house-slash-meat market. On a part-time salary, I was happy to get in free instead of paying the $1.50 bleacher-ticket fee. I would make no waves and attract no attention—not this tiny mammal scurrying under cover of darkness. But unexpected courage seized me as I decided to go beyond the daily credentials restrictions and sneak into the clubhouse. Nobody stopped me.

Kingman was the most controversial Cub of the day, having zipped his lips to the media despite racking up an amazing 48-homer season in 1979. But the following season, as the Iran hostage crisis dragged on and double-digit inflation raged, was a disaster for both Kingman and his teammates. A 10-6 start—which another woe-begotten Cubs team would mimic 26 years later—quickly degenerated into weeks upon weeks of pratfalls. Kingman hurt his shoulder, and his outfield starts became more sporadic.

He made news off the field, though. Unprovoked, right out of his own special left field, he dumped a bucket of ice water on mild-mannered Arlington Heights *Daily Herald* sportswriter Don Friske in spring training. A ghostwritten *Chicago Tribune* column quickly became the object of derision, drawing special ire from *Sun-Times* columnist Mike Royko. Rumors also persisted that Kingman had tossed a WMAQ-TV female producer off his boat into Lake Michigan.

I tiptoed in the direction of Kingman, sitting by his cubicle near the back of the sparsely furnished locker room. Wire cages comprised players' lockers. Kingman was not in a talkative mood, but I kept approaching. He eyed me. Keeping the stutter to a minimum, I extended a kind of olive branch.

"Not all media are out to get you," I said nervously. "I would like to try to understand you a little better."

I can't remember his mumbled response, but I wouldn't stick around to feel the wrath of the Cubs' Moby Dick. Like a petitioner disengaging himself from a meeting with royalty or papacy, I back-stepped through the small room, then swiveled and dashed out the door near the left-field corner.

Not assigned to cover the Cubs on a daily basis spared me much of the on-the-job aggravation I'd experience several decades later. The group of Cubs was a sour collection—even as they stayed in contention into late August 1979. Kingman was the worst, but he had plenty of company starting in 1978 with the likes of Bill Buckner, Ted Sizemore, Barry Foote, and Mike Vail.

I thought Lenny Randle was similarly fearsome, especially after he had punched out Frank Lucchesi, his Texas Rangers manager, three years previously. But when I approached Randle to pose with the Cubs batboy—the kid was the subject of a Lerner Newspapers "local angle" feature since he was from nearby St. Benedict High School—I received nothing but cooperation. Ditto when I dared approach the sour-faced Vail by the dugout.

From a generation-later vantage point, Randle—an impresario of sports camps around the world—claimed to be Kingman's cheer-up guy. "I kept Kingman loose," he said. "I got him going to Comedy Store. We did a lot of fundraisers there after hours. Dave's thing was boating and fishing. He was a little bit of Ted Williams, a little bit of Anthony Perkins. Writers made him nervous. The New York media had hurt him."

Ken Holtzman, who had thrown two no-hitters during his first Cubs incarnation between 1965 and 1971, finished his career back at Wrigley Field in 1978-79. The supposedly sour dispositions weren't out of the ordinary.

"I don't think there was anything concerning that team that didn't exist on other teams," said Holtzman, now a teacher in the St. Louis area. "The only player that kind of danced to his own music was Kingman; and, actually, he wasn't that bad. A lot of the negativity concerning him was his relationship with the media, not the other players."

Oddly enough, Kingman said more than a decade later that some of his best friends were sportswriters.

"It wasn't all bad moods there," Randle said of the left-field cubbyhole. "You had guys like Dick Tidrow and Steve Dillard being funny. They'd bring dummies in the clubhouse, do pranks. [Catcher] Tim Blackwell brought in his guitar."

Years later, I discovered the 1980 pitchers considered themselves a close-knit group, including Tidrow, Rick Reuschel, Bruce Sutter, Mike Krukow, and Dennis Lamp.

Now used as a groundskeepers' locker room, the cozy clubhouse somehow hosted 40-plus oversized Bears players and their equipment for both practices and games in the old days. For 25 ballplayers, it was tight enough. Gary Nicholson, team trainer during the 1970s, recalled how the players had to shower in shifts, barely cooling off in the poorly ventilated room. Broadcaster Steve Stone, a Cub from 1974 to 1976, said that, in the height of summer, the clubhouse was warmer than the outside climes.

Clubhouse caudillo Yosh Kawano squeezed September callups into a dungeon-like equipment room, where they shared quarters with rodents. Odors stayed. One time, Dick Butkus fingered Bears linebacker Doug Buffone and his cubicle as a foul-stench source. Despite washing his sneakers and other equipment, the odor remained. Buffone poked at the false ceiling with a broom, and out fell a deceased rat, true source of the olfactory offense.

"The clubhouse was like being in the stock market [trading floor]— no elbow room," Randle recalled.

Kawano also tried to starve his players. There was no food spread before or after games. Players had to import their breakfast of champions from Yum-Yum Donuts or McDonald's. "Guess Yosh felt we should be eating at home after the game," 1980s catcher Jody Davis said. "We still had to wait around there to avoid [the postgame] traffic." Still working in the visiting clubhouse in 2006, the diminutive Kawano—now an octogenarian—explained that he thought players preferred to chew tobacco rather than eat.

"I didn't want to worry about food," Randle said. "Cubby Bear took care of me. I liked Carson's Ribs." Randle sensed something was amiss above the level of acerbic, defensive Cubs general manager Bob Kennedy. He was right. Cubs owner Bill Wrigley was hammered by inheritance taxes (eventually totaling $40 million) due to the 1977 deaths of his parents, Philip and Helen Wrigley. The younger Wrigley, determined not to have the core gum business affected, began trimming costs, and the Cubs rapidly declined as a result. Wrigley rejected a $450,000 salary for Sutter for 1980 that Kennedy had negotiated, then lost an arbitration case in which Sutter was awarded $700,000. Sutter was dealt to the Cardinals after the '80 season.

Wrigley quietly began to look into selling the team. Chicago sports power broker Andy McKenna picked up on the vibes and informed real estate maven Jerry Reinsdorf, then dickering for the White Sox, that another team in town might be for sale.

Nobody figured Wrigley would ever let go of the Cubs, even as sportscaster Chet Coppock handed me a story in the spring of 1981—as Kennedy was forced out—about how a group of North Side and north-suburban businessmen who made an offer to buy the team. Kennedy successor Herman Franks told us the team was not for sale. The nouveau-riche bidders were told a similar tale. A definite change was needed after the Cubs got off to a 6-28 start in 1981. When the boys in blue finally broke a 12-game losing streak—prompting WGN Radio to play its slump-busting "Hallelujah Chorus"—I decided to enter the cramped clubhouse. Media swarmed all over the cubbyhole to get a reaction. "Did we win the World Series?" asked incredulous manager Joey Amalfitano.

Baseball soon took an enforced two-month break due to a strike. But right after the stoppage, Wrigley's quiet negotiations, shepherded by McKenna, resulted in the sale of the franchise and Wrigley Field to Tribune Company. The immediate reaction was a collective sigh of relief. Now the Cubs would be run by a growing media company, possessed of deep pockets with the simple motivation of a better team to bolster decades-long programming on corporate-owned WGN-TV and radio. Tribune Company was freed a decade earlier from the moss-covered, Colonel McCormick-era management. On an early September off-day at Wrigley Field, McKenna and Tribune Company bossman Stanton Cook held an outdoor press conference, with mikes set up on the field by the Cubs' on-deck circle, to explain their expectations of building the Cubs into a winner.

Nobody in the box seats watching the press conference could have predicted that, eventually, this light at the end of the tunnel would prove to be an oncoming freight train. Far more drama and comedy—plenty of ethos and pathos—were fated to take place in the generation to come.

one

NEW TRADITION, BUT SAME RESULTS

DALLAS GREEN loudly trumpeted his "new tradition" when he blew into town to seize control of the Cubs in the fall of 1981. He swept out much of the old Wrigley family cobwebs and patronage-style employees, but retained such warhorses as park operations expert Salty Saltwell, scouting exec Vedie Himsl, and assistant general manager John Cox. He offered a job to junior exec Andy MacPhail, but he'd already accepted an assistant general manager's position in Houston.

While the bombastic Green began banging the drum not-so-slowly for the installation of lights for Wrigley Field—immediately drawing community and political opposition to the Philly import—the quaint, old-style atmosphere around the Cubs did not change radically for years, except for one element of humor the Wrigley family would have never tolerated. After a two-inch overnight snowfall and amid 34-degree game-time temperatures, Green allowed the Billy Goat Tavern's Sam Sianis, nephew of 1945 hex-caster William Sianis, to bring his mascot goat on the field to break the curse on Opening Day, 1982.The media had fun with the animal's appearance. But the almost exclusively boys club of the baseball press was a lot more fun, period, in those days. Reporters and executives had long mixed as one. During one down spell in the late 1970s, manager Herman Franks suggested the writers might as well make out the lineup during a slump. So after huddling after hours in a bar, the scribes handed in their batting order with Bill Buckner hitting cleanup.

1

Buckner, who did not do well in the game, discovered the writers' handiwork and screamed at Franks. Then, after Franks came out of retirement again to succeed Bob Kennedy as general manager in May 1981, he allowed *Chicago Tribune* beat writer Dave Nightengale to sit in his office while he discussed the trade of ace Rick Reuschel to the Yankees. When the Cubs flew to San Diego on their ill-fated playoff excursion in 1984, Green allowed the media to fly on the team plane, as they did in the regular season.

Even as late as 1988, seven seasons into Tribune Company stewardship of the team, I simply could walk the length of the front office, past the GM's digs, without being stopped—after entering through the Pink Poodle media lunchroom. In mid-summer 1988, media relations chief Ned Colletti, the first former left-field bleacher bum to become a general manager (with the Dodgers in 2006), caught me in the Poodle and asked me what I would need in terms of credentials for the first scheduled Wrigley Field night game, which was scheduled for August 8 of that year. As sports editor for Lerner Newspapers, I was being asked whether multiple passes were needed, as I'd be joining a then-record regular-season 556 media representatives for the historic event. He would not have asked a similar question 15 years later.

Until Green ordered the excavation under the left-field stands to create a new clubhouse after the 1983 season, the Cubs continued to dress in their cramped quarters in the left-field corner. In that loser's walk from the dugout down the line to the locker room on April 29, 1983, the grist for the most famous postgame rant in sports history was provided.

Fans could subject Cubs players to all kinds of humiliations in that trek down the line after every loss. They were particularly rough on this day, when the Cubs' record dropped to 5-14 after closer Lee Smith had coughed up a save against the Dodgers. But the difference between then and now is that there were few witnesses and just one recording device to commit to history the verbal volcano that spewed from manager Lee Elia's lips.

Television cameras were in such quantity amid a burgeoning media horde that they were barred from the pregame Wrigley Field clubhouse starting in 2004. Postgame, up to seven TV cameras recorded the manager's press conference in the "Black Hole of Calcutta" interview room near the Cubs dugout. But in 1983, only the stray mini-cam

New Tradition, But Same Results

ventured near the locker room. Only a cozy group of writers and microphone jockeys prowled the tiny clubhouse. When Elia learned that fans had dumped beer on Larry Bowa, Ron Cey, and Keith Moreland as they made the losers' walk to the left-field clubhouse, the *Chicago Tribune's* Robert Markus, the *Chicago Sun-Times'* Joel Bierig, and the *Daily Herald's* Don Friske were there to jot down his expletive-deleted-filled, fuming explosion. WLS-Radio's Les Grobstein, armed with his cassette recorder, was the only broadcast representative in the manager's tiny office, up a flight of stairs from the locker room. All other media were distracted in the Dodgers' clubhouse, interviewing former Buffalo Grove high school star Mike Marshall on his first game back in his hometown.

Grobstein immediately knew he had one for the ages when Elia blew up, using variations of the F-bomb seemingly every third word as the incomparable rant centered on the concept that 85 percent of the world is working, the other 15 percent were at Wrigley Field. Elia got his logic from the news that the national unemployment rate had surpassed 10 percent for part of 1982. Fellow radiomen David Shuster, Pat Benkowski, and Rich King arrived mid-rant, so Grobstein had the only complete audio record.

For the next 24 years, Grobstein always would mark the anniversary of Elia's rant, which developed cult status, and quickly would produce the recording, copied umpteen times, whenever asked. Grobstein tried several times to give Elia an exit to cut the rant, but the emotional manager—well-liked by players and media at all other times—did not take the hint.

"The Cubs of '83 were basically a good group, but they just didn't win," Grobstein said. "Lee was an excellent interview, a good guy and everybody liked him. There were very few guys who were as easy to deal with as him. I thought the players on the team were willing to run through a wall for him. Lee was not angry at *all* fans, but at a few idiots who were throwing crap. He wasn't saying all these fans in Chicago were bad. He was mad at a few. He was referring to the idiots."

The rant, still played on the air and during dull pressbox moments a generation later, was like a scarlet letter for Elia. He did not want to talk about his Cubs managerial days. "It changed my life [for the worse]," Elia said while working in his latest incarnation as Baltimore Orioles bench coach in 2006. Although Elia was fired later in 1983 after explaining he was unfamiliar with the Braves' Gerald Perry, who had beaten the Cubs with a homer, he was hired four years later to manage the Phillies, and had otherwise continual employment as a coach with assorted teams.

The on-field performance caught up with the positive clubhouse when the Cubs pulled off their unexpected National League East run in 1984. The arrival of straw-stirring-the-drink Gary Matthews as "The Sarge" did wonders on and off the field. Riotous, triple X-rated clubhouse byplay was provided by closer Lee Smith and running mate Leon "Bull" Durham, whose verbal antics and exhibitionist body English would not play in a more politically correct, proper-language-sensitive time. Female reporters, barred from the clubhouse by Bob Kennedy as late as 1979, had to have a strong stomach and a high threshold of being offended listening and watching both the spoken word and physical contortions of Smitty and the Bull. Moreland was Texas tough and blunt, although at one point he asked the location of his in-season home in Deerfield not be revealed. He didn't even want any published hints he lived in Chicago's northern suburbs. Seems fans would arrive in downtown Deerfield, asked about Moreland, and find their way to his front door.

Manager Jim Frey could spew blue words with the best of them as well. His everyday language was peppered with F-bombs. Only 15 years had passed since the then-greatest collapse in team history, the 1969 Cubs, and comparison questions invariably were brought to Frey, who was profanely puzzled. "Fuck 1969," he'd respond, end of conversation. The mere mention of 1969 also caused Tribune suit Don Grenesko, put in charge of business operations before being promoted to team president in 1987, to cringe.

The symbol of the revived Cubs was Ryne Sandberg, square-jawed, disciplined, and doing his talking on the field instead of the clubhouse. Ryno could not fill a notebook throughout his entire career. He finally could put his phenomenal 1984 actions into words two decades later, when his memorable Hall of Fame induction speech summed up both his tunnel-vision work ethic and disdain of steroids and other short-cuts latter-day players had taken to succeed. It was as if Sandberg was so focused that he could not both articulate and play at a Cooperstown level at the same time.

"It just makes the 'Sandberg Game' even more special now, having him go in as a Hall of Famer," Ryno said of the 2006 induction of Bruce

New Tradition, But Same Results

Sutter, who served up his pair of game-tying homers on June 23, 1984, in one of the most memorable games in Cubs history.

"At that time, he was the toughest reliever out there," Sandberg continued. "He was total ground-ball pitcher and how I was able to lift two balls for game-tying home runs in those situations ... I still remember the swings in almost disbelief myself."

The spectacle that day was just as improbable to any observer. Covering the game for the *Decatur Herald*, I recall twice leaving the old pressbox that hung from the Wrigley Field upper deck to do postgame interviews in the Cardinals locker room—and twice retracing my steps after Sandberg connected.

One of the underrated contributors to the 1984 Cubs never wore a uniform. Instead, he looked like he was born in a finely tailored suit. That season, Jim Finks, who already had put the building blocks in place for the eventual Super Bowl XX champion Chicago Bears, was serving as Cubs president in an unusual sabbatical from pro football. I remember meeting Finks one hot Sunday in the pressbox. Despite the humidity, the suit was impeccably pressed without a bead of perspiration apparent. Behind the scenes, Finks was more vital than anyone could imagine as a buffer between the voluble Dallas Green and stuffed-shirted Tribune Company executives. Finks, a former NFL quarterback, could move comfortably among both the corporate crowd and the *jockocracy*. He even hoisted a couple with anti-lights activists at a saloon across the street from Wrigley Field. When Finks departed—it's unclear whether he was jumped or pushed after just a year on the job—after the 1984 season, it signaled trouble ahead.

Newly promoted to team president in place of Finks, Green, who was able to maintain his role as general manager, now dealt directly with the men in Tribune Tower along with corporate bean counter Don Grenesko, who was installed as the Cubs' business operations chief.

The magic of 1984 disintegrated on the field after Finks' departure. Pitching injuries unraveled Green's best-laid plans and no doubt drew both raised eyebrows and hushed conferences among the powers in the Tower. In the clubhouse, the mood turned fouler. Players increasingly grumbled about Frey, who had his negative side. One day, lefty Ray Fontenot, who had pitched a creditable game, allowing two runs in six or seven innings, alternated between usable quotes and angry profanity, seemingly sentence by sentence, in the locker room. Lee Smith's jolly mood went sour as he drew some boos after blowing saves, making him feel he was the scapegoat while the fans regarded Sandberg as the fair-haired kid.

As the 1984 starting rotation struggled to recover its form, someone approached Frey by the dugout to suggest a novel approach: shift sidearming starter Dennis Eckersley to the bullpen. Frey huffed at the idea. After Eckersley departed the Cubs for Oakland in early 1987, Tony La Russa was open-minded about the bullpen shift of his new acquisition. The rest was history, all the way to the Hall of Fame.

Frey was fired in June 1986, and then returned six months later as a Cubs radio color analyst, just in time to take mental notes of a disgruntled Smith profanely complaining about his working conditions. Booking a few minutes of Smith's time in the dugout for Opening Day 1987 at Wrigley Field required tremendous machinations with Brian David, his agent at the time.

Green always thought Frey was planted in his new job—he had no previous radio experience—as a spy by Tribune Company brass eager to build a case against him. But rising above such petty politics and counterbalancing Smith's crabbiness was an oak tree of dignity taking root in the locker room. Andre Dawson had been beckoned by bleacher fans to sign with the Cubs the previous two seasons while playing a Gold Glove right field with the Montreal Expos. Finally, he signed for a $500,000 base salary in spring training 1987 as baseball owners tried to collude in restraining salaries.

His surgically repaired knees getting reinvigorated on natural turf, Dawson immediately produced, became a favorite of fans who "salaamed" to him in the bleachers, and proved he was an old-school personality, if not having invented the school himself. Almost as verbally low-key as Sandberg with an intensity that prevented much smiling, Dawson nevertheless made almost every word count with profound, sensible statements. His word was his bond. If he had committed to doing an interview, "Hawk" was there at the appointed time and place. I would end up doing two interviews at Dawson's Miami-area home in 1992 and 1995. He was a moderating, older-brother influence on motor-mouthed, trash-talking shortstop Shawon Dunston; with his physical strength, Dawson could even lift Dunston off the ground. No wonder

New Traditions, But Same Results

Yosh Kawano, still running the clubhouse with an iron fist, called Dawson the best man he ever had in the locker room in a half-century span.

When Dawson was accorded a standing ovation on his final Wrigley Field at-bat of the 1987 season, the crowd imploring him to connect one more time, he obliged with his 47th homer—then an enormous number—off Cardinals reliever Bill Dawley. The welcome he had received from Chicago made Dawson adopt the city as his second home, and he'd always make sure he traveled with the Marlins during their trips to Chicago after his career.

"I do have a lot of ties, a lot of friends here," he said years later. "I always look for situations to get back to the city. I can't really just sit here and say what this city did for me. It was phenomenal. Had it been anywhere else, I don't think I would have had the same reaction. This city did a lot for me in transforming me not as a player but my whole life. I'm forever going to be grateful for that."

During his Chicago days, Dawson also turned on several caution lights that would prove prescient for ensuing years.

For one, he had no desire to manage because younger players—this is the cusp of the 1990s, remember—weren't as dedicated as when he came up in the mid-1970s. Then, discussing his own team, Hawk said teams in New York, Chicago, and Los Angeles should always be in contention because of the big-market resources available to them.

Soon others joined Dawson and Sandberg as dominant Cubs personalities. Greg Maddux came up at the end of 1986, was placed in the rotation for good the following year, and quietly began building his portfolio as baseball's smartest player. Maddux would assume a low profile as long as Rick Sutcliffe was ace.

Mark Grace also appeared on the scene early in 1988 as the most glamorous Cub, his left-handed, line-drive, .300-hitting style and blond shock of hair appealing to all ages and sexes. Grace was the most hailed homegrown hitting prospect in a generation, and he did not disappoint with a .297 rookie average.

He soon had a seemingly dream marriage to the fetching Michelle Messer, whom he met while playing for the Class-A Peoria Chiefs. The couple moved into a four-story townhouse a mile south of Wrigley Field, on Wolfram and Halsted. Their cat could safely stroll across the stove since it was never used with all the dinner invitations they accepted. Alas, the union would not last all that long. Michelle Grace wanted to pursue a career in Hollywood. Obliging, her husband bought a $1 million home in Pacific Palisades as her base of operations. They tried to be a dual-city couple with Mrs. Grace in Tinseltown, getting a part in Goldie Hawn's *Death Becomes Her* that ended up on the cutting-room floor. Grace stayed in Chicago. The long-distance marriage sounded like it wouldn't work, and it didn't. Michelle got the Pacific Palisades home while Mark stayed in the townhouse. He celebrated aloud a few years later when he no longer had to pay support to his ex-wife, but he could not avoid additional Hollywood glamour. Grace dated *Northern Exposure's* Janine Turner in the summer of 1993, laughed when every female star coming to Chicago was linked to him, and expressed a liking for Helen Hunt that went unanswered. Meanwhile, Michelle Grace re-married. Her new spouse was Ray Liotta, the wrong-side-swinging Shoeless Joe Jackson from *Field of Dreams,* and the couple formed their own production company.

Managing Sandberg, Dawson, Maddux, and Grace by now was Don Zimmer, who alternated a fiery temper with his impish "Popeye" personality. Zimmer became a media favorite and entertained all while his youthful "Boys of Zimmer," many products of Dallas Green's farm system, won a surprise NL East title in 1989 as the manager's hunches all seemed to work out. Zimmer had practically been run out of Boston, but he became one of the more popular Cubs skippers of all time based on his near-cuddly public persona.

A legend filtering through the decades alleged that Zimmer had a metal plate in his head from a 1953 minor-league beaning. But in a telling 1990 interview in his office, Zimmer revealed that he had metal "buttons" implanted to hold the old skull injury together. He also said he woke up from the beaning thinking it was the next day, but in reality it was a week later. Zimmer would forget this session nine years later when, as a Yankees coach, he barked at me in the visitors dugout at U.S. Cellular Field when my radio microphone got too close to him: "I been telling you to stay away from me for 15 years!" Many of his players reported such Jekyll-and-Hyde Zimmer behavior. Zimmer took an immediate dislike to third-year lefty Jamie Moyer, who lost a bunch of low-scoring games in 1988 and fashioned a losing record. Eighteen years later, Moyer, ranked as one of the most admired big leaguers around, was still pitching at 42. Outfielder Dwight Smith, runner-up to teammate Jerome Walton for 1989 rookie of the year honors, quickly became disenchanted under Zimmer as well.

While the Cubs' big names made headlines and Harry Caray served as the night-crawling, seventh-inning warbling maestro of all the fun, an insidious rot began to take hold of the Cubs organization behind the scenes. Zimmer's childhood buddy, Jim Frey, ascended from the broadcast booth to take Green's place as GM, although he had no major front-office experience. He would later admit he was too quick on the trigger on deals. With Zimmer in agreement, Frey traded Lee Smith, whom he abhorred, in half an hour to the Boston Red Sox for what seemed like the first two names BoSox GM Lou Gorman tossed his way—ne'er-do-well pitchers Calvin Schiraldi and Al Nipper. Similarly peeved at promising outfielder Davey Martinez, Frey dispatched him to Montreal, prompting never-ending rumors about the real reason for the trade. Dissatisfied at Rafael Palmeiro's slow progress to develop power, the .300-hitting Palmeiro was dealt to Texas to get reliever Mitch Williams, part of the domino effect of trying to replace Smith. Frey first thought of Schiraldi, then signed an overripe Goose Gossage, got one hair-raising season out of Williams, and finally inked a washed-up Dave Smith to the closer's role.

But even worse, Frey presided over a sharp decline in the scouting and farm systems. He had foolishly fired Green's right-hand man, the courtly, highly respected Gordon Goldsberry, who had run the only consistently effective Cubs player-development effort in franchise history—one that produced Grace, Dunston, Rafael Palmeiro, Greg Maddux, Jamie Moyer, Davey Martinez, Joe Girardi, Jerome Walton, Dwight Smith, and other highly regarded players. Frey craved power hitters and was upset at the preponderance of the speedy outfielder types Goldsberry had signed, calling them "midgets." He also disliked Goldsberry's taking credit for the homegrown talent flow in a September 1988 article in *VineLine*, the Cubs' monthly magazine. A disagreement over firing one of Goldsberry's scouts was apparently the last straw.

Frey prided himself on turning Ryne Sandberg into a long-ball threat with his coaching tips. Zimmer practically adopted Dunston, a kindred soul as a shortstop, Popeye's old position. Catcher Joe Girardi, a rookie in

Entangled In Ivy

1989, had positive remembrances of Zimmer's stewardship from the vantage point of his own Florida Marlins manager's job in 2006. But insidiously—mostly away from public view and the media's positive spin on Zimmer—negative reinforcement from the brass became the order of the day, contrasting to the encouragement of good-cop Goldsberry. "What you couldn't do instead of what you can do," was the description of the Frey-Don Grenesko regime by homegrown catcher Damon Berryhill, whose Cubs career was eventually cut short by injuries.

Above Frey, the Cubs were drawing ever closer to the clutches of Tribune Tower's executive mind-set. As team president, Grenesko cast off the perceived spending excesses of the Green regime. Staff and player payroll were cut while profits were maximized. The starched-shirt Grenesko suggested that writers covering the team wear ties to the ballpark since that was their workplace. Spotting me one day in the pressbox lunchroom, he called me "Inspector Clouseau." But it was the president and the front office who would do the bumbling over the next few years.

Grenesko usurped Frey's authority by firing Zimmer in the spring of 1991, and Frey's days were numbered. A power vacuum then seemed to ensue in Cubs baseball operations. At mid-summer 1991, Maddux told me he and his wife, Kathy, would purchase a home in the Chicago area if he would be signed to a long-term deal the following winter, heading into his free-agent season. He never intended to leave Chicago, but Maddux became back-burner material as Frey was pushed aside. Grenesko shifted back to Tribune Tower, and former Tribune Company CEO Stanton Cook—who had declined to take retirement at 65—was placed in charge of the Cubs as chairman. Former White Sox GM Larry Himes was hired to replace Frey. In that process of executive shuffling, crafty Toronto Blue Jays GM Pat Gillick turned down a top Cubs job because he did not detect a thirst to win in his interview with Cook. Seizing control of baseball operations for a while, Cook bestowed baseball's then-richest contract on Ryne Sandberg. Almost as an afterthought, a deal was proposed to Maddux. He mulled over a five-year, $25 million contract, then agreed to terms while dropping his no-trade clause. But he did not provide his "yes" answer in time to satisfy Cook or his hired-gun attorney. The contract offer was withdrawn, so Maddux and tough-guy agent Scott Boras decided to play out the pitcher's option.

New Tradition, But Same Results

It was the perfect storm. Not long after busting the production unions at the *Chicago Tribune*, Cook squeezed the Cubs like never before. Himes later confirmed the Cubs had to show a certain profit level to the Tower, and his baseball operations budget was crafted accordingly. He was hamstrung, though—Himes said he could not strip the Cubs down and rebuild in the same manner as with the White Sox in the late 1980s because of advertising commitments and ratings expectations at WGN-TV and radio. The franchise would embark on a course of mid-level talent that they could not shake for years.

After losing his Sox job for his inability to get along with chairman Jerry Reinsdorf, Himes—never an office politician—lacked the people skills to undo Cook's damage with Maddux. Neither Cook nor Himes really knew of the towering baseball intellect they were about to let get away. With Sutcliffe finally gone, Maddux, still just 26, assumed leadership of the Cubs pitching staff in 1992. Pitching well enough himself to have won up to 25 games (actual record 20-11, 2.18 ERA, just seven homers allowed) with better run support, Maddux even called pitches for rookie right-hander Frank Castillo through a secret set of signs flashed from the dugout. Mike Morgan, who had signed to pitch with his buddy Maddux, even demonstrated the set of signs years later. Then-manager Jim Lefebvre confirmed the signs. Maddux denied it then, and again debunked the story 12 years later upon his return to the Cubs. Magicians don't reveal their tricks, but apparent to all but Stanton Cook and his acolytes, the Cubs had developed the ace of aces, and let him escape for no good reason.

"From the pitching point of view, we were consistently short," said 1994 manager Tom Trebelhorn, factoring in other injuries to Jose Guzman and Mike Morgan. "Too many times, we had a fourth, fifth, and spot starter going up against a one, two, and three. At home, the other team's best was going up against spot starters."

Under Himes, the clubhouse fractured as never before. Himes had imported a young, undisciplined Sammy Sosa from the White Sox in his first big trade at the end of spring training 1992. Sosa was almost immediately perceived as a teacher's pet. Andre Dawson was miffed that, after all his accomplishments, Himes would brush by him in the clubhouse without a word to make a beeline for Sosa. A faction led by Grace, who in future years would repeatedly call Himes "Satan," set up in dissent of the GM's actions. Maddux just shook his head at the bickering. When a last-minute Maddux bid to stay with the Cubs was rejected by Himes after the 1992 season, morale plunged even lower. In 1993, outfielder Willie Wilson, a Himes import that season, had set up an easy chair for himself in front of his locker. Wilson, once involved in a big baseball drug scandal in Kansas City, engaged in a shouting match with two teammates in the shower that could be heard all over the clubhouse. Lefebvre was seen dashing out of his office into the off-limits-to-media area to break up the budding fracas. Also in 1993, Grace claimed Himes only talked to Sosa and Greg Hibbard, one of his old White Sox pitchers spending his only season on the North Side.

The clubhouse mess continued into 1994.

"I had no complaints when we went out to play," Trebelhorn recalled. "I don't think the clubhouse was more fractured than any of them are when you're not playing the way you want to play. Everything is overexposed, and every problem is reacted to too strongly."

Sosa became the first Cub to slug 30 homers and steal 30 bases in 1993, prompting the showboating outfielder to wear jewelry honoring the 30-30 feat. That did not sit well with the anti-Himes faction. Meanwhile, up in the broadcast booth, media lunchroom, and even the men's room, an increasingly infirm Harry Caray conducted additional off-the-air complaining about players' jewelry, this time Shawon Dunston's gold chains.

After firing Lefebvre, to whom the prevailing player clique was loyal, Cook ordered the GM to pare down his payroll in the winter of 1993-94 in anticipation of a possible players' strike. He also cut player development expenditures, a critical blow to a struggling farm system. Non-people person Himes did not mingle with the media in the Wrigley Field press lunchroom as successors Ed Lynch, Andy MacPhail, and Jim Hendry would. Oddly enough, though, Himes had good media phone manners, returning calls to me faster than any of the successors did, leaving me with at least half a loaf of information on which to chew. Taking advantage of such a relationship, I met with Himes one mid-winter day in the clubhouse as he was working out on a treadmill in the weight room. I told him he was falling on his sword by shaving talent from the Cubs, and that would eventually cost him his job. Himes shrugged off the analysis, apparently determined to be loyal to the end to Cook, who'd rescued him from the management scrap heap.

Himes' shrunken roster took the field for Opening Day 1994 at Wrigley Field before an audience that included First Lady Hillary Clinton, attending her first Cubs game since the 1984 playoffs. Despite Tuffy Rhodes' record-breaking three homers, the Cubs would lose the first of 12 consecutive home games, putting Lefebvre successor Trebelhorn, perceived as a Himes loyalist, under the gun. After the Cubs had gone on a road trip and beaten the Astros 5-3 in Houston on April 28, 1994, Trebelhorn suggested he'd meet with the fans at the firehouse behind the left-field wall at Wrigley Field the next day if his team did not record their first home win.

"I said I don't anticipate having to do this because I think we're going to win," Trebelhorn recalled. He didn't check the date of the home game against the Rockies in question. It was 11 years to the day that Lee Elia let loose his all-time rant. And both games were on a Friday, with the Cubs enduring late-inning frustration in each instance.

This time, the Cubs lost 6-5 to the Rockies for the ninth loss in a row in the un-Friendly Confines. Trebelhorn stood atop a park bench by Engine Company No. 78. A crowd of 200 gathered, a copy of the *Tribune* was set on fire on Waveland Avenue, fans chanted that the erstwhile world's greatest newspaper "sucks," and Trebelhorn had to summon all his trademark wit to soothe the fans.

"It was interesting," Trebelhorn said. "ESPN wanted to re-create it the next day, but I said no. They had a chance to tape it, but didn't. I answered a number of questions. I had a nice half-hour, 45 minutes out there."

One fan asked Trebelhorn when the Cubs next would win at home. "Tomorrow," he proclaimed. "Now, go have another beer."

Like Elia's speech, that sound bite would be played into the next century on entertainment-panting sports-talk radio.

The Cubs would go on to lose three more in a row at home until Thursday, May 4. With the Reds in town, Chicago's WMAQ-Radio commissioned some Wisconsin seminarians to bring their billy goat to Wrigley Field to break another hex. The guards barred the animal until the party ran into Mr. Cub, Ernie Banks, leaving for a golf date. Banks used his pull and got Cubs marketing chief John McDonough to admit the group. Goat and handlers entered half an hour before gametime through the double doors down the right-field line and paraded all around the warning track, picking up mini-cams and still photographers along the way. Then they all made a left turn and headed toward home plate, disrupting Cubs starter Steve Trachsel's warmup routine.

"The goat was kind of in my way," Trachsel said at the time. "It didn't set too well with me. It was a distraction."

Trebelhorn took the goat for what it was worth—a laugh.

"The saloon [Billy Goat's] was famous," he said in 2006. "The owner was famous. So I'm sure the goat was famous. So to have this famous goat, or symbol of this famous goat, parading around this famous field trying to get rid of this famous hex, or curse, I thought it was famous. And it's become infamous now."

Angered but also apparently de-hexed, the increasingly famous Trachsel took it out on the Cincinnati Reds, winning 5-2 and breaking the home losing streak at an even dozen. The goat's effect wore off quickly, though, despite Trebelhorn toting around a toy goat on road trips for a while. His team found its level of talent at 15 games under .500.

Trebelhorn remembered his catchphrase from his firehouse talk.

"As long as you have tomorrow, you're okay," he said. "We got to a point with the strike [starting August 13] that we had no tomorrows. Then in October, [new GM] Ed Lynch said I had no tomorrow here."

Eventually, Lynch wouldn't have another day in power, either. For even while the management structure of the Cubs changed as the rest of baseball shut down due to the strike, the promise of tomorrow would often become nothing less than a rehash of yesterday.

two

SLOW, STEADY, AND UNSPECTACULAR

THE MEDIA ate well at Wrigley Field's special productions during 1994, but baseball public was starving for their favorite game due to the catastrophic strike that began in August. But a string of press conferences in the ballpark's Stadium Club down the right-field line featured delectable, free lunches compared to the mystery meat in lifeless gravy served up by a cantankerous chef named Aaron in the media dining room. At least the latter was also on the house—for now.

First of the confabs took place on a humid Monday, June 12. Reporters and photographers practically pushed in line to get at the bill o' fare. Three hot entrees, including cheesy chicken, were appropriated quickly as Ryne Sandberg made his startling announcement: he was retiring at 34. Media tongues, doing double duty as they scarfed down chicken, clucked at the sight of Sandberg's then-wife, Cindy. Garbed in her infamous corncob-pattern mini-sundress, Mrs. Sandberg stood to the side of the lectern, from which her husband, adorned in a funeral-dark suit, spoke to the audience. Off to the side, Cubs broadcaster Ron Santo told of an earlier phone call to Sandberg in which the second baseman gave him the retirement news. He also informed Santo there was more to the story than he could reveal at the time. A week later, the Sandbergs initiated divorce proceedings, a major factor in the retirement announcement.

Entangled In Ivy

The scribes, microphone jockeys and camera operators were at Aaron's culinary mercy, then on their own in the search for vittles when the strike began—until Friday, September 9. Rumblings of a big Cubs management change began to surface in the vacuum of non-labor baseball news. Behind the scenes, Tribune Company broadcast division chief Jim Dowdle had wrested control of the team away from Cook. He looked around for a dynamic baseball executive who could run a more autonomous Cubs operation as Dowdle sought to "cut the cord" of corporate micromanaging of the team.

"They needed an active president who really understood the game," Dowdle recalled in 1999. "My role was to basically ask questions, to have the president ask me questions. The two of us would set the payroll."

Decades-worth weight of the family's good name and recent successes with limited resources in Minnesota led Dowdle to recruit Minnesota Twins general manager Andy MacPhail, more than 12 years removed from his last Cubs front-office tenure. The only other candidate on Dowdle's "A" list was Atlanta Braves general manager John Schuerholz. After Twins owner Carl Pohlad was persuaded to let MacPhail out of the last two years of his contract—with the proviso he could not make a lateral move to a GM's job for five years—Dowdle appointed MacPhail Cubs president. The Stadium Club kitchen and bar revved up again after their summer break.

But on this day, Larry Himes was not interested in eating. He cradled a glass of vodka, standing behind WGN-TV sportscaster Rich King, near the back of the room while MacPhail was introduced as president. With his own three-year contract running out in weeks, Himes gazed straight ahead at the end of his GM days.

Intellectual, reserved, and philosophically conservative, MacPhail gave no FDR-style, 1933 rally-the-troops speech as he was introduced. He would adopt a "solid, slow, unspectacular" method of grooming homegrown players. In another interview a few weeks later, he would amend that statement to "slow, steady, unspectacular." A few years later the ball club's slogan was "We're working on it." MacPhail branded "throwing a lot of money at free agents … the lazy man's way" of improving the Cubs.

While MacPhail's success in rounding out two World Series winners with the Twins in 1987 and 1991 was the big lure to Dowdle and the top angle at the press conference, the story-behind-the-story would not be evident for years. MacPhail did not bring his own crew of front-office employees from the Twins. There were some skilled player development types on hand, starting with his top aide, Terry Ryan, who would earn notoriety as Minnesota GM when his farm system produced a bumper crop of home-grown players in upcoming years.

Also not arriving at Wrigley Field was Florida Marlins GM Dave Dombrowski, a rumored candidate for the Cubs' GM job on September 9, 1994. Dombrowski had built a competitive franchise in Montreal, constructed a World Series winner in Florida, and revived the Detroit Tigers in 2006, only three years after a 119-defeat season. Instead, MacPhail would hire relatively inexperienced people with whom he did not have strong personal connections, contrary to the accepted procedure in baseball front-office politics. The game's most notable executives would not be drawing Cubs paychecks under MacPhail.

The free Stadium Club lunches continued during the third press conference on October 10, 1994, when the first of MacPhail's lesser-known appointees—former ne'er-do-well Cubs pitcher Ed Lynch—was announced as Larry Himes' replacement at GM. Lynch, 37, had just four years' front-office experience with the San Diego Padres and New York Mets before MacPhail decided to train him. "Andy assured me that I'll be the GM; but he'll be here to assist me," Lynch said during the press conference, doing little to dissuade doubters of the chain of command. MacPhail had met Lynch only once previously, at a general managers meeting. Even so, he did not invite other candidates for interviews. There would be no new GM with a track record of building a winner working for a team in dire need of such experience.

"Our situation was different than other clubs," MacPhail said while introducing Lynch. "Their presidents were not exposed to people like I was at GM's meetings. I didn't want to go through an elaborate process if I was not 100-percent satisfied [with job applicants]. I have a lot of friends in the game, but I didn't want to lead them on."

Joe McIlvaine, a front-office heavyweight of the era, recommended Lynch, which seemed to sway MacPhail. Running both the Padres and Mets, McIlvaine took Lynch under his wing almost directly out of the University of Miami law school.

Entangled In Ivy

"That gave Ed a little credibility—to have been hired by McIlvaine," recalled Jim Riggleman, who became Lynch's first managerial hire. "Andy's thinking was that Ed was farm director under Joe, and the San Diego system was well-regarded."

Rather than totally cleaning out the old front office, MacPhail actually retained Himes, well regarded for his ability in lower-level scouting positions, as an Arizona-based scout. He tendered Himes a three-year contract. Himes would eventually renew the deal for another three years before moving on to join old buddy Syd Thrift with the Baltimore Orioles before retiring.

MacPhail also retained Himes' top aide, Al Goldis, as scouting director, but took farm-system responsibilities away from him. MacPhail did not know Goldis, who worked in different baseball circles. Goldis had tried to distance himself from Himes in the weeks before the strike, realizing change was in the air.

In the wake of his first two Cubs June drafts, which would turn out to be utterly unproductive, Goldis had practically begged to keep his job in a phone interview. Once Lynch was installed as GM, he hired another relatively inexperienced man as farm director. Jim Hendry would make a Cubs reputation for himself, good and bad, about a decade later. But in 1994, Hendry had on his resume just three years in pro baseball with the Marlins—as a scout, low-A minor-league manager, and special assistant to Dave Dombrowski. He had won national coach of the year honors in 1991, guiding Creighton to a third-place finish in the College World Series, yet such experience was not quite the same as heading up a pro team's player-development system.

"Jim Hendry was a baseball junkie, and he had been entrenched in [college] recruiting and scouting his entire life," Riggleman said.

Nevertheless, MacPhail seemed more interested in training young executives in his own philosophy rather than importing a proven collection of executives and development people to give the Cubs the jolt they needed. The strategies of the previous dozen years, when Dallas Green imported en masse those who ran the successful Philadelphia farm system of the 1970s, would not be employed.

The string of free Stadium Club lunches—a fact finally acknowledged by the new bosses as they walked into the room—ended on Friday, October 21, 1994, the only baseball event in hundreds of miles

Slow, Steady, and Unspectacular

with the World Series canceled due to the strike. The search for the first manager of the MacPhail-Lynch era did not last long. Having run the San Diego Padres' farm system for one season, Lynch recalled former Las Vegas manager Riggleman bravely accepting the parent club's job even though he knew the talent had been stripped down to lower payroll. One year after his Padres lost 100 games, Riggleman got the job of directing the Cubs out of the muck and mire. Although he had been a key coach under Whitey Herzog at the end of the latter's Cardinals tenure, Riggleman's record did not excite always-skeptical fans. One sports talk show caller termed him "Jim Wrigleyman."

"He took it like a man," Lynch said, speaking on Riggleman's composure with Padres management, who gave him a reduced talent base that led to a 112-179 record over his two seasons in San Diego. "He didn't point upstairs. He understood the constraints. He's not a self-pity guy."

While Riggleman took his bows, MacPhail would prove prophetic when he revealed another philosophical bent. "It's a failing of the front office when you fire a manager," he said.

Little did Lynch know that his and MacPhail's comments would ultimately describe the conditions under which their first manager would operate. Riggleman would not be taking a radical step up in class. In the immediate post-strike era, MacPhail refused to open up the financial spigot. He was no deficit spender, and pointed to losses of $14 million in a *Chicago Magazine* article in the summer of 1996. He was determined to repay debts incurred by the strike while staunching publicly proclaimed yearly revenue deficits. There would be no "lazy man's" effort to stock up on free agents, but no compensatory help would rise from a farm system whose cupboard had become increasingly bare since the Jim Frey era.

Years later, MacPhail said he rejected the idea of stripping down the Cubs and starting from scratch, ala the 1980s Braves. His reasoning: after so much losing and front-office upheaval, the franchise could not take another "broadside." At the time, MacPhail also expressed the same sentiment to Riggleman.

"Andy mentioned to me that he really wanted to strip it down and start over," he said. "But it couldn't be like Atlanta (which drew slim crowds in the 1980s). [The Cubs] were putting in 30,000 or 40,000 a night, so part of him felt you couldn't put a Triple-A team in there. You can't wait for the team to get good."

Apparently, MacPhail had not heard of the old pro basketball axiom: the worst thing you can do is be a .500 team. The middle-of-the-pack franchise can't get the top draft choices by being lousy, and is still far from the elite. The only direction such wheels-spinning could go was down.

Riggleman was true to the scouting report of his Padres days. He did not hang crepe over the middle-ground approach.

"That's where [experience] managing in the minor leagues is crucial," Riggleman said. "You take the team you're given, you go to the city you're playing in, and you compete. These are the players you have, and you do the best you can. You don't look at things like, 'Woe is me, how are we going to win?'"

MacPhail's first payroll in 1995 was $36.8 million. That dropped to $32.6 million in 1996. By 1997, the payroll was down to $30.7 million. MacPhail made out the payroll and ran it past Jim Dowdle, who rubber-stamped the numbers. He simply installed his own salary cap, but did not verbalize strategy in meetings.

"It never really was an issue," Riggleman said of the payroll. "We never had a conversation where it was said, 'Here's a concrete number—this is where the payroll is.' We might have a conversation about [acquiring] a player, and it was said we're not able to do that."

In 1997, the major-market Cubs ranked No. 23 out of 28 teams in payroll. MacPhail equated the Cubs' ranking in attendance, ticket prices, and overall revenues with all teams in baseball. If they were in the middle of the pack or lower, that's where payroll and player development spending would correspondingly rank. A traditionalist through and through, MacPhail dumped weird gizmos and training techniques such as balance beams and vectograms (eye tests) instituted under the Himes regime by Goldis and Syd Thrift for the minor-league system. Instead, the players "… would just go out and play," MacPhail said. New-era baseball analysts like Bill James would be kept at arm's length.

No grand upgrade of the Cubs' talent pool would occur. Middle-level players making moderate salaries were the *modus operandi*. Sammy Sosa, moving to another level of power production with 119 RBIs in 144 games in 1995, would become frustrated as the only legitimate long-ball threat in the Cubs' lineup. Continuing a phenomenon from 1994,

Slow, Steady, and Unspectacular

visiting teams often would out-homer the Cubs in Wrigley Field. MacPhail and Lynch talked about being "competitive." Nowhere was the World Series mentioned in such proclamations.

"Sometimes it's a matter of semantics," Riggleman said. "The point is to get into the postseason. If you can get into the postseason, anything can happen. It's not that we didn't want to win the world championship."

Riggleman's viewpoints were voiced a decade too early, but during his managerial tenure, with one exception, he never complained about the limitations imposed upon him. Instead, as the last Cubs manager permitting long, one-on-one media visits in his office before games, he waxed on the intricacies of the game along with the challenges of single fatherhood, among other non-baseball topics. "Good ol' Riggs," as he came to be called, was an eminently decent man working in an inherently political, arrogant, backstabbing sport. He would go on to take unfair knocks as a waffling, mild-mannered manager—columnist Jay Mariotti called him "Ragdoll Riggs"—but those who talked to him knew otherwise. He faced down Sosa and Navarro when they acted up or violated baseball etiquette. When Lance Johnson and Benito Santiago sulked during a massive nosedive in 1999, Riggleman reamed them out privately in his office. The media would not find out for months—as it should have been.

Riggleman also tried to protect his players. Rookie lefty Ramon Tatis hit Cardinals third baseman Gary Gaetti in the eighth inning of an 11-5 loss on July 13, 1997, after Gaetti had slugged four homers and drove in seven runs amid a 9-for-17 spree in a four-game weekend series at Wrigley Field. Riggleman thought the plunking was a rogue action, risking hard-boiled Cards manager Tony La Russa retaliating by throwing at Sosa. Riggleman was ripped in the media again for refusing to mandate a bean-ball battle.

"I'm embarrassed when you see stuff like that," he said that day of Tatis. "If you're good enough to brush someone back, you're good enough to make good pitches."

Unfortunately, Riggleman didn't have enough pitchers with such talents. His boss started off quickly, faded fast, rallied, and then stumbled in his general manager's tenure as five years would go to waste in building a consistent contender.

Entangled In Ivy

During and immediately after the strike, Lynch proved surprisingly aggressive in acquiring new, "B-list" talent. He picked up centerfielder Brian McRae in a good deal with Kansas City, signed pitcher Jaime Navarro as a free agent, and then landed outfielder Luis Gonzalez and catcher Scott Servais in a trade with Houston. After the latter deal, Lynch called out, while leaving Wrigley Field after a night game, "Good deal, wasn't it?" Professional hitter Todd Zeile also was acquired in a rare trade with the archrival Cardinals. But Lynch also let strongman outfielder Glenallen Hill go before the 1995 season to save money. At the San Francisco Giants spring training camp that year in Scottsdale, Arizona, Hill came up to me, gave me a bear hug, and exclaimed, "What happened?" Hill eventually came back to the Cubs in 1998—and again embraced me long after that, at the 2005 Cubs Convention.

An amazingly strong finish to an otherwise mediocre 1995 season fooled all the brass. Stumbling into the first-ever NL wild-card race at 65-69 with more than a week to go, the Cubs won eight in a row against the Pirates, Cardinals, and Astros at Wrigley Field—the last two dramatic victories—to hang around playoff contention. Frank Castillo was one strike away from throwing a no-hitter against the Cards when Bernard Gilkey slashed a triple just out of Sosa's reach in right field. The starting five of Castillo, Navarro, Steve Trachsel, Kevin Foster, and Jim Bullinger had some promising moments, but were still inconsistent, with none rating as "ace" material. Management overrated the group, and passed up on free agent Kevin Brown, whose hard sinker was perfectly suited for Wrigley Field. Brown later said he seriously would have considered the Cubs, while MacPhail admitted "in retrospect" the Cubs should have pursued Brown.

Pitching problems would plague the Cubs the rest of the 1990s. From the standpoint of a decade later, now watching the game as an Arizona Diamondbacks television analyst, Mark Grace said there just weren't enough quality arms in the rotation.

"I remember after [Greg] Maddux left, the Opening Day starters were guys like Mike Morgan, Jamie Navarro," he said. "That's how you win in this game. That's just the recipe for success, starting pitching. There were some good pitchers, but not enough. Or they got hurt. That's the bottom line. There were plenty of good position players here over the years—from [Ryne] Sandberg to myself to Sammy [Sosa] to [Andre]

Slow, Steady, and Unspectacular

Dawson to George Bell to Shawon Dunston. You just can't continue to try to out-slug people."

The fast '95 finish also further reinvigorated Sandberg. His divorce completed, he re-married Phoenix neighbor Margaret Koehnemann in late summer. The newlyweds came back to Wrigley Field and caught wind of the excitement of the season-ending Astros series. Koehnemann was bussed by Harry Caray in the broadcast booth while Sandberg was treated like a returning hero. He regained the itch to play even with his 36th birthday approaching. When MacPhail and Lynch were informed of Sandberg's desire, they had to take back the Cubs icon. Problem is, during the final Astros series, Houston second baseman Craig Biggio— one of the game's best lineup sparkplugs—expressed a love of Wrigley Field while suggesting he'd consider playing in Chicago with his free agency approaching. Biggio would have been a grand statement, a positive (and more expensive) spur in rebuilding the Cubs. As many fans would have lauded Biggio's arrival as welcomed Sandberg back. But the brass took the path of least resistance in reinstalling Sandberg at second base. Despite a 25-homer output in 1996, he would not prove to be a Michael Jordan in his return from sabbatical. The comeback would fade out after just two seasons.

Behind the scenes, at the root of the organization, MacPhail's goal of turning around the player development operation became stuck in the mud for two years. Al Goldis was beaming like a proud papa in the Stadium Club—this time sans hot entrees—on the afternoon of June 1, 1995. He had snared 17-year-old Dallas-area fire-balling phenom Kerry Wood with the fourth pick in the draft, the Cubs' reward for their 49-65 strike-shortened finish in 1994. "How's it goin', y'all?" Wood said via conference call to the reporters laboring on empty stomachs. "I don't really know too much about the Cubs. I know the wind blows out at Wrigley Field a lot."

Goldis dropped names. "If Dwight Gooden was in this draft, I would have taken Wood over him." Events and consequences would eventually play out much greater than Wood's and Goldis' wild dreams.

Further down the draft list, none of Goldis' picks would enjoy more than a cameo appearance in the majors. As 1995 wore on, the fast-talking Goldis would say the wrong things to the wrong people about his new bosses. Later in the year, he would be demoted from his scouting director's job and eventually would disappear from the Cubs organization. With just four years' pro experience—and in the middle of the annual scouting cycle—farm director Jim Hendry replaced Goldis. Hendry would do his best, but later admitted his 1996 draft left much to be desired as a result of his own midstream job transition. He miscalculated second-round pick Quincy Carter's dedication to baseball compared to his pro future as a quarterback. Carter took the Cubs' money, played three indifferent years as a minor-league outfielder, then opted for the NFL. The first two amateur drafts under MacPhail—with the exception of Wood—would turn out to be a waste.

Hendry also discovered the Cubs' attempts to tap the burgeoning Caribbean-talent goldmine lagged far behind the competition. "We were last in the league in Latin America," he would say years later. The Cubs' first home-grown Dominican Republic product to have made the majors, pitcher Amaury Telemaco, made his debut with the parent club in 1996, many years after most teams had tapped the talent-rich island nation. The team had never put much emphasis on Latin scouting, even during the otherwise player-development-savvy Dallas Green regime. Some modest improvements would be forthcoming, but it would take the turn of a millennium for homegrown Latin players to begin contributing in any numbers.

Meanwhile, Lynch's early aggressiveness had petered out. The quickest he moved was on the gas pedal. After one Sunday night game at Wrigley Field, I happened to trail him going westbound on Irving Park Road and onto the northbound Kennedy and Edens expressways. I zoomed up to 65 mph, but Lynch's truck shot forward at far greater speed and disappeared into the darkness on his way home to Lake Forest.

Whether it was payroll constraints or MacPhail's management style being imprinted on him, Lynch quickly evolved into an overly cautious general manager. His general lack of movement aggravated all corners of the Cubs organization. Word began circulating in the baseball community that Lynch was far from his colleagues' favorite GM with whom to discuss trades. His communication skills were seen as lacking in dealing with other GMs, agents, players, and fellow Cubs front-office workers. Indeed, Lynch could frost a room through his mere presence, and he would display such a persona the remainder of his GM days.

Slow, Steady, and Unspectacular

By mid-summer 1996, with the parent club marginally in contention, clubhouse grumbling from Brian McRae and Mark Grace, by now good chums, centered on the absence of midseason deals to improve the team. Even Riggleman privately wondered what his boss was doing. In response to the dissent downstairs, Lynch and MacPhail, contacted while discussing a minor league call-up, proclaimed they were upset that their uniformed personnel were upset. All the while, the favored status of Sosa and his own *prima donna* behavior continued to upset Grace—and other teammates—privately.

The atmosphere was not conducive for instilling the long-sought winning attitude for a franchise perceived as cursed. The lack of a talent base really bit the Cubs as Sosa, on a 52-homer season pace, was lost for the season when his wrist was broken by a pitch from the Marlins' Mark Hutton with six weeks to go in 1996. The middle-ground management strategy was playing out according to the historical trend: downward. After hanging in around .500 until mid-September, the Cubs lost 14 of their last 16 games—the first of a number of mega-slumps under the MacPhail Administration—to finish 76-86. The chief scapegoat, fired on the '96 season's final day, was pitching coach Fergie Jenkins, an all-time Cubs favorite finally working for his old team five years after he was inducted into the Hall of Fame. The pitchers had backslid from 1995, but the top brass thought the affable, fan-friendly Jenkins had spent too much time signing autographs in lieu of his coaching duties. Little did they realize Jenkins would have been perfect as the team's community relations director.

The Cubs passed on an opportunity to deal for Braves outfielder David Justice in the upcoming winter. MacPhail and Lynch did acquire free agents Kevin Tapani, a former Twin, from the White Sox, and closer Mel Rojas from the Expos. But with no winning tradition from which to draw, the spring training atmosphere in 1997 was guarded, even fearful. A string of 11 straight games starting the season against the powerful Braves and beefed-up Marlins beckoned, and assorted Cubs worried about the matchups. Sosa's hot spring training was voided by a back injury that ruined his timing at the plate. Tapani was injured. The spoken worries about the opponents turned into on-field results. Out of the gate, the Cubs lost a record-breaking 14 in a row. The season was over in the snap of a finger.

Entangled In Ivy

The composite record was 2-28 since mid-September of 1996. The pitching did not improve. Rojas coughed up a series of saves that evoked boos from the Wrigley Field faithful. Sandberg showed his age, and left field became a revolving door of homegrown players who would leave much to be desired. Since 1995, the Cubs had two platoons of outfield hopefuls in the guise of slugging prospect Brooks Kieschnick, converted first baseman Brant Brown, Ozzie Timmons, Robin Jennings, and Pedro Valdes. With the exception of a half-season of production from Brown in 1998, none would ever pan out as more than bit-part players. Eventually, the last man installed in left, speedy Doug Glanville, became the regular and the player with the longest-running career, later attaining near-star status for several seasons in Philadelphia.

The skimping on payroll finally came home to roost. In a sub-par year, Sosa had 36 homers. Grace and Sandberg were next with 13 and 12 homers, respectively. Slapped across the face with embarrassment at their parsimonious roster construction, management had to take action. An early August waiver trade dispatched McRae and (unfortunately) colorful setup man Turk Wendell to the Mets, with starter Mark Clark and center fielder Lance Johnson coming in return. With the fans still faithfully packing Wrigley Field for many games, MacPhail was pushed to bump up the payroll more than $20 million. Incoming were outfielder Henry Rodriguez with his feast-or-famine power bat, plucky second baseman Mickey Morandini, veteran shortstop Jeff Blauser, and pear-shaped, hirsute closer Rod Beck. After his minor-league apprenticeship, Kerry Wood was scheduled for near-future delivery to the majors.

The cause-and-effect process worked. The 1998 Cubs got off to a good start, won a series of memorable games, and rode Wood's spectacular pitching in the wake of his unprecedented 20-strikeout conquest of the Houston Astros—perhaps the best game ever pitched in Wrigley Field history. I continually asked Cubs assistant pitching coach Rick Kranitz for Wood's top speed on his radar gun. At times, Wood would touch 99 mph on his final pitch of the outing, when he knew Riggleman was coming to hook him. I dashed into the coaches' room beyond the manager's office to get Kranitz's reading after games. Such journeys also would soon be off-limits.

Sammy Sosa proved to be a one-two punch with Wood. After listening to hitting coach Jeff Pentland, who preached more patience and

Slow, Steady, and Unspectacular

better plate coverage, Sosa caught fire in June with a record 20 homers in a month. Finally, the longtime clubhouse whispers and backbiting about the moody right fielder died down. He was a more patient hitter, coming through in the clutch—enough so that any questions about artificial stimulants contributing to his massive power surge died down, too. (Sosa claimed all he took were "Flintstone vitamins.") The entire country was spellbound by Sosa's home-run race with Mark McGwire that ostensibly revived a sport hindered for three years by the strike.

Understated along with the Sosa-Wood headliners was a clubhouse camaraderie rarely seen at Wrigley Field. Beck, who joined the fans at Bernie's Tavern at Clark and Waveland after games, warmed up for such sessions by holding court in his skivvies at his locker, beer and cigarette handy, as reporters filed in for postgame interviews. Joining him for the baseball bull sessions—a staple of the game's previous generation—were Grace, Mulholland, Blauser, and several others. Tapani entertained with his dry, deadpan Michigan upper-peninsula wit, while Morandini greeted me by flipping the bird when I approached to do his weekly column for the *Times of Northwest Indiana*. Bash-man Glenallen Hill only added to the good mix when he was reacquired at midseason.

The Cubs made only incremental improvements at the trading deadline. While the front-running Houston Astros reeled in the biggest fish, literally, in Randy Johnson, Lynch traded his previous two years' No. 1 draft picks in Jon Garland and Todd Noel to land, respectively, relievers Matt Karchner of the White Sox and Felix Heredia of the Marlins. MacPhail couldn't believe the Karchner deal and years later rued the fact he did not pull rank to stop the transaction. The Sox were more than eager to dump Karchner, who had lost his closer's job to Bobby Howry. Karchner turned out to be a total bust as a Cub, and Heredia was little better.

Worse yet, Lynch did not try to block Johnson from going to the team the Cubs were chasing. When I mentioned that fact in a book on Sosa the following off-season, Lynch was furious. He called me into his Fitch Park office in spring training in Mesa, Arizona, in 1999, roaring that he did not have the likes of pitcher Freddy Garcia and infielder Carlos Guillen to dangle to the Mariners for Johnson, as the Astros did. Lynch repeated Garcia's and Guillen's names, but he never explained why he did not have prime talent to offer for Johnson.

Entangled In Ivy

Despite the failure to land Johnson, the usual roster flaws, continued uneven pitching and the portent of Wood being shut down in September due to a sore elbow, Riggleman steered the Cubs to an 87-67 record amid the hoopla of the Sosa-McGwire home-run race. Sosa's postgame chats began the system of limited-access press conferences for players and managers at Wrigley Field. A Lynch move that did pan out was the August signing of 39-year-old third baseman Gary Gaetti, recently cut from the Cardinals a year after he had single-handedly destroyed the Cubs in the weekend series that ended in the Ramon Tatis hit-batsman incident. Gaetti supplemented Sosa's power with his own clutch hitting. But a 2-6 pratfall, starting with the lowly Reds' three-game sweep at Wrigley Field, put the Cubs' wild-card hopes in jeopardy. Brant Brown dropped an infamous game-ending fly ball that instead turned into a Brewers victory at old County Stadium in Milwaukee. Ron Santo buried his head on the radio booth table, leading partner Pat Hughes to believe, momentarily, that he had "expired."

The Cubs actually played their way out of the wild-card spot with a season-ending loss in Houston, but were saved in overtime when Neifi Perez of the Rockies hit a game-winning homer against the Giants, forcing a wild-card tiebreaker in Wrigley Field on the night of September 28.

The tiebreaker, prompting a literal rush on the Wrigley Field ticket office the previous day, was one of the most memorable games in Wrigley Field history. Gaetti homered, Steve Trachsel had a no-hitter into the sixth, and Terry Mulholland volunteered for relief duty a day after he threw more than 120 pitches in the season-ending start in Houston. The rubber-armed lefty indeed was summoned, and he proceeded to get Barry Bonds to fly out to the warning track in his final at-bat. The Cubs made the postseason for the first time in nine years with the 5-3 victory. Players and fans were beside themselves in celebration. Sosa sprayed champagne into the bleachers. Utility infielder Manny Alexander nailed me three times with ice water in the uproarious clubhouse.

The emotional scene was the apogee of the first half of MacPhail's administration. The downslide would be swift and sure, starting with the Braves' three-game sweep of the Cubs in the National League Division Series. The time bomb in Wood's elbow was ticking, and the Cubs drew fire for starting him in a near-lost cause in Game 3 at Wrigley Field.

Slow, Steady, and Unspectacular

The 1998 playoff appearance did not have the positive bump one might have expected. Only Sosa's Most Valuable Player award provided a momentary afterglow. Instead of making big-splash moves in the off-season with attendance and revenue soaring, Lynch and MacPhail reverted to their more conservative tendencies. Falling in love with his season-ending splurge—and no doubt remembering his long-ago service to MacPhail's Twins—the Cubs re-signed Gaetti as their regular third baseman. All the while, they chose to ignore the free-agent availability of White Sox third baseman Robin Ventura. In fact, MacPhail and Lynch told conflicting stories on whether the team had even talked to Ventura's agent. Lynch traded the star-crossed Brant Brown to the Pirates for right-hander Jon Lieber and acquired veteran catcher Benito Santiago.

A pall was cast on the season when the other shoe finally dropped on Wood's aching elbow. Pain in an early spring training start in 1999 led to Tommy John surgery a month later for Kid K. The atmosphere was anything but positive. Lynch verbally dueled with *Chicago Tribune* Cubs beat writer Paul Sullivan in a Houston tavern over who was the better closer—Lynch backed Rod Beck, and Sullivan endorsed the Astros' Billy Wagner.

Although the Cubs jumped off to a 32-24 start, they were swept in a three-game series at Wrigley Field by the low-rated, cross-town White Sox, who featured light-hitting shortstop Mike Caruso belting a game-busting homer in the broom-wielding. As summer began, the losing fed on itself. Producers from the previous season simply disappeared as the season spun downward out of control. The Cubs endured a record-worst 6-24 August—part of an overall 8-34 collapse that surely ranked as one of the top two or three downslides in team history to that date.

Although Sosa was squarely on the way to his second straight 60-homer season, he began making noises about an enriched contract to replace the one he had signed only two years earlier. Steroid insinuations only nipped at his edges, even though Sosa had reported to spring training with a bull neck and a linebacker's build. Sosa always claimed he had bulked himself up through weightlifting, but that was hard to believe. He was never seen going into the Wrigley Field weight room to work out. Jim Riggleman said Sosa never stayed in one place in the off-season, and he was busier than ever in the winter of 1998-99, flitting off to Japan and sitting with Hillary Clinton at the State of the Union address, among other celebrity activities. That scarcely left time for an active weight-training program. In a midseason manager's-office chat in 1999, Riggleman reported that Sosa's arm strength in scout's ratings had declined from a "seven"—good—to a mediocre "four." His quickly bulked-up frame cut down on some of Sosa's five-tool talents.

The clubhouse sniping that began at Sosa upon his arrival never totally relented, even amidst his spectacular 1998-forward successes. To this day, some who played with him believed Larry Himes and successive top management turned a garden-variety monster into a ferocious, hard-to-satisfy beast totally preoccupied with himself. Sosa was considered "the worst teammate" and the "No. 1 asshole" in baseball by these Cubs. I never saw Sosa as a disruptive force, but then that was only from the perspective gleaned during media-access time. He'd often keep to himself by his locker, eating a ham sandwich after batting practice. More often than not, he was cooperative with the media, never threatening like Albert Belle and not standoffish like Barry Bonds. However, the Cubs did not enforce a rigorous team concept early on with Sosa and began catering to most of his needs, beginning with the home-run race in 1998. The team allowed Julian Martinez, his personal assistant, full clubhouse access at all times home and road until post-9/11 restrictions forced Martinez into a made-up job of running a radar gun during games. Eventually, Martinez was banished altogether after an altercation with a parking lot attendant outside the ballpark.

Rebecca Polihronis, now manager of Cubs Care, had handled Sosa's image and off-the-field affairs from his arrival. She was joined by media relations chief Sharon Pannozzo as a Sosa handler in the home-run race.

"I'm first generation [U.S]," Polihronis said. "My father is Greek, and my mother Mexican. I really understood the Latin culture. I understood his problems with English. Instead of saying, 'I was really excited that happened,' he'd say, 'I'm very proud of myself.' Here, that doesn't sound as nice. The verbs change in the different language. It hit so fast. He was excited about it.

"Baseball's a very small fraternity. Everybody knows what everyone else is doing, which can be good and bad. He was one of those guys who didn't want to get into the gossip and all the drama. He wanted the drama on the field. He kind of stayed to himself. It wasn't being unfriendly. He liked to keep everything lighthearted."

Slow, Steady, and Unspectacular

In spite of his growing baggage, Sosa was the least of the Cubs' problems in 1999. Off the field, the front office practically collapsed onto itself. Even with the inevitable public relations fallout, Jim Hendry drafted pitcher Ben Christensen of Wichita State despite Christensen's beaning of Evansville hitter Anthony Molina in the eye while he timed Christensen's pitchers from the on-deck circle. Agitated by the negative aura over the Christensen selection, the top brass had rabbit ears. MacPhail was upset at my *Times of Northwest Indiana* article that, in his cursory reading, implied he and Lynch hid from the fans while Riggleman absorbed the faithful's boos when he went to the mound.

On Tuesday, August 23, management ordered the 7 p.m. Wrigley Field game with the Giants delayed because of an impending rainstorm. No rain actually inundated the ballpark until 9 p.m.—a time frame in which an official game could have been played. WGN-TV weather guru Tom Skilling said the storm took an unexpected turn sideways before it arrived at Clark and Addison. Giants owner Peter Magowan ripped Cubs management for the dry delay. Paul Sullivan, asked to kill time on the game telecast with Chip Caray and Steve Stone during the delay, put his own baseball-writing career in jeopardy by suggesting that MacPhail and Lynch were to blame for the team's problems.

In the season's closing weeks, a mood of resignation permeated the clubhouse. Riggleman figured he was a goner. Lynch lowered the temperature even further in his locker-room forays. Mickey Morandini and pitching coach Marty DeMerritt said Lynch did not speak to them when he passed through the clubhouse.

The only light at the end of the tunnel shone more than 200 miles northeast in Lansing, Michigan. Hendry's drafting and scouting efforts over the past few years had produced a well-rated crop of youngsters, led by center fielder Corey Patterson and first baseman Hee Seop Choi. Third baseman David Kelton and Jeff Goldbach were touted as well. Lesser known was a strapping 18-year-old flamethrower named Carlos Zambrano. After a decade-long dry spell in producing everyday players, the Cubs farm system seemed to be in revival, with management pointing to this effort. Frustrated fans even called the Lansing ballpark to plead that Patterson, turning 20 near the end of the season and a year out of high school, be promoted to the parent club just to catch the ball in center field. The over-hyping and crushing pressure that would hinder Patterson over the next five years was underway in earnest.

The season dribbled to its dreary 95-defeat conclusion with loyal soldier Riggleman fired after his five-year tenure, the longest by a Cubs manager since Leo Durocher. Even more changes beckoned in the upcoming millennium season. But, unknown to the brass, they would be setting the wheels in motion that would provide the ultimate ecstasy and agony in Cubs history, far dwarfing what they had just experienced in the last two years of the 20th Century.

three

CUBS GET IN AND OUT OF THEIR 'GROOVE'

THE INK was hardly dry on Jim Riggleman's pink slip when Andy MacPhail and Ed Lynch went manager hunting. Their search didn't last long. They zeroed in on Don Baylor, hitting coach of the Atlanta Braves. The bigger attraction was Baylor having guided the expansion Colorado Rockies to a wild-card playoff berth in 1995, the franchise's third season, creating a consistently competitive team despite the pitching-unfriendly confines of Denver's Coors Field.

Nicknamed "Groove," Baylor's tough-guy persona as a player—having been beaned a record 267 times—along with his leadership reputation were top lures for the Cubs. He had played on World Series teams in Boston and Minnesota, the latter for then-young GM MacPhail in 1987. Also on his resume was service for contenders in Baltimore and Anaheim. Although he liked Riggleman, MacPhail believed he was upgrading his manager with a premium candidate as he and Lynch went to Atlanta to interview Baylor on October 11, 1999.

"We wanted him," Lynch said later. "I was interested in what he had to say. He said a lot of the things he said here today that I believed in. I was ready to reach across the table after the interview that Monday and offer him the job."

Lynch thus was beaming at the side of the podium, appearing five years younger than his haggard midseason-1999 look, when Baylor and his four-year, $1.3 million annual deal were unveiled at a lunch-less

Entangled In Ivy

Stadium Club press conference on November 1, 1999. That lent some positives to an otherwise negative day on which Walter Payton died of a liver disease. Baylor asked the assembled to pray for Payton.

Baylor, the past winner, talked about that quality before anything else.

"This franchise is a great franchise with the support they get," Baylor pointed out. "I want to change that into a positive, where we can start thinking about winning. Once you get into the second half of the season starts [as a non-contender], guys are talking about setting up [off-season] hunting trips, fishing trips. That's the part of the season I hate the most—when you're out of it. I want them thinking about winning. It will take work in spring training. It won't be going through the motions."

Baylor's reputation had been everything to his allure. All baseball minds contacted praised Baylor's baseball personality and the Rockies' intensity while playing for him. And yet one little statement of reaction, from Rockies beat writer Mike Klis of the *Denver Post*, would prove to be telling.

"He keeps his distance a bit from the players," Klis said. "You would not classify him as a disciplinarian. He deals with the mental part of the game."

Baylor did talk a good game in the Stadium Club, though. He vowed to tighten up clubhouse discipline. He said he'd ban cellular phones from locker rooms and stress a stricter guidance of player behavior.

On the field?

"The one thing I hate the most is double plays," Baylor said. "I like to get the guys started in motion. I want to get in position to score more runs. On long fly balls, I want them to tag up and advance. I don't want to stand around and wait for the three-run homer."

Cubs players who would later change their opinions endorsed Baylor.

"I'm excited about playing for Don Baylor," said Mark Grace, playing for his seventh Cubs manager. "I know what a quality player and quality manager he is. He'll finally get to manage real baseball because Coors Field isn't real baseball. He's been watching Bobby Cox while he's worked for the Braves, and I consider Bobby Cox the best manager in baseball."

"He was the type of guy who let the guys go out and play," said starting pitcher Jon Lieber. "He gets guys ready to go and play every day."

Cubs Get In and Out of Their 'Groove'

Baylor also could look forward to a long-awaited bump of homegrown talent in the future, led by center fielder Corey Patterson. Given Patterson's first exposure in a big-league camp in spring training 2000, Baylor was impressed. When asked which present-day player reminded him of himself when younger, he quickly replied, "Patterson."

But like most of his predecessors, Baylor would soon get a healthy dose of realism to temper his initial optimism. Although Lynch had snared a new double-play combo of second baseman Eric Young and shortstop Ricky Gutierrez—both good clubhouse guys—his No. 1 pitching acquisition, Ismael Valdes, frequently encamped in the trainer's room with blisters. The bullpen was comprised of aging closer Rick Aguilera, acquired the previous summer, and a bunch of no-names like Danny Young and Brian Williams. Shane Andrews bombed out at third base and was replaced by .200-hitter Willie Greene. Damon Buford, son of big-leaguer Don Buford, had holes in his swing, but manned centerfield. Old Cubs like Brant Brown and Davey Martinez came back for cameo appearances. Behind the scenes, Baylor quickly became disenchanted with Lynch's roster construction.

"That's why pitchers shouldn't become general managers," he said in a rare candid moment in his office early in the 2000 season.

Several months later, an anonymous Cubs player confirmed two divergent opinions between GM and manager. "Ed was attached to some players Don no longer wants," he said.

I was lucky to get that rare moment of candor from Baylor. Gaining access to his office was a feat. Baylor withdrew from easy contact with the media. He was determined to spend as little time as possible in dugout chitchat. His office generally was off-limits to reporters—a 180-degree turn from Riggleman. Media were now discouraged from entering the adjoining coaches' room, in which I had spent numerous hours in before and during the Riggleman era talking baseball with the likes of Billy Williams, Tony Muser, Rick Kranitz, Lester Strode, and others. Baylor's pregame media chats, held before batting practice, were as brief as possible. One morning, I asked all three pregame questions of Baylor, who then happily exited stage left. And in a postgame Sunday session, I asked the first question about his handling of the bullpen that contributed to an extra-inning defeat. When the inexperienced group of television station interns and radio reporters failed to ask a follow-up question quickly, Baylor turned around and started up the stairs to his office before being stopped by fast-arriving sportswriters. He sometimes leaned away from media groups to whom he was forced to speak, like a track guy on the starting blocks. Baylor's style was in stark contrast to several old pros on his team like Grace and Aguilera, the latter of whom stood at his locker, waiting patiently for the media to arrive after a blown save while his manager finished his postgame talk at the other end of the clubhouse.

Curious as to why, after being raised in an old-school environment where media and baseball types more easily mixed, I finally asked Baylor flat-out why he bordered on the standoffish. His response: he had once played for manager Dave Garcia on the Angels. Garcia spent more time schmoozing with the media than talking to his players, and the Angels resented him for that. Problem is, Baylor didn't talk much to his players, either. He would make a pronouncement about the playing status of a Cub, and then the media horde would head for that player for a reaction. Many times, it was the first time the player had heard the news.

Long before the end of the 2000 season, the likes of Grace and Eric Young, who had played for Baylor in Denver, confirmed that Baylor had communication problems with his players. Sportswriter Mike Klis had called it correctly. The mystery was why Baylor, the team leader as a player, turned into such a shrinking violet as a manager.

"I don't think Don was the best communicator I've been around," said former infielder Ron Coomer, a Cub in 2001. "There's a couple of different things being a tough player and tough guy [manager]. Donnie didn't like confrontation one on one."

Baylor would indulge just a couple of favorites. The talented but raw Gary Matthews Jr. was one. Baylor personally supervised Matthews' sessions in the batting cage. In one pregame media chat, I asked Baylor what specifically he was working on with Matthews. "You wouldn't understand, George," he replied.

That begged for a reply: "Don, I've been following the Cubs for nearly four decades as a fan and reporter, and I think I've learned a little bit about baseball through that time."

Baylor's style led to an oil-and-water situation with Sammy Sosa as 2000 began. Seeing the slugger's outfielding and baserunning skills erode as his body bulked up, Baylor publicly proclaimed he wanted Sosa to be a more complete player. Sosa's ego was hurt, and relations between the men quickly chilled. Sosa also got increasingly dissatisfied with not getting an enriched contract to replace a $42.5-million deal originally signed in 1997, which would expire after 2001. At some point, the Cubs began exploring trading their new icon. Eyeing Sosa's star power in the Big Apple, which also featured the country's biggest Domincan community, Yankees owner George Steinbrenner began a dialogue with Andy MacPhail, who took personal charge of trade talks. Top Yankees position-player prospect Alfonso Soriano and their best homegrown young pitchers were bandied about as a return package to the Cubs. However, Steinbrenner's baseball brain trust eventually talked him out of dealing for Sosa, arguing the price would be too high—both in the slugger's salary and the players to be shipped to the Cubs. They recommended Juan Gonzalez of the Detroit Tigers. By the end of June 2000, the Sosa deal was dead, and the Yankees eventually settled on David Justice of the Indians. The move turned out to be correct, with the Yankees winning the World Series over the cross-town Mets.

A month after the Yankees pulled out of the Sosa trade talks, Lynch publicly pulled the plug on his general manager's career. The official line was that he desired to step down as GM in May 16, same day as the near-riot in Wrigley Field over a fan stealing Dodgers catcher Chad Kreuter's hat. But MacPhail urged his usual caution to evaluate the situation better. "The one thing I told Ed is, when I decide it was a good idea [to quit], I'll let you know," MacPhail said, leaving open the concept that the resignation might have been forced. The five-year period forbidding MacPhail from taking a GM's job had passed, so he added that job to his plate. Continuing his pattern from the beginning of his presidency in 1994 of keeping top purged execs in the organization, MacPhail made Lynch a Scottsdale, Arizona-based scout. Like Larry Himes before him, he would serve the Cubs longer as a scout than he did as GM. At the same time, MacPhail promoted Hendry to assistant GM, again ostensibly training him as he did with Lynch.

With the Cubs' train wreck continuing, I asked MacPhail at the July 20 press conference: "Andy, many people say you don't have a plan. Now that you are general manager, what is your plan?"

Entangled In Ivy

Bristling, MacPhail cut me off three questions later in an attempt at a follow-up query. In nearly the same breath, MacPhail rationalized the Lynch era.

"If you evaluate the trades individually, with maybe one exception, they were all either favorable to our club or at least neutral," MacPhail said, "which is a percentage any general manager would be proud of."

Then he put into words what had been broached when he became Cubs president nearly six years previously and prematurely retired from general manager's work at 41. "We're not going to have any confusion at to who's responsible from here on out," he said. "It's going to be me."

MacPhail also confirmed that he would not blow things up and start over, as had been suggested before and after his descent from the president's chair.

"There's part of me that would be very tempted to say that we're going to go younger, and that we're going to see a much younger, more aggressive team out there," MacPhail said. "But it completely ignores the reality of the game today. There are, by nature of the economic restraints on certain clubs, a lot of good players who are arbitration-eligible who become available every year. And if you make a decision to go way young, you might be taking some opportunities away from yourself prematurely."

Finally, in concluding the buck (in more ways than one) stopped at his desk, MacPhail said he ultimately would be held accountable. The impact of the statement would fade through the years, along with all the subsequent controversies and other scapegoats, but they are entered into the record.

"I feel I have an obligation to the fans—to Tribune Company—to let there be no misunderstanding," he said. "If it doesn't get done in the end, I'll be responsible. There won't be two people [to fire]."

Little did MacPhail know on this afternoon that his own day would come, although much later than projected and in a different situation than envisioned.

In 2000, MacPhail vowed to conjure up some immediate trade action, and he came through. He dealt outfielder Glenallen Hill to the Yankees. He also swung a trade viewed favorably, obtaining athletic outfielder Rondell White from the Expos for young left-hander Scott Downs. Of course, White almost immediately got hurt, becoming an

Cubs Get In and Out of Their 'Groove'

authentic Cub. Yet, a healthy White could have not stopped another mega-slump in which the Cubs now specialized. Mimicking the time of the season and severity of 1999's collapse, the Cubs went 7-32 in August and September and finished with 97 losses, most since 1980. Changing managers had no effect on this horrific historical trend.

A 13-season era came to an end when Mark Grace was allowed to walk as a free agent with top slugging prospect Hee Seop Choi, considered ready for big-league delivery at first base within a season. Grace was upset at MacPhail for supposedly not returning a call from Barry Axelrod, his agent. Already an off-season Paradise Valley, Arizona, resident, Grace signed with the Diamondbacks. Although Grace has diplomatic relations with other longtime members of the Cubs organization, he could not, even in 2006, bear to talk about MacPhail's stewardship. He offered a rare "no comment."

While Grace was let go, MacPhail kept stirring the pot in the following off-season to get the Cubs out of the mud. He added Jason Bere and Julian Tavarez to the rotation, replaced Rick Aguilera with Flash Gordon as the closer, obtained crafty lefty Jeff Fassero for the bullpen, and traded for heady third baseman Bill Mueller from the Giants. But his biggest, most expensive move would turn out to be a total fiasco—and it became the first in a long series of transactions that called into question the ability of MacPhail and his front office to evaluate talent and character properly.

Outwardly, MacPhail and his new protégé, Jim Hendry, could not quibble with catcher Todd Hundley's desire to play for them. After all, Hundley was a second-generation big leaguer, son of 1969-era Cubs catcher and certified hero Randy Hundley, one of the franchise's truly distinguished names. Todd had grown up in and around the Cubs in northwest suburban Palatine. He had caught future relief ace Lee Smith in the bullpen at age 10 at Class AA Midland in 1979 as his father taught him to conquer his fear of the baseball on the receiving end of Smith's often-errant pitches. Nearly from the day Todd broke in with the New York Mets in the early-1990s, he never lost sight of his goal of playing for his old man's team as he set the big-league record for homers by a catcher with 41. His 24 homers in only 90 games in 2000 overrode any other drawbacks in his game for MacPhail, by no means a gambler of a baseball honcho.

Entangled In Ivy

"He told me, 'I want to be with the Cubs,'" Randy Hundley said. "He said, 'I don't want to be with anybody but the Cubs.' I don't think I realized how much he wanted to be a Chicago Cub."

And there was a special, personal reason to come home this time. Todd's mother, Betty, had died the previous August after a long battle with cancer.

Once again, the action shifted to the Stadium Club, serving only beverages to press conference attendees. On December 13, 2000, fresh from escaping the Dodgers by signing a four-year, $23.5-million free-agent deal, Todd Hundley put into his own words his homecoming desires.

"Probably for the last four or five years, once I established myself, it was, 'How can I get to Chicago?'" he said. Hundley repeated the Cubs goal several times.

But even during the press conference, there were some warning signs that Hundley could not easily come home again. Even though it was early winter and the room wasn't particularly toasty despite the television lights, he was perspiring heavily. Perhaps it was nerves, but as Hundley adjourned to a side room to continue the conversation after the formal part of the press conference was over, he broke out a cigarette and asked, "Mind if I smoke?"

MacPhail and Co. had to know Hundley was semi-damaged goods after the catcher had reconstructive elbow surgery three years previously. In 2000, he threw out only 20 percent of baserunners attempting to steal. Immediate talk suggested he'd split his time behind the plate and at first base.

But behind the scenes, in the category of the "sixth tool"—*character*—that the best organizations like the Braves had long emphasized, there were warning signs. Hundley had been long rumored to have a fondness for the grape. He was a smoker, not a good habit for any ballplayer, let alone the physically taxing position of catcher. He had some personal behavior issues that had red-flagged some scouts going all the way back to Fremd High School. Yet, if the Cubs scouts really wanted to dig deep, they might have picked up on a built-in schism in the Hundley family itself.

Father and son were almost opposite personalities. Randy was an old-school taskmaster type, a teetotaler who did not use profanity, but could

Cubs Get In and Out of Their 'Groove'

nevertheless drive umpires crazy with his dogged, drawling verbiage. Junior was more laid-back in personality. Like most players, profanities wandered in and out of his streams of consciousness. Randy Hundley was overjoyed his son was a Cub. But on a day-to-day basis, there would be behind-the-scenes tensions. Tiffany Hundley, Todd's then-wife who was with him from Day One in pro baseball, said later she urged her husband to sign with the Giants instead of the Cubs. There would be too much potential conflict with father and son in the same city. Proof of that problem came in spring training 2001, when Randy Hundley worked as a catching instructor for the Cubs. Spying Todd puffing away on a cigarette while taking a break from workouts, Randy expressed the frustration of a parent having long nagged his kid to stop smoking.

Don Baylor was rumored to have disliked the Hundley signing. He already had a favored catcher in place in veteran Joe Girardi, an original Cub who had played for him in Colorado. On Opening Day, 2001, Baylor got Hundley's homecoming off on the wrong foot by starting Girardi. Hundley went straight downhill from there and never recovered as the homecoming became a nightmare. The strikeouts mounted, and the boos began thundering in from all parts of Wrigley Field. In his first 46 games of 2001, Hundley batted just .179 with four homers.

Curiously, Baylor said he'd have to be careful catching Hundley on 85-degree-plus, humid days because the catcher got dehydrated. The sweating episode at his introductory press conference correlated. No major leaguer in prime condition logically would have to be watched for dehydration in hot weather, a staple of most of the season in almost all big-league cities. The questions kept on coming, and they certainly did not stop when the Cubs sent Hundley home from St. Louis on June 19, 2001, putting him on the 15-day disabled list officially for a lower-back muscular strain. Three days later, Hundley was given clearance to rehabilitate on his own, away from the team and Wrigley Field—an unusual move for a short-term disablement.

Hundley's bosses stonewalled on his condition, only fueling speculation further. Their top free-agent signee was a troubled man from whom they wanted to remove the spotlight.

"All I can tell you is, he's doing it off-site," Baylor said, "end of story. He's on the disabled list. I won't talk about it."

Entangled In Ivy

MacPhail declined comment and would not say when he expected Hundley to return. When players encounter serious personal problems—and Hundley also had four children occupying his concern—they often are given extended off time with misdirecting cover stories. After disappearing for a few weeks, Hundley eventually resurfaced in a 15-game minor-league rehab assignment, finally making it back to the Cubs roster near the end of July. At the end of the 2002 season, it was learned Todd and Tiffany Hundley had separated. No one knows what would have happened had Hundley signed with another team instead.

While Hundley remained his No. 1 dilemma, Sosa suddenly kissed and made up with Baylor. Initially, Sosa declined to attend the 2001 Cubs Convention, then changed his mind. Very soon, he had his enriched contract—a $72-million deal running through 2005 that the Cubs eventually would regret. But for now, Sosa was as happy as he was in 1998—and even more effective at the plate. He arguably had a better season in 2001 than three years earlier. Sosa was virtually a model citizen in baseball that season. His performance as a run-producer turned out to be virtually unparalleled in Cubs history—and that of baseball, too.

Sosa was the Cubs' standout. But what made 2001 special for four-plus months was the right mix of personalities complementing his one-man RBI machine in the clubhouse. Mark Grace had been shown the door unceremoniously the previous winter—his age and declining production along with the presence of slugging prospect Hee Seop Choi a convenient out for MacPhail. He imported role players Ron Coomer and Matt Stairs to platoon at first to keep the position warm until Choi's projected arrival. Eric Young and Ricky Gutierrez held forth as the double-play combination, and MacPhail dealt for aggressive-hitting third baseman Bill Mueller of the Giants. Despite his continual injuries, this time a groin problem, left fielder Rondell White was a popular man who fit in with the group. Joe Girardi, another model baseball citizen, was behind the plate when Hundley was unable to play. The pitching staff, led by Kerry Wood, Jon Lieber, and Kevin Tapani, was close and loyal to pitching coach Oscar Acosta. Coomer, Stairs, Young, and Gutierrez were at the center of a loose, upbeat clubhouse—a relative rarity in Cubs history. Only the 1998 Cubs had approached the chemistry of this group of players assembled from all over baseball.

Cubs Get In and Out of Their 'Groove'

Most jolly of the group were first baseman-outfielder Stairs and infielder Coomer. Both were husky men who were compared to park-league softball players due to their physiques and down-to-earth personalities. Stairs, in fact, displayed a flair for the comedic. One time, he strolled through the clubhouse adorned just in a jockstrap and Santa hat.

"Guys were excited to come to the ballpark," said Coomer, now a part-time baseball television analyst in both Minneapolis and Chicago. "We always had someone different stirring it up in the locker room, making noise. Kevin Tapani was a quiet guy, but the biggest quipster on the team. We had a great group of team guys who'd dig in for each other."

Even with the eclectic, but positive mix, Baylor believed the Cubs could use an attitude boost with all the negativity around the franchise. He had a nearly $200,000 personal fund to hire an advance scout reporting directly to him and to fund "… a gadget, a gizmo, it could have been a scouting service," said MacPhail, who approved the fund. The use of "gizmo" was interesting since MacPhail had banished the eye-test vectrograms and balance beams of the Syd Thrift-Al Goldis minor-league days of 1994.

Baylor put part of the fund toward hiring martial arts-fitness guru-motivational instructor Mack Newton, whom he met while playing in Oakland in 1988. The manager added to Newton's fee out of his own pocket. In addition to putting the Cubs through strenuous workouts in spring training camp and periodically during the season, the Phoenix-based Newton would try to purge the losing attitude from the franchise. Given examples of defeatist actions of past Cubs regimes, Newton had the answer to turn things around. He expounded on his philosophy in Mesa during a break from those workouts.

"I always ask myself the question, 'What am I going to do about it now?'" Newton said. "I'm not concerned about whose fault it is. What I'm going to do about it is think, talk, and act with positive expectations every single minute I'm around a Cubs player. In fact, that's what I do all the time anyway. In the past, the Cubs have had negative talk, losing talk, [which] has led to extended mediocrity that has extended out to the generations."

A Vietnam veteran and black belt, Newton put the Cubs through their workout paces in the mornings. A loudspeaker blared upbeat music.

Baylor and Hall of Famer Billy Williams joined in the contortionist acts stretching on the grass. Sammy Sosa listened with rapt attention as Newton addressed the Cubs.

"Hang out with successful people," he lectured one morning. "If you catch something negative coming out of your mouth, just stop it. Anything less [than success], I don't give a rat's butt about it."

Preaching "last to first" in one season, Newton said of the world-champion Yankees: "Losing is simply not tolerated. If they don't go to the World Series this year, someone's going to lose their job. They expect to win."

Sosa praised Newton after the workouts. So did Coomer. Kerry Wood and pitching coach Oscar Acosta even attended one of Newton's local workout classes to get a flavor of the system and seemed to come away impressed.

Most of their attitudes toward Newton would soon change. But developing a positive attitude wasn't hard after an unexpectedly hot start in 2001. The Cubs won 12 in a row starting May 19, on the strength of exceptionally strong starting pitching and Jeff Fassero's fill-in work for an injured Flash Gordon at closer. Lieber and Wood threw back-to-back one-hitters at Wrigley Field against the Reds and Brewers, respectively, on May 24 and 25. The streak took place in spite of Todd Hundley's slump and the loss of Bill Mueller to a broken kneecap, which he injured crashing into the left-field wall at Busch Stadium chasing a pop foul. The pitching boosted an underproductive lineup, but the collective good attitude and acceptance of roles held firm. The good luck extended to the June amateur draft. Watching their pennies, the top-picking Minnesota Twins passed on Southern Cal's Mark Prior, allowing the Cubs to pick the phenom.

The Cubs took over first place on May 29 and held it through the All-Star break. Adhering to his philosophy of adding on when his team played well at midseason, MacPhail began to make deals. He acquired outfielder Michael Tucker, infielder-outfielder Delino DeShields, and reliever David Weathers. Then, in early July, MacPhail went after the biggest fish: first baseman Fred McGriff of the Devil Rays. At first McGriff turned down the trade because he wanted to play at home to be with his family. Then talks resumed, and the McGriff watch was on. The Cubs quipsters had a field day.

Cubs Get In and Out of Their 'Groove'

"Barry Bonds is coming next," Stairs shouted at media from the tiny Wrigley Field team lunchroom.

McGriff, pleading that originally he had been asked to rush into a decision, finally agreed to the trade near the end of July.

But behind the scenes, the chemistry-stirring started to go in the wrong direction.

"Freddy did not want to come to Chicago, and they were trying to get him the whole month [of July 2001]," Coomer said. "I don't think he wanted to play in Chicago, his heart wasn't in it. With those trades, we lost some of our chemistry. You bring in a bunch of new guys jumping into the starting lineup. If things could have been different, maybe you don't make those deals. Hindsight may be 20-20. But you had a group of guys who molded together."

The quiet McGriff was accorded a hero's welcome from a capacity crowd in his first two Cubs at-bats on an ESPN Sunday night game against the Cardinals on July 29. But he slugged just two homers in his first 22 Chicago games, when the Cubs needed him the most.

After reaching a season high point of 62-43 on July 31, the Cubs started treading water while the Astros and Cardinals got hot. Wood reported a sore shoulder after an August 3 victory in Los Angeles. A long soap opera began about the fireballer's real condition. Wood did not throw on the morning of August 12 as scheduled. After the loss to the Giants, Baylor opened his media briefing by answering several game-related questions. The Cubs seemed in no hurry to make any announcements.

"Have you given any thought to putting Wood on the disabled list?" I asked the manager.

Baylor finally came clean, confirming Wood's disablement. Six days later, the Cubs fell out of first place for good in Phoenix, where their 1999 downfall began. By the time the season was interrupted for one week due to the September 11 terrorist attacks, the Cubs had fallen to third place, six games back—slipping out of the wild-card race.

When the season resumed, the behind-the-scenes schisms that had been growing tore apart the team. On October 3, Baylor forced Oscar Acosta to resign as pitching coach. The manager revealed Baylor had clashed with Acosta in his first season as pitching coach, but decided to give it another go in 2001. "I just didn't see going another year," Baylor said. But Acosta had a Svengali-type hold on his pitchers, who were in almost open rebellion after crediting the coach with cutting the team ERA by a full run from 2000's inflated total. Wood threatened not to make his final season start on October 4 at Wrigley Field. Jim Hendry had to come down from the front office to talk Wood into taking the mound. "It seems like it's biting off the arm that's feeding you," Kevin Tapani said. Normally mild-mannered in his comments, Lieber uttered a profanity in a broadcast interview on WGN-Radio. Acosta could be given to fits of anger, and one report said the Cubs wanted Acosta to go through anger management counseling. Acosta almost worked as shadow management in the clubhouse. One time, he peered around the corner from the coaches' room and beckoned across the clubhouse to beat writers Mike Kiley of the *Chicago Sun-Times* and Bruce Miles of the *Daily Herald*. Both scribes rarely left each other's side at the ballpark. I followed Kiley and Miles, and an Associated Press reporter followed me, to the entrance of the coaches' room. Acosta was cueing his two main media conduits about his feelings on Wood. He would later inform Kiley and Miles that he was being forced out.

On the same day as Acosta's ouster, I revealed in the *Times of Northwest Indiana* an earlier player rebellion had taken place—against Mack Newton. The fitness guru had shown up periodically in the first couple of months. "We will be in first place in June, July, and August," he had correctly predicted on May 5. As late as July 17, he was seen at Wrigley Field. "As far as Houston or the Cardinals, that's not something to worry about," he proclaimed, less accurately. After that date, I had not seen Newton. None of the traveling beat writers had penned anything about his whereabouts. So I called Newton at his Phoenix office on October 1. I got an earful.

"The players did not want me there after a time," he said, adding he rejected a Baylor suggestion to visit the team at a recent series in Houston. "I feel very strongly that, if I was allowed to continue the things I wanted to do, the team wouldn't be in the position it is now. My whole thing is about success. It is about positives, teamwork, openness. It is not about backbiting and jealousy. Certain members of the team thought that I was taking credit for their success."

Cubs Get In and Out of Their 'Groove'

But those optimistic player comments in the spring masked a healthy skepticism from the players that only grew bigger in the regular season, when Newton appeared to be trolling for publicity and fan adulation.

"You don't walk into the stands in uniform and sign autographs," Ron Coomer recalled. "It rubbed the guys the wrong way."

Newton and Baylor had sensed they had lost the players as far back as Mesa. Eric Young, Kevin Tapani, and Matt Stairs confirmed they did not want to continue Newton's workouts. Acosta and Newton also clashed over the overly aggressive workouts for the pitchers. "If there was any friction, it was from Oscar to me, not me to Oscar," Newton said, adding he would have never worked with the Cubs if he knew Acosta would react to him in that manner. No doubt, Acosta's vitriolic rejection of Newton added to Baylor's aggravation with the pitching coach.

"In spring training, the workouts were tough, and we were gassed," Coomer said. "Was that going to help us in September? Nobody understands the daily grind except the people around the club. You can't be an absentee guy who's a motivator. If you're trying to get in good with the players, you can't come in for two, three games and fall all over yourself that you're our savior."

More negative news hammered the Cubs on the season's final day on October 7. Beloved television producer-director Arne Harris had dropped dead the night before waiting to get a table in a restaurant with announcer Chip Caray. The Cubs finished 88-74, oddly enough the same record with which they would win the National League Central two years later. But after all the promise through August, the season seemed like a failure. Baylor also felt he had lost big in the clubhouse and executive suite.

MacPhail thought otherwise. He opened up his checkbook to sign free-agent outfielder Moises Alou on December 19. But another injury to Flash Gordon forced MacPhail, with Hendry helping out in his training ground as a near-future GM, to trade on March 27, 2002, for closer Antonio Alfonseca from the Marlins. Starter Matt Clement was a secondary product of the deal. Little known was the left-handed pitching prospect MacPhail and Hendry included in the return package to Florida: Class A pitcher Dontrelle Willis.

The 2002 season started out poorly and got worse. Alou strained his calf, was disabled till April 15 and hobbled for awhile afterward. He batted just .184 in his first 39 games, finished the season 0-for-19 and drove in just 61 runs on 15 homers. Apparently unaware he was being paid $8 million for day differential, the night-crawling Alou complained about having to get up early for Wrigley Field afternoon games. But even for night games, he often arrived 15 to 25 minutes late to the clubhouse when the mandate said players had to be dressed at 4 p.m.

Other slow-starting players like Delino DeShields, handed the second-base job over rookie Bobby Hill, were booed at Wrigley Field. Angered, DeShields pulled an Albert Belle routine after he belted a two-run game-deciding homer in the seventh inning on June 24. I reached DeShields before any other reporter.

"I've got nothing to say, man," he said. "Nothing to say. We won the game."

Alfonseca, who gave up more hits than innings pitched as the Marlins' closer, was pummeled even harder as a Cub, ruining many good starting outings, particularly by Wood and Clement. He clicked on his first seven save opportunities, but was just 12-for-21 afterward. Whenever the media came around the six-fingered Alfonseca seeking comment after another ninth-inning disaster, he would shake his hand and gesture to go away. That zipped-lipped attitude upset Cubs officials.

Even with more than a year to go on his contract, the rug had been pulled from beneath Baylor. He knew he was walking on eggshells. Before a July 4 loss to Atlanta that dropped the Cubs to 34-49, Baylor did his usual group briefing with traveling beat writers. He gave no hint of his despair nor was he asked the same. Minutes later, though, an Associated Press reporter got Baylor to open up one on one. He bemoaned the lack of support he got when he had to cut Oscar Acosta the previous October.

The next night, both MacPhail and Hendry donned their best suits in the southern summer swelter. They fired Baylor, the timing convenient on a Friday on the road with only the small cadre of traveling writers to clamor for information and at the low point of the weekly news cycle. Baylor departed without comment. I tried to talk to him via phone after the season, and he hung up before a question could be asked. Obviously embittered, Baylor to this day has not commented on why he was fired or his closing relationship with MacPhail and Hendry.

MacPhail used the Baylor firing as a clean break from the general manager's job. He handed the position officially over to Hendry, who had

Cubs Get In and Out of Their 'Groove'

been performing many GM tasks anyway. In turn, Hendry promoted Triple-A Iowa manager Bruce Kimm to succeed Baylor.

The Cubs started out 8-4 under Kimm, but it was only the shortest of sugar fixes. They resumed plummeting downward with all due speed. The only drama was seeing how good rookie Mark Prior could become.

He was better than most on August 4 at Wrigley Field, mowing down the Rockies. But Kimm left Prior, only a year out of college, in to record his first complete game. He threw 136 pitches in a 4-1 win. Prior was "kind of surprised" he went back out for the ninth. Kimm had said previously that he'd limit his starters to 120 pitches. Prior had reached that threshold in the eighth. But the manager's justification was that Prior was getting five days' rest after the start.

Kimm tried to let the veterans police themselves, which was akin to letting the inmates run the asylum. For one 12:15 p.m. Saturday national Fox telecast, Kimm canceled mandatory batting practice, allowing the players an 11 a.m. reporting time. That was given as an absolute drop-dead arrival time—good form would have meant an earlier arrival, if just to loll about the clubhouse. But Todd Hundley, still fighting to hit his weight, came in at 11:02 followed on his heels by Moises Alou. On September 9, the team-mandated on-field stretch time was 4:20 p.m. Hundley walked into the clubhouse at 4:15.

Then, as an early-warning signal of the events that would lead to the end of his Cubs career, Sammy Sosa was asked on September 9 what the Cubs needed for improvement. "They've got to clean the house," he said. Sosa was also asked what he personally could do to improve. He seemed taken aback. "Get better players around me," he replied.

By that date, Kimm pretty much knew he had no chance of being re-upped for 2003. Before the season's finale at Wrigley Field on Sunday, September 29, Hendry gave Kimm the bad news. The manager was supposed to wait until after the game for the announcement, but the Cedar Rapids, Iowa, resident could not hold it in. He wore dark, wrap-around sunglasses, gathered the media in the dugout in mid-morning, and broke the news, trying to compose himself in the process.

Once again, the Cubs were in chaos. It would be far from the last time, too. But at that moment, in an effort to restore order, Hendry looked West for his beacon of light. The man in his hiring crosshairs would prove prophetic when he protested that he was a mortal man, not a messiah.

The craziest day in Cubs history was just one year away.

four

IT WASN'T BARTMAN'S FAULT

AROUND 11 P.M. ON WEDNESDAY, October 15, 2003, the Cubs locker room in Wrigley Field—and all of the far-flung representatives of Cubdom, for that matter—reflected the pallor of a *M*A*S*H** unit. Players, coaches, front-office executives, team employees in the ballpark, and fans all over the planet comprised the walking wounded, but bled internally. This time it was mental and emotional. Injuries to the mind, to the heart, are much harder to mend than those to the body.

Off in a locker-room corner, Kerry Wood tried to absorb the pain of so many. "I choked," said the man who could not hold a 5-3 Cubs lead— partially fashioned by his own ballpark-shaking three-run homer—in the eventual 9-6 Florida Marlins victory that propelled them into the World Series, a destination that seemed a lock for the Cubs just three days earlier. Amidst the dazed survivors making their way around the locker room was Cubs pitching coach Larry Rothschild, who had helped bottle the immense talent of Wood and fellow young ace Mark Prior. As a native Chicagoan, the astounding collapse cut Rothschild as deeply as anyone, yet he had a second to cull a positive spin out of the baseball tragedy.

"I think they drained their tanks for us," a reflective Rothschild said of Wood and Prior. "It's the first time either one of them has pitched this long. Now they tasted it, so hopefully in the future this helps, and we can take the next couple steps."

Entangled In Ivy

The pitching pair and their supposedly gilded arms seemed to have a far better chance of recovering from the shock than one diehard Cubs fan. Out of sight, sequestered in his suburban home about 22 miles north of Wrigley Field, Steve Bartman most likely endured his own private hell. The only consolation was that Bartman escaped unharmed physically. Twenty-five hours earlier, he wasn't so sure he would be that lucky. Bartman had become the greatest scapegoat in modern sports history, and his physical well-being was threatened by fans infuriated over his mere deflection of a foul ball. He could scarcely show his face in public, let alone Wrigley Field.

The cryin' shame was that it never had to come to this—much of Steve Bartman's life in ruins because he reflexively went after a foul fly that Cubs left fielder Moises Alou had a dubious chance of catching anyway. And when Alou failed to snare the ball—hit by the Marlins' Luis Castillo against Prior—for what would have been the second out of the eighth inning with just one Marlin on base, a domino effect like nothing else in sports was set into motion. Minutes later, the Marlins had snatched the sure Fall Classic berth away from the Cubs with an eight-run inning that scarcely made any sense. To be sure, the Cubs had another game with Wood going the next night, but the pure shock of the "Bartman Game" created a funereal atmosphere before the deciding Game 7 of the National League Championship Series.

In reality, the house of cards started many months, if not one and a half years, earlier. And when cards fell one by one, their relentless tumbling swept up Steve Bartman and forever became the seminal moment of Cubs history.

If you listed a dozen scapegoats for the Cubs' failure to put away the Marlins, reach the World Series, and avoid a massive emotional hangover that fully permeated the championship-starved franchise over the next three seasons, Bartman would rank no higher than No. 13.

The tipped foul—a ball other fans pursued and an unidentified attorney eventually grabbed and made out, in fact, like a bandit financially—would have meant nothing had Cubs manager Dusty Baker possessed a half-reliable bullpen to call upon as Prior steadily weakened in the following moments. Alex Gonzalez also booted a potential double-play grounder two batters after Bartman and Alou tussled. The Marlins had a powerful but underrated lineup that viewed adversity as a motivation, so a 3-0 deficit with five outs to go wasn't the worst they could have faced.

A number of factors beyond Bartman's control unfairly consigned him to infamy. In the end, every member of Cubs management and a gaggle of players needed to somehow make amends to the man. They haven't. So the only justice that can be applied three and a half years later is to backtrack and reexamine exactly how the Cubs let their best opportunity to end their World Series drought slip away.

The opportunistic, irrepressible Marlins might have found a way to pull it out anyway, no matter how the Cubs played, but as a Runyonesque-bookie-type once told me in the right-field bleachers, "You've got to lose honestly." The right man had to be inserted in the right position at the right time to stave off the Marlins. And if they still won, you could tip your hats to the better team.

The Cubs did not lose honestly in the eighth inning of Game 6 on October 14, 2003. They offered up a tiring Prior and a shortened bullpen to a Marlins lineup so strong that savvy manager Jack McKeon could bench right-fielder Juan Encarnacion and his 94 RBIs in favor of Miguel Cabrera, who was pushed off third base by Mike Lowell's return from injury.

The roots of the all-time fiasco might have been planted 25 months earlier. Cubs closer Tom "Flash" Gordon's arm had gone bad near the end of the 9/11-interrupted 2001 season. When Gordon was slow to recover, then-general manager Andy MacPhail, assisted by Jim Hendry, his successor-in-training, dealt a package of players, headed by veteran pitcher Julian Tavarez and a minor-league left-hander named Dontrelle Willis to the Marlins, a favorite Cubs trading partner. In exchange, the Cubs received six-fingered and -toed closer Antonio Alfonseca and starter Matt Clement.

But Alfonseca had baggage on his resume. Sometimes a standoffish type who did not handle failure as professionally as the game's best closers, Alfonseca was a too-easy-to-hit ninth-inning man. Even while racking up 45 saves for the Marlins in 2000, Alfonseca allowed 82 hits in 70 innings with a 4.04 ERA. In each of his four and a half Marlins seasons, Alfonseca allowed more hits than innings pitched. Defenders pointed to batters making contact with his hard sinker and his supposedly good control, but effective closers cannot be hit so freely.

Entangled In Ivy

Tipping the scales on the far end of his listed 250 pounds, Alfonseca also had weight problems that aggravated Marlins management. He offered up some comic byplay one day when Florida conditioning man Dale Torborg, son of former manager Jeff Torborg and a part-time pro wrestler, tried to corner Alfonseca to weigh him accurately. The reliever—nicknamed "El Pulpo" ("The Octopus") due to the extra digits on his hand—led Torborg on a merry chase through Marlins offices in an effort to avoid tipping the scales at a weight well above the team's desired goal.

Once a Cub, Alfonseca took a turn for the worse. Although he saved his first seven opportunities in 2002, he finished the season nailing down only 12 of his next 21. Alfonseca's shoddy late-inning work probably cost Kerry Wood an extra three victories in an eventual 12-11 campaign. He also upset management by shooing away inquiring media after most of the ninth-inning pratfalls.

Alfonseca lost his closer's job due to a spring-training injury in 2003, then did little more than take up space as a middle-inning reliever when he returned, sporting a 5.83 ERA that was as hefty as his frame. Typical was one midseason five-inning stretch over six games in which he gave up 11 runs.

But he had an important backer in the organization, which perhaps forestalled Alfonseca being put on waivers. One day in the clubhouse during '03, Alfonseca stood next to Gary Hughes, Jim Hendry's mentor when he broke into pro baseball with the Marlins in the early 1990s, who was now his top advisor as a pro scout. Hughes had been scouting director in Montreal when Alfonseca was first signed out of the Dominican Republic. On this afternoon, the pitcher turned to Hughes and proclaimed, "He's my daddy." So with that kind of support, the Cubs weren't going to cut Alfonseca to make room for a more effective reliever.

The rest of the bullpen, with the exception of journeyman Joe Borowski, was ineffective in 2002, so Hendry, by now fully general manager in title, opened up the checkbook to snare free agent Mike Remlinger, perhaps the NL's best lefty reliever in '02, for a three-year deal. The move appeared brilliant. Remlinger had a 1.99 ERA in Atlanta the previous season, giving up only 48 hits (including just three homers) in 68 innings.

For additional veteran insurance, Hendry also signed right-hander Dave Veres, who had a decent year as a setup guy with the Cardinals in

It Wasn't Bartman's Fault

2002. Veres also possessed closer's experience, having saved 60 games with the Cardinals and Rockies in 1999 and 2000.

The GM even welcomed an old hero back. Although Rod Beck had lost the 2002 season due to Tommy John surgery, Hendry tendered a minor-league contract to the savior of 51 games back in the wild-card 1998 Cubs season. Beck could start to work his way back into shape at Triple-A Iowa. If no opening cropped up in the parent club's bullpen, Beck would be free by June 1, 2003, to leave and seek another big-league deal.

A holdover reliever was the talented but enigmatic Kyle Farnsworth. The homegrown right-hander was lights out as a setup man in 2001, but upset the brass by falling asleep in the clubhouse during a game the following season and developing a night crawler's reputation. Farnsworth's 100-mph fastball and youth, however, kept management coming back for more.

Hendry's best-laid plans for the bullpen were undone soon after the team left Mesa that spring. Alfonseca was out with a pulled hamstring. Borowski was tried as closer and took to the job immediately, his New Jersey stout-heartedness making up for any shortcomings in stuff. More trouble ensued when Veres had to go on the disabled list April 15 due to a sore shoulder.

"There's some sort of impingement, something in there," Veres told me in mid-spring. He defined it as a "hook," or a kind of bony protrusion that would require surgery after the 2003 season. "They're going to have to get rid of it through surgery eventually, shave it down and make it smooth again," he said. Eventually, Veres worked his way back to the Cubs with an 88-mph fastball, but was consigned to the back of the bullpen with Alfonseca. He'd eventually appear in just 31 games, posting a 4.68 ERA.

Meanwhile, Remlinger was nowhere near as consistent compared to 2002 with the Braves. His walks and homers-allowed totals were way up. He would go on to pitch well down the stretch—more on guts and knowledge than vintage great stuff. There was good reason for the drop-off in performance. "Yeah, my arm was sore," Remlinger said. "But it doesn't hurt quite as much when you win. Having a sore arm and pitching is part of being a pitcher."

Entangled In Ivy

After the 2003 season, Remlinger had arthroscopic surgery on his rotator cuff.

The combination of the bullpen's grab-bag performance in getting the game to Borowski for the ninth-inning and revelations by Veres prompted several midseason queries to Hendry about adding an arm or two to the bullpen. After all, he was in the buying mood for more talent anyway since the Cubs were in the National League Central race. Twice, Hendry responded, "I like my bullpen."

More than three years later, as he finished a salad at Bar Louie's near Wrigley Field in a wide-ranging discussion on the state of the Cubs, Hendry applied hindsight to his lack of midseason moves for the 2003 bullpen even while he traded for three lineup regulars in Aramis Ramirez, Kenny Lofton, and Randall Simon.

"I looked into improving everything," Hendry said. "I certainly wouldn't tell people I wasn't happy with my bullpen. I'm not going to make disparaging remarks about the guys running out there. I knew Veres was struggling. Rem was a guy who pitched with a lot of pain and tried to suck it up, and probably wouldn't tell me, or a lot of people, if he was hurting. He wasn't hurting bad enough to where it would affect him."

But at least one 2003 Cubs regular believed Hendry should have imported bullpen reinforcements.

"Absolutely no question," said then-second baseman Mark Grudzielanek, now with the Royals. "No question we needed at least one, and probably it would have been better to get two veteran arms in there in the middle, and possibly to close, games. We didn't even have anybody to come in. It was very, very shaky to go to the bullpen at any time. For us not to do something to get at least one arm out there that's healthy, who could throw in a big situation; we didn't do that and that cost us."

Borowski tried to understand Hendry's logic at the time. "Most people said, 'You're going to need your pitching in the playoffs,'" he said. "I don't think that was our glaring need at midseason. Our need was offense. I don't think he [Hendry] envisioned our struggles in the bullpen would continue that long. We had [veteran] guys who had been in that [playoff] situation all the time."

One possible addition was right under the Cubs' nose. Rod Beck had gained notoriety for living in a camper outside Sec Taylor Stadium in Des Moines. He'd invite fans to stop in for postgame refreshments and conversation. That was simply an updating of Beck's man-of-the-people postgame jaunts into Bernie's, one-half block west of Wrigley Field, after games in 1998 and 1999. Beck's fastball had not been at his vintage velocity in 1998 anyway. But in his post-surgery rehab in the spring of 2003, he was clocked at just 82 to 85 mph. After Beck got his release, he signed with the San Diego Padres, a team in dire need of a closer due to an injury to Trevor Hoffman.

"The scouting reports were all bad," said Gary Hughes, who recommended Beck to Padres GM Kevin Towers. But Towers responded that Beck surely couldn't do any worse than the relievers who tried to fill in for Hoffman. He was right, and then some. Beck went on to save 20 games in 20 opportunities the rest of the season. With his slowpoke stuff, Beck allowed just 25 hits in 35 2/3 innings, struck out 32, walked just 11, and had a 1.78 ERA. Hendry claimed Beck wanted to close games. But he loved the Cubs and Wrigley Field so much he would have settled for a setup role for Borowski. The Cubs actually told Beck they'd consider welcoming him back after the 2003 season, even though they believed their bullpen roster was full when he left for San Diego.

"We had a numbers game—what are you going to do?" asked Cubs manager Dusty Baker at the time. "I have no second thoughts. I'm glad for 'Shooter.' He called me before he made his decision. I told him, 'You gotta go for it; you got to take care of yourself at this point.' I hope he saves 40 of 'em, I really do. There's always a chance [of re-uniting], brother."

Hendry had a slightly different take from his vantage point in 2006.

"You have to remember, even though Rod left here and pitched okay," he said, "after a very successful [three] months in San Diego, which obviously didn't lead to any World Series, Rod wasn't to be heard from again.

"I'm sure he [Beck] would have helped, maybe; but that wasn't the premise of the deal. The deal was by June 1 [2003], if he wasn't in the big leagues, and somebody wanted him, it was up to him. At the time, when San Diego called, we weren't beat up, and Borowski was doing fine. Rod wasn't going to hang around to hope someone was going to get hurt and we'd be in the postseason."

With the bullpen already beat up to a degree, situational lefty Mark Guthrie went south down the stretch. The culmination of his failures was serving up Mike Lowell's game-winning homer in the 11th inning of Game 1 of the NLCS. At that point, Guthrie had given up five runs, including two homers, in his last four appearances. He had his worst monthly ERA (5.87) in September, a far contrast from his hot stretch from June 20 to August 14, when Guthrie had a 24-outing, 14 1/3-inning scoreless string.

Pitching coach Larry Rothschild tried to "clean up his delivery a bit."

And Borowski gutted out the rest of the season after falling on his right shoulder trying to field a grounder in a mid-September game. The bullpen was full, but lame and halt going into the postseason.

"Where were all the relievers that got traded who helped that year?" Hendry asked in 2003. "[Ugueth] Urbina was traded [to the Marlins] before our guys got hurt. Guthrie pitched well until September. I can't get upset Guthrie pitched well all year, then stunk in September or Borowski got hurt after getting [33] saves."

But Baker had to adopt a strategy-via-necessity going into the playoffs. Before Game 7 of the NLCS, he revealed that he had intentionally shortened his bullpen. He would only trust Borowski, Remlinger, and Farnsworth. Alfonseca, Veres, and Guthrie would mop up at best. Juan Cruz would gather dust in the bullpen.

"These guys are throwing their best," Baker said of his cozy group of relievers while leaning on the batting cage amid the weird pregame atmosphere of Game 7. "You shorten the bullpen because certain guys are working well. It can work if your starters go deep in games."

That was Baker's motivation for handling Prior and Wood throughout the postseason. He'd let them go longer simply because he had fewer alternatives to shorten the game to five or six innings. Baker got support three years later from his cross-town colleague, White Sox manager Ozzie Guillen, who in 2003 was the Marlins' third-base coach.

"That's the best guy they had," Guillen said of the Cubs' starters. "Dusty and his pitching coach decided, 'It's the best guy we have, we'd rather lose with him than someone else.'"

But it turned out to be a recipe for disaster.

The Cubs had to face both their history and the devil-may-care Marlins. They got a false sense of security in taking Games 3 and 4 to go up three games to one in Pro Player Stadium, a football-shaped arena set in a wasteland on the northwest fringe of Miami. After the Cubs moved

It Wasn't Bartman's Fault

to within one game of clinching the World Series after Game 4, I spied Kerry Wood sitting in a lounge chair, watching television in the clubhouse. I started to ask him about the feeling of being on the threshold of the Cubs' Holy Grail.

"Believe it," Wood responded, careful to say no more.

Yet, the Marlins weren't hanging crepe by any means. Manager Jack McKeon, an old-school chap who loved rubbing shoulders with the media, showed up a couple of hours later at the postgame media party in a large tent by the stadium. "Trader Jack" easily moved among the clumps of reporters, practically dancing about, telling stories, and wielding his cigar like a baton. Then he got up on the bandstand and helped croon a couple of tunes. Like his players, he had faced adversity before in the 2003 season and overcame it, so why mope around now?

"We were supposed to fall over and play dead," McKeon would say after Game 6. Once again, he would lead his team to defy expectations. McKeon had come back down to the dugout at age 72 on May 11 to replace Jeff Torborg. The Marlins were 17-22. Eleven days later, they sunk to 19-29. But with his calm hand guiding the mix of talented young veterans and kids like Dontrelle Willis making their first big-league impression, the Marlins steadily stormed from behind to win the NL wild card. By August 2, they had recovered to a 60-50 record and finished 91-71, playing the best baseball in the NL.

"We trained ourselves from May on," recalled Derrek Lee, then the Florida first baseman. "We learned we could come back under any situation. We learned that if the other team gave us extra outs, we'd take advantage of it. Just by doing it throughout that whole season. We learned how to play baseball. It seemed like every break went our way. We took advantage of every break. That's what happens when you play good baseball. It doesn't just happen—you have to train yourself to do it."

True to form, the Marlins played best when backed to the wall. Josh Beckett, at the high point of his young career, shut out the Cubs in Game 5 to send the NLCS back to Chicago with Prior and Wood waiting. The odds still seemed daunting to all but the Marlins themselves.

"That's what we mainly focused on, going pitch by pitch and inning by inning, whatever lay ahead," Beckett recalled. "We all packed [going to Chicago] also ready to go to the World Series. There wasn't any of us who thought we were going to lose the first game [after being down 3-1] or even the second game, Game 6, *or* Game 7. We thought it was a tough task facing Mark Prior and Kerry Wood, but I think we were up to the task.

"We still stayed pretty optimistic (going into Game 6)," Beckett continued. "We knew we could do a lot of things to score runs. We could hit a home run. We could steal a couple of bases, get a single. We could put a lot of pressure on defenses. You get the breaks—the lucky breaks go your way. They don't go the other person's way. That's kind of where we were at. Every mistake the other team made, we capitalized on."

And the Marlins realized another way to combat Prior and Wood.

"When we were facing the Cubs, I told the players we have to beat Kerry and Prior if we want to go to the next level," Guillen said. "They were throwing the ball well. One thing the Marlins did, we make him [Prior] throw a lot of pitches. That worked for us. That was strategy. Be patient on him. He'd be on a pitch count. They did a good job."

Matt Clement agreed with Guillen. "Taking pitches was a good strategy," he said. "They took a lot of pitches or swung early to avoid [my] slider."

Mind you, the Cubs were not overconfident the way their forebears had been on the plane heading to San Diego, up 2-0 over the Padres in the five-game NLCS of 1984.

"We felt pretty good about our chances," Clement said. "But at 3-2, anything can happen. We respected the Marlins. We had high confidence, but not overconfidence."

While McKeon was absent from the postgame party after Game 5, Paul Hagen, national baseball writer for the *Philadelphia Daily News*, was present and accounted for. After a few beers, Hagen showed an old newshound's guttural prescience. He proclaimed that if the Cubs did not win Game 6, they'd possess "tight assholes" going into the final, deciding contest.

Three years later, Hagen—who had covered a generation of postseasons—explained his well-lubricated reasoning.

"This is an extreme example: The 'Denkinger Game' [Game 6 of the 1985 World Series]," he said. "You just knew they [the Cardinals] weren't going to bounce back from that. When you have a team that hasn't won in so long and now they're coming home, they're trying to wrap it up at home. If you don't win in Game 6, that puts a tremendous amount of pressure to win in Game 7. I think that's what you see in winning teams. It's the chicken and egg, what comes first. Winning teams take advantage of other teams' mistakes. They play loose. They play like it doesn't matter even though it does."

The issue then became Mark Prior's ability to dominate the Marlins and how far he could effectively go in Game 6. After missing three weeks in July when he collided with the Braves' Marcus Giles while running between first and second, Prior recovered to go 10-1 down the stretch, finishing 18-6. But he amassed a large number of high-pitch count games, running up the pitches in outings of less than eight innings. In the NL Central-clinching first game of a doubleheader on September 27, Prior threw a whopping 133 pitches in just 6 ⅔ innings. "I didn't realize I had thrown that many," he'd later say. Baker already drew fire for letting Prior pitch eight innings instead of pulling him an inning earlier to save his arm in the blowout 11-3 victory over the Marlins in Game 2 at Wrigley Field.

Prior tried to re-create both his physical condition and mind-set three years later, sitting in the Wrigley Field dugout amid his thoroughly lost 2006 season. He would not talk about his present status—speaking about constant injuries had completely bummed him out—but was candid about his first and only journey into the postseason.

"When you've been around one, two, or even 10 years, there's obviously a fatigue factor," Prior said. "But you're in a pennant race. I couldn't tell you exactly how I felt. You pitch a lot on adrenaline and a lot in the situation. I'm sure I was pitching primarily on what the moment was and where we were in the season.

"I think I threw 170 total innings [actually 167 ⅔] my first year, majors and minors, to 230 [actually 211 ⅓] innings in my second year. There was a jump. I'm sure there was some sort of fatigue. I was pitching off adrenaline and the intensity of what your team's situation is dictating."

Prior claimed the pitch-count total is not always an accurate barometer of how effective a pitcher is or how tired he has become.

"At 115 pitches, was I cruising?" he said. "If you're talking the first week in April, it's obviously ludicrous to be out there for that amount of pitches. There's a sense of sometimes when you get late in the game, you're forced to mentally concentrate a little harder, your body reacts probably and starts working a little more efficiently.

"A sinker-ball pitcher, early in game they're so strong. That can happen a whole lot later in the game, too; in rhythm, you're forced to relax and really concentrate on executing pitches. And you can rattle off a stretch of 30-40 pitches where you're in such a groove. Sometimes that comes out early in the games, guys start out hot early in the game.

Sometimes it comes out late, sometimes it's 90 to 130 [pitches], where you're in that groove," Prior continued. "A lot of those decisions [pitch counts] were based on the situations. Were those games where I was cruising along and ran into trouble late in game, and that's why my pitch count spiked? Is it a situation where I had a lot of pitches early, then I got in a groove and I was able to get a lot deeper in the game? Me and Woody were throwing the ball well late in the year in '03, and that's just kind of what we had to do. Unfortunately, it's the nature of the game. You can protect [pitchers' arms] so much; but if you have a chance to win, you have to go for it."

Prior indeed seemed to be going for it in an otherwise uneventful Game 6, through seven innings. He had throttled the Marlins 3-0 as the excitement level rose pitch by pitch both in and outside Wrigley Field, where ticket-less fans had gathered by the thousands on the surrounding streets to join in what was projected to be the greatest party thrown in Chicago, perhaps, since V-J Day in 1945.

Inside the Cubs clubhouse, Fox Sports had set up a stage for the pennant presentation and interviews of the World Series-bound home team. And in the auxiliary press area on the right-field side of the upstairs pressbox, I asked Brian C. Hedger and Jeff Carroll, my colleagues from the *Times of Northwest Indiana*, if I should chance on writing my game-story lead with the ever-cruel first deadline not all that far away. "Go for it," Hedger said. Having long thought of what I'd write if the Cubs ever got that far, I quickly laid down about 400 words of imagery of thunderbolts emanating from Prior's strong right arm, ghosts being cast out of Wrigley Field, and evening-up for the trades of Lou Brock, Rafael Palmeiro, and Lee Smith.

Down on the field, no Cub had an inkling that lead wouldn't be used. From his vantage point at second, Mark Grudzielanek saw no reason why

It Wasn't Bartman's Fault

Baker should even be concerned about tapping a bullpen about which both had serious questions.

"He was working very well the whole game," Grudzielanek said. "He was throwing the ball extremely well. In the past few months, [Baker] kept starters in there longer. Our bullpen was a little beat up and a little hurt. No question, he was trying to stretch him one more inning, at least a few more batters. The way he threw in previous games in the playoffs, I just thought he threw the ball extremely well. He earned [going long] that game. It was a question that could have gone either way. I didn't think he'd go to our bullpen because of the way the bullpen had performed the last few weeks into the playoffs. It was in very bad shape. I would have been surprised if he went to bullpen that early. He gave those two guys [Prior and Wood] the opportunity to do their thing and pitch the way they did all year."

Prior himself also was confident—but with some perspective.

"The game was 3-0," he said. "Especially in this ballpark, nothing's out of reach. Anything's possible. Obviously, things were looking good. But you're making a 3-0 game sound like it's 10-0. It's a lead, but it's not like it's substantial."

Prior was approaching the 100-pitch mark as the eighth inning began.

"If I felt like I was done, that I was going to be a detriment to the team, I would have told them I was done," he said. "I felt good, but you got to understand, the eighth and ninth inning, the intensity of the playoffs is easily two or three times more than a regular-season game. The intensity of the eighth and ninth inning of a playoff game is about three or four times as much as it is in the first two or three innings. That's why closing ballgames is so tough. Everybody says, 'If you can set up, why can't you close?' It's a different mentality—especially with that [Marlins] team. They were a team that had a lot of scrappy ballplayers. Their mentality was, 'We don't give up and don't give a crap what the score is.' You knew you were in that fight. They weren't just going to roll over and think they were done."

Interestingly, the Marlins players knew about the banged-up Cubs bullpen. Before the game, according to second baseman Luis Castillo, they figured starter Matt Clement would be the first reliever in the game if Prior could not make it to the ninth, and planned accordingly.

Entangled In Ivy

Although Clement had battled a groin injury to gingerly make all his late-season and playoff starts, he claimed he had his spikes on in the dugout in the eighth inning, ready to warm up if needed.

Juan Pierre reached on a one-out double, but things still appeared to be in hand. Castillo, the No. 2 hitter, began battling Prior with his bat control.

"He [Castillo] was battling," Prior said. "I had him 1-2, 2-2, and he just kept fighting off … fighting off pitches."

On a full-count pitch, Castillo sliced a long fly down the line into the seats where Steve Bartman and fans surrounding him braced to catch the popup. At the same time, leftfielder Moises Alou leaped and thought his glove was in position to catch the foul before Bartman, a youth baseball coach and consulting firm worker, by the luck of the draw was the one among a scrum of fans to deflect the ball.

"Even a local fireman who was sitting two or three seats down from Bartman made a comment that he came down to catch the ball, too, and the replay showed that," said Thom Brennaman, who handled the television play-by-play of the game for Fox. "It just so happened that Bartman was the guy that touched that."

Meanwhile, as the rhubarb flared a few feet away, an unnamed attorney snared the ball when it finally crashed to the ground, hoarding it until he sold it to Harry Caray's restaurant, where it was ceremoniously blown up the next year.

Alou threw a fit like a child whose toys had been yanked away. Prior pointed to left field, claiming fan interference. But the ball was clearly in the stands and was ruled "no play" by the umpires. Alou claimed he had a 100-percent shot at the ball. So did many others. But the truth was, the sore-kneed, slow-running Alou was no Torii Hunter in climbing outfield walls. He was hardly a lock to make the catch, even if Bartman had leaned back to make room.

"It was a pop fly," said Brennaman. "There's still great debate at least for me, that Alou catches that ball. We're not talking about a multi-Gold Glove winner who's climbing the bricks down the line."

The popular feeling was Prior, just 23, was rattled as he walked Castillo on the next offering, which got away from catcher Paul Bako.

"I don't think think it broke my concentration that much," Prior said. "I've seen the replays. I looked out. I pointed. I thought it was fan interference. But I don't think it affected my concentration. Everybody says, 'You ended up walking the guy.' The foul ball might have been the ninth pitch of the at-bat anyway. It wasn't as if it was a foul ball on the first pitch, and I threw four balls and walked the guy."

Baker would counter years of criticism for not striding to the mound to calm down Prior.

"Usually, the manager doesn't go out," Baker said. "Usually, it's the pitching coach [Larry Rothschild]. I'll go out to make the decision to take them out or not. I thought my pitching coach was better suited to tell him about the situation and what to expect than the manager."

Neither Baker nor Rothschild came out after the Bartman deflection because, according to Prior, no such visit was needed. "That's one thing for sure there was no reason to come out there. What was he going to say? I don't know what Larry would have told me out there."

Clement is still Prior's best friend in the game—the buddies text-message each other even though they're on different teams—and he said that he would have reacted in the same manner. "He doesn't have to settle him down," he said of Baker or Rothschild. "Any pitcher would have gestured. I never made a whole lot of it. He [Bartman] didn't reach onto the field."

Far above the gesturing and the pointing, in the press box, Paul Hagen, the Nostradamus of the scribes, had that funny feeling. He realized what team he was covering and its proximity to a Fall Classic berth.

"After the play happened, we all sat there and looked at each other and said, 'Oh, my God, is this how it starts?'" Hagen recalled.

Almost out of sight and mind among the hubbub was Kyle Farnsworth. As Castillo's foul touched Bartman's hands behind him, set-up man Farnsworth was warming up in the bullpen. Baker and Rothschild obviously had a Plan B cooking in case Prior faltered.

But Prior still felt confident facing the tying run in Pudge Rodriguez, the Marlins' best clutch hitter in the NLCS. He ran the count to 0-and-2. Amazingly, he did not waste a pitch and ran a breaking ball too close to Rodriguez's hitting zone. The catcher lined the ball into left, and Pierre scored the first Marlins run.

"I don't think it was that bad of a pitch, and I don't think it was that great of a pitch," Prior said. "If I remember, he was kind of out in front of it and just kind of hooked it into left field. It wasn't as if he yanked it and pulled it. Obviously, if I would have executed perfectly, it would have been in the dirt. But nobody executes 100 percent of the time. It still wasn't that bad of a pitch, and it was on the outside part of the plate. I could have buried it, but you run the risk of runners moving up from first and second."

At this point Baker had to make a decision. Prior still was throwing well, but he was only in his first full year in the majors. He had never faced such pressure. And with just five outs to go—even after limiting his bullpen in pressure situations—wouldn't it have been better to pull a pitcher one batter too soon than one too late?

Clement was the only 2003 Cub with a semi-dissenting view.

"I think Mark was at the end of his rope at that point," he said. "He was not used to being in that situation. But I can see Dusty's point: If I'm going down with the ship, I'm going down with Mark and Woody."

Farnsworth continued heating up in the bullpen, but received no summons; nor did a call come for closer Joe Borowski to warm up. Even though he had been pained a bit from landing on his shoulder a few weeks earlier, Borowski had pitched 2 ⅓ innings in Game 3. He had three days off. The next night, before Game 7, Borowski claimed he was ready to go as long as necessary.

"He got his set-up guy in the bullpen," Borowski said. "He was probably thinking, 'Mark is still dealing.' Mark up to that point was absolutely cruising. It's too easy of a scapegoat to say it should have been done that way. You've got to go with your workhorse and the man who got you there. There were so many ways we could have gotten out of that inning."

What was Prior thinking?

"I was in a game where I was pretty much pitching good all game and still pitching good. Pudge gets that single, I'm like, 'Okay, next pitch was a ground ball to short. Two outs changes the situation; three outs changes a lot.' You're asking almost on semantics, was I done? I don't know. I'm not going to say I'm done in that situation. I felt fine physically. If you want to take me out and bring someone in with more experience, who might be able to handle the situation, I don't have an answer to that. You have to ask Dusty or Larry. Those are things I never really thought about."

It Wasn't Bartman's Fault

The Rodriguez single inflamed the crowd beyond the bullpen, around Bartman, seated with his old-fashioned headphones. They began hurling verbal jibes at the Cubs loyalist. The abuse would only get worse, paralleling the on-field situation.

In the Marlins dugout, confidence welled when no move to pull Prior was made. Luis Castillo confirmed that the longer Prior stayed in, the more confident the Marlins became.

Prior steadied himself and got Miguel Cabrera to slap a grounder right at sure-handed shortstop Alex Gonzalez. The popular image was a tailor-made double-play ball. However, official scorers never assume a twin killing on such balls. If handled perfectly, the grounder might have yielded the magical third out on the relay, but an extra bounce created a shred of doubt. If fielded cleanly, the second out of the inning would have surely been made, slowing momentum for the Marlins. It was not.

Gonzalez bobbled the grounder, leaving all hands safe.

"Gonzo was about as sure-handed a shortstop we've had here since I've been here," Prior said. "If he has a ball 10 times hit at him, he makes that play nine or 10 times. If he catches it and throws it, it's a guaranteed double play. Cabrera can't run that well. It's a three-hopper right at him. He doesn't make the play, so you move on. It happens. It was not like he was trying to make an error."

The miscue meant extra pitches from an overworked Prior arm that seemed desperate to punch the clock. Farnsworth still warmed in the bullpen as Baker allowed Prior to face Derrek Lee with the bases loaded. He doubled to tie the game 3-3.

By now, the Marlins had become an emotional express train. Castillo was right-on when he related how his teammates feasted on a tiring Prior like hungry sharks.

"You could see it," Mark Grudzielanek said of the Marlins' confidence. "Each hit got bigger and bigger. You could see the life and the energy, and just the total atmosphere of the game shifted."

Baker had no choice but to yank Prior at this point. The well-warmed Farnsworth came in, gave up a go-ahead sacrifice fly to Jeff Conine, then a three-run double to Mike Mordecai that made it 7-3. Pierre's RBI single completed the eight-run shocker.

"There were some fluke things that happened," Grudzielanek said. "We needed to keep the lead for one more inning, and it didn't happen.

"I don't think 'choke' is the right word," Mordecai said of the Cubs after the game. "You're basically giving a major-league team five outs in an inning, that's almost two innings' worth of outs."

All hell broke loose in the box seats near Bartman. Fellow fans tossed threats, threw garbage, and doused him with beverages.

"We couldn't see everything that was going on," Borowski said. "It was kind of getting the impression of what was happening. It was a damn shame."

Brennaman and the Fox crew had a clearer view.

"We were privy to seeing stuff not shown on the air, what exactly was going on down that left-field line," he said. "You knew immediately where we sat that this guy was in big trouble with the fans. It was despicable."

Brian C. Hedger hurried down the ramps to where Bartman sat. By the time the top of the ninth rolled around, Cubs security escorted Bartman out for his own safety. Hedger said fans were trying to climb over the cordon of Bartman protectors to get at the poor guy, who pulled his sweater over his face as he was whisked out through the main concourse into the security office.

All the evidence pointed to poor roster construction, overconfidence in a 23-year-old pitcher to carry the load, and failure to execute on the field. But Bartman went up on baseball's cross for the sins of others, a little more than a year before Baker's turn.

"People like to talk about the Bartman incident," Brennaman said. "To think that a team scores eight runs in an inning—an error by the shortstop; you have a pitcher in Prior, who was best pitcher that year. You can't get two more outs? At the end of the day, there was one guy on with one out, and the Marlins scored eight runs. Now, that has nothing to do with Steve Bartman."

But the fan's life was wrecked, at least for the near future. A Judas character in his life leaked his name out quickly. By the next morning, Steve Bartman was outed in print and broadcast accounts.

"I'll never forget it as long as I live—that was one of the most disturbing moments I've ever had in my life," Brennaman said of Bartman's name being disclosed. By the time I woke up at 6:30 a.m. the next day, I'm looking at a helicopter shot where he lived. It's exposed to the world where he lives, he works. ... Does he have a family? C'mon, this is a baseball game. This isn't a killer, for cryin' out loud."

Eventually, Bartman would go into hiding, and his video and still-photo images of the tipped foul ball remain the most lasting of the greatest collapse of Cubs history. Rumors abounded that the north suburbanite moved about in disguise or that he was offered a transfer to Great Britain by his employer. Through relatives, he turned down all interview requests. Undeterred, in 2005, a writer for ESPN.com stalked Bartman, following him from his home to office, then waited for the chap to come to his car in the parking lot at day's end. A very short conversation ensued. Bartman still rooted for the Cubs. The franchise did not deserve a fraction of that after what he endured.

Bartman still gets the blame that should fall on others.

"We have the most gory mistake of '03, and it wasn't even made by a player, which of course is poetry," celebrity-profile author Bill Zehme said in *Wait 'Til Next Year*, a 2006 HBO documentary on the Cubs. "It was one of us. *We* did it."

Zehme spent much of 2004 at Wrigley Field trolling for a possible Cubs book before disappearing when the team went into the tank the next season. He should have known better, based on his own journalistic experience. Zehme offered up the typical simplistic fan's explanation. Game 6 was a Cubs organizational house of cards waiting to topple, and an untimely deflection could not have prevented that from taking place.

Of course, the Cubs had another game to provide consolation to Bartman with Kerry Wood on the mound.

"That's what you do in the postseason, go hard," Wood said. "You pitch the whole season, then pitch into October and ultimately try to win the World Series. There has to be some kind of workload there, and you handle it. Before [Game 7] started, I felt great. I felt great when I was throwing in the game. Going into the game, I didn't feel any different than in the previous series in Atlanta [when Wood won two games]."

But the same bullpen problems overwhelmed Baker when Wood simply lost staying power after slugging his Friendly Confines-shaking three-run homer.

"I've never been in a wilder atmosphere than when Woody hit the home run," Clement said. "I'm thinking, no way we're going to lose."

Entangled In Ivy

A whole host of Cubs believed that, despite the shocking ending to the playoff run, 2003 was a mere starting point.

"We're going to make some improvements for next year," Baker said after the Game 7 defeat. "In my mind this is just the beginning of good things to come for us for many years."

"No doubt, I felt, 'Next year, we are going to win,'" Clement said.

Baseball's most valuable lesson, though, went unlearned: "Tomorrow is never promised." Nothing can be bottled. When all the sun, moon, and starts are properly aligned, the moment must be seized. The right alignment may not appear again for 10, 20, 30, or maybe even *100* years.

Sure enough, the Cubs have had one long hangover, one crazy thing after another taking place in their universe since the bullpen stayed quiet too long on October 14, 2003.

"I'm not a big 'what-if' guy, especially if you're looking at history," 2003 Cubs reliever Mike Remlinger said as a 2006 Brave, his second tenure in Atlanta. "Baseball's a game you win with what you have on that day. If you're a player, and you get caught up looking at reasons why you're not going to win, you're probably going to lose. If you have the attitude, 'Whoever we have is going to be good enough to win the game,' then you'll have a better chance of winning.

"A hangover? Let's say we won the World Series and then we had the (three increasingly bad) years we ended up having. It's still a failure and a letdown. The monkey is off the franchise, but it's still a failure for the players. What '03 got was a higher level of expectation by the fans. But in '03, we weren't expected to win, which is part of what helped us. The '04 [failure] was bigger."

Befitting their differing vantage points of that night, the three main Cubs characters of the Bartman Game don't have the same take on what happened with some time in between to reflect.

"Lately, it's been so bad," GM Jim Hendry said of more recent pratfalls. "Every now and then [he thinks about it]. If we had won Game 1, we would have swept them. We got five off Beckett in the first, but we couldn't hold the lead.

"I've let it go. It didn't happen. We were close, and it didn't happen. The Marlins played better. I have as many regrets about '04; I thought we were a much better club coming to camp. I was very happy about what happened between the end of '03 and the beginning of '04. It just didn't

It Wasn't Bartman's Fault

work. It was a heck of a team that got off the plane coming off spring training."

The lesson Hendry learned? "The game is very humbling," he said.

Dusty Baker narrowly missed taking two different teams to consecutive World Series after his Giants lost in seven games in 2002.

"The plays speak for themselves," he said, "the [Alex Gonzalez] error. … If they want to put me up on the cross, they can do so. Nobody expected us to be in that situation in the first place, No. 1. And then when you get there, you're going to blame somebody for not going all the way? I thought we did a heck of a job winning as many games as we did, especially with our bullpen and our young pitchers. Next year, we won one more game and ended up worse [in the standings].

"I have no regrets and no remorse about anything that I did other than us not getting to the World Series. The only thing we can do is to get back to that point and go further."

Prior gets to finish in a manner he did not on October 14, 2003.

"How much are you going to overanalyze it?" he said. "Are you going to analyze it to the tenth degree about what should have been done or what shouldn't have been done? Just play the game. The game was played, and it didn't work out for us. Move on.

"I never understood why they [Marlins] didn't get the credit they deserved. They were down three games to one. They came back. They won. They beat us. Did we play our best ball at the end? No. They came back and won. They went to New York [in the World Series] and beat New York. Everybody said New York lost, but somebody had to beat them, so obviously they were a good team."

But were they better than a Cubs team that could have closed its gaping holes in the seventh and eighth innings?

five

THE PARADOXES OF
ANDY MacPHAIL

A FULL 12 YEARS had passed before I heard the words pass from Andy MacPhail's lips.

"You can make the case that the best thing [for baseball] is for the Cubs to win three championships in a row," he said. "It would be great for ratings and it would make [good for] the game. Nothing would be better for baseball than to have the Cubs be world champions next year. It wouldn't matter [if the World Series opponent was the Yankees or the Red Sox]. Go back and look at postseason TV ratings, none were higher than the 2003 NLCS."

A shorter statement was indicative of what I knew MacPhail believed.

"If you don't win on the field, you're going to suffer at the gate, it's inevitable," he said.

MacPhail had saved his best for last. He finally pushed his verbal advocacy full-throttle, departing from the lukewarm proclamations of the previous decade-plus. Too bad he had not swooped in with such a grand—and true—analysis when, adorned with slightly longer hair and larger glasses on that day early in the 1994-95 strike, he had first assumed the Cubs presidency.

"Slow, steady, and unspectacular," "We're working on it," and "being competitive" were his mantras.

Now it was early afternoon on Saturday, September 16, 2006. MacPhail had just dashed back from New York that morning, where he had participated on management's side in ongoing talks for a new Collective Bargaining Agreement. MacPhail and I sat down in his private booth in the Wrigley Field press box while the Cincinnati Reds took batting practice. Unknown to me, the chat was very, very late in his Cubs presidency. Amid perhaps the most disastrous season during his tenure, he had already proffered his resignation to Tribune Company top brass, and it had been accepted. His forced departure would be announced 15 days later.

Broadcaster Jack Brickhouse had a catchphrase for nearly every baseball situation. In this case, MacPhail's envisioning of the Cubs as baseball's flagship team was akin to the "horse already out of the barn," in Brickhouse vernacular. Had MacPhail possessed such great vision from Day One, our conversation probably would have focused on—in past tense—multiple playoff appearances and, no doubt, the long-detoured World Series appearance. Instead, the emphasis was on the "why" of what went wrong and an attempt to mine MacPhail's logic for all that had transpired.

That was the paradox of MacPhail—multiple paradoxes, in fact. Scion of a baseball royal family, MacPhail's grandfather, and later his father, had developed winners. The youngest of the trio had put the finishing touches on a fine homegrown nucleus by fashioning two World Series winners with the Minnesota Twins—a feat that led to MacPhail's recruitment for the Cubs in 1994 by Tribune Company executive Jim Dowdle. Armed with perhaps three times the resources in Chicago, however, MacPhail failed to develop a winner. In fact, the trend was much the opposite. A smattering of contending or playoff teams were overwhelmed by incessant depressions in performance—five seasons of 94 or more losses—unprecedented for a modern big-market, big-budget franchise.

MacPhail, who aggressively wielded a finely tuned player-development plan for creating a winner in Minnesota, turned into a passive, almost defensive executive in Chicago. He lacked any kind of clear vision to make the Cubs baseball's No. 1 organization. There was no articulated "Cubs Way" of running baseball operations in the manner of other successful franchises. While achieving smashing success in marketing, attendance, and other financial yardsticks, the Cubs would lag behind other big-market teams in player payroll, position players produced by the farm system, and baseball-operations staffing, which could've provided better player evaluation.

The MacPhail who could wax eloquently his thoughts one on one to those he allowed into his confidence was contrasted with a pay-no-attention-to-that-man-behind-the-curtain public image. He was a man who could have articulated his plan, if he possessed one, and had the Cubs' far-flung fandom following him to hell and back. However, he preferred his subordinates speaking for him, abhorred sports talk shows, and chose to funnel his thoughts to a small group of traveling newspaper beat writers through whom he could control his message.

An executive who recoiled when informed of the Wrigley family ownership's worst management slapstick ended up with results too much like Phil Wrigley. MacPhail ran the Cubs longer than anyone else aside from gum magnate Wrigley. Since he had fiduciary power over the franchise, he held an owner's power. Yet, save for a couple of playoff appearances that were lacking under the Wrigley post-1945 era, his record was just as poor as the bad ol' days.

To determine the cause of these paradoxes, a personal profile of MacPhail had to be created. But that was a challenge, since MacPhail opted for a reserved, low-key personality—he stayed out of the gossip pages, and carefully rationed his public exposure and message.

I posed the question about the concept of ego to MacPhail in his private box. Almost all successful sports executives possessed a special kind of ego that led them to beat their chests and crave victory without holding anything in. I wondered if MacPhail possessed even a remote resemblance of that championship-thirsting ego.

"I definitely think you have to remind yourself that it's not about you," he said. "MacPhail as a GM was a much more volatile personality. For me, that's okay as a GM. I don't know that's really appropriate for the president. Everybody's got an ego. This game is primarily about the players. That's who the people come to see. No one's ever paid a dollar to watch me work at my desk, nor is anyone likely to. The game's about the players. When our attention gets away from the players, I think the game suffers. The people want to hear from the manager, the general manager; they want to hear what the field strategy is or about player acquisitions. Occasionally, they want to hear from the owner or the president or whatever. I really think you ought to have one voice. Occasionally it's very appropriate that I take a public position on something. But it should come much more frequently from the GM or the manager."

Interestingly, for part of his tenure, MacPhail had a GM, Ed Lynch, who was a cold fish in communicating with both media and baseball colleagues. One of his managers, Don Baylor, couldn't wait to end his daily media sessions and had mediocre communication skills with his players. On the other hand, he had expert public communicators in manager Jim Riggleman and GM Jim Hendry. But they did not set the payroll or shape the scope and direction of the Cubs organization as a whole.

The only way to explain MacPhail's actions, and their effect on the Cubs, was to somehow re-create his own personality. Over the 12 years of his presidency, I gained some peeks into MacPhail the man—good and bad. The former outweighed the latter. On a personal level, he was decent and honorable, dignified, and even personable. To be sure, he could boil into several fits of arrogance and anger, but generally did not hold grudges. Mark Grace might disagree.

MacPhail was not a gentleman who had to struggle to make his way. He was like the son of an executive who dutifully works every job in the factory from the bottom up before being promoted to run the company. MacPhail served similar apprenticeships—in the Cubs and Astros front offices from 1976 to 1985—before being hired as Twins general manager at age 33.

Several clues to his personality were revealed in the first-ever radio interview of Lee and Andy MacPhail together, which I featured on my weekly baseball radio show—then called *Chicago Baseball Review*—during the darkest days of the strike. Airdate of the program was January 21, 1995.

"I think he was qualified to move along and do whatever he wanted to do," Lee MacPhail said at the time. "The only thing I did for him is expose him to baseball, to see how a club was run, and to work for a club."

The younger MacPhail's ambition coming out of Dickinson College in Pennsylvania was simple. "I was more interested in just working somewhere in a baseball operations department of a major league team," Andy said. "I never quite honestly—even recently—aspired to be a president of anything.

The Paradoxes of Andy MacPhail

"Being exposed to the game, one thing I learned in a hurry is that those people who were involved in the game were enjoying themselves. At that stage, I was trying to make a cognizant decision to get into a field where the financial rewards were not as great. The people were enjoying what they were doing. The hours may be a little longer, but they seemed to be fulfilled. At that time, I thought I'd be sacrificing finances; and as it turned out, I've probably done better economically than I ever anticipated in my life. Quite honestly, the enjoyment level of a baseball executive in the [1990s] isn't quite what my father enjoyed in the 1950s, 1960s, and 1970s."

Lee MacPhail was one of the most admired baseball executives of his era. He served as general manager of the Orioles, president of the Yankees, and president of the American League. He almost had enough clout and respect to forge a settlement of a short strike in 1985 with player concessions before then-commissioner Peter Ueberroth decided to impose his own deal.

However, Lee's personality couldn't be more opposite to that of his mercurial father, two-fisted drinker Larry MacPhail, who was nicknamed the "Roaring Redhead." The eldest MacPhail had introduced night baseball to the majors in Cincinnati in 1935; then brought radio to New York baseball in 1939 with the Dodgers, whom he built into a winner. Later, he ran the Yankees. One longtime story had Larry MacPhail wheedling second baseman Billy Herman away from Cubs general manager Jim Gallagher by (amazingly) staying sober while Gallagher got drunk. Larry MacPhail supposedly excused himself every few minutes to pour out his glass of liquor in a nearby toilet.

"I can guarantee that's not a true story," Lee MacPhail said on the radio show. "I can prove it by one thing. There's no way my father would ever pour liquor down the drain. It was a great trade for the Dodgers, so I can understand [the story]. He and [Red Sox owner] Tom Yawkey were drinking companions, and one time they had a little too much to drink. My father was with the Yankees. They agreed to trade Joe DiMaggio for Ted Williams. You can imagine how Ted would have been in Yankee Stadium with the short right field and Joe in Fenway with the short left-field wall. The next morning, they both sobered up, and I think it was Yawkey who called off the deal."

Entangled In Ivy

The sins of Larry MacPhail, the father, would not besiege Lee MacPhail, the son, though, or his line of descendants.

"My grandfather was very volatile," Andy MacPhail said. "If anything, my father kind of reacted the other way and took steps to be extraordinarily un-volatile. Different times, the dynamics were different. No question, the personalities were quite diverse."

Andy MacPhail took after his father, but a bit of Larry MacPhail's emotionalism latently lingered, bubbling up only when provoked.

"He was a very unusual person," Lee MacPhail said of Larry MacPhail. "There was no one else quite like him. I was nowhere close to the kind of person that he was. I think Andy is maybe between us, but a little bit toward me, my type."

Fast-forward 11 years to 2006. Remembering that interview, I asked MacPhail the Third a question many had speculated about for years. Since he was the latest of this baseball royal line, he seemed destined to be commissioner when Bud Selig stepped down. He begged to disagree.

"I do not have any ambitions," MacPhail said. "I have an understanding of what that job entails. You'd think a team would get a record above .500 before they are anointing me commissioner. Our current commissioner has done an extraordinary job reshaping this job—the wild-card system, interleague play, getting revenue up, revenue sharing—there have been a lot of meaningful changes done on his watch. He had the first labor agreement in, I don't know how long, without a strike. He still gets criticized despite clear black-and-white indications of being very effective in his job. When you find out, let me know [why MacPhail should be commissioner]. It's a mystery to me.

"My father was more qualified [for commissioner]. No doubt about it. Never in my life have I ever had a job where I was looking at the next one. The next one always has come as a surprise to me."

Little did I know that MacPhail would officially be looking for his next job in two weeks. Assuming he would continue amidst the latest Cubs nightmare and reviewing his entire resume in Chicago, I asked MacPhail if he was conservative by nature and upbringing. I reminded MacPhail of the radio interview and the statement about personal restraint in comparison to the unhinged Larry MacPhail style. In addition, I asked Andy MacPhail for his definition of conservative,

The Paradoxes of Andy MacPhail

which, like anything else in our superficial society, is subject to stereotypes, real and imagined.

"I would say that, in most cases, it's a fairly reasonable evaluation," MacPhail said. "I am reasonably conservative. People make a lot of assumptions as a result of that, which I really don't think are accurate.

"Conservative to me—don't let it take on a political tone—I'd like to think it doesn't necessarily, when you get down to it, have to impact the approach you have on building your franchise. We've done a lot of things that could have been considered radical [with Wrigley Field's appearance]. We made a lot of changes, things you never dreamed of back in 1994. We've done it in a conservative-building manner. We added [seats] behind the plate, first base, bleachers, a batter's eye suite, advertising in the ballpark [in the dugout and in the upper deck by the pitch-speed display boards]. It's a pretty conservative approach, but conservative doesn't have to mean you're averse to change."

Interestingly, the comment on conservatism—and MacPhail skillfully avoided being pinned to a specific personal philosophy while distancing himself from some obvious political bents—hardly mentioned the baseball, and troubled, end of the Cubs.

Other aspects of his existence weren't rock-ribbed conservative.

MacPhail employed back-to-back African-American managers in Don Baylor and Dusty Baker, with minor-league skipper Bruce Kimm serving a two-plus-month interim bridge between the two. A hint of his early attitude came from Bill Harford, a longtime friend starting in their junior-employee days together in the Cubs front office in the late 1970s.

Harford and future [now ex-] wife Judy introduced MacPhail to his wife, Lark, who was a roommate and fellow United Airlines flight attendant with Judy. Bill and Judy thought Lark would be "good" for Andy. However, when both Harford and MacPhail were single, they went out on the town after hours one early-season night in 1979. They bumped into Cubs outfielder Sam Mejias, a Dominican. All attempted to enter a bar. Mejias was barred admission because of the color of his skin. MacPhail suggested to Harford that they all leave at once.

A few years before our 2006 interview, I told MacPhail that, due to rainouts, the Cubs were forced to play four consecutive doubleheaders over the Labor Day weekend in 1967 at Wrigley Field. "That's why you needed the Players Association," he said.

Entangled In Ivy

MacPhail was shocked when told old-school Dallas-based scout Bill Capps' story of Phil Wrigley's 1962 order prohibiting the signing of any new high school or college players in the era prior to the June amateur draft. Apparently, Wrigley was upset because of bonus money being flushed down the drain on failed prospects. Eventually, Wrigley was talked out of his suicidal stance, but the Cubs signed just six players the rest of '62, prompting a devastating effect on the farm system for years to come.

MacPhail also cringed when I told him of a 1963 kinescope of Brickhouse introducing Col. Robert Whitlow as baseball's first, and only, "athletic director" to run the Cubs. The mere thought of Wrigley's wacky ideas disturbed him.

Yet MacPhail was condemned to repeat history through errors of omission on his baseball operations side. That contrasted with Wrigley, whose miscues of commission and desire to be different overwhelmed the need to strengthen the organization's basics in adhering to the standards of successful opponents. Raised in Baltimore and New York, MacPhail simply did not understand the Cubs situation from the inside out, and thus lacked a sense of urgency to catapult the team out of its seemingly perpetual doldrums. MacPhail had never suffered continual heartbreak in the manner of his fans. He was in New York doing what teenage boys desire to do best in 1969, when the ecstasy and agony visited Wrigley Field. He did not possess the institutional memory to learn from the few examples of Cubs successes through the years.

Perhaps he did not listen closely enough to his own father in the 1995 radio interview.

"He's very knowledgeable, works very hard," Lee MacPhail said of his son. "You have to rely on people working for you. You have to get some good opinions of players from those people. I hope he has that type of organization in Chicago. If he doesn't have it now, I know he soon will have."

MacPhail would hire the inexperienced, indecisive, uncommunicative Lynch as his first GM, but would permit the understaffing of his front office, shorting the operation of enough qualified baseball minds throughout his presidency. There was no grand plan other than to make the Cubs a "player development"-oriented organization—the goal of 29 other teams.

The Paradoxes of Andy MacPhail

That was the ultimate paradox in comparison to MacPhail's management style in Minnesota. Red Mottlow, my late co-host when the radio show's title changed to *Diamond Gems*, always nicked the MacPhail reputation by insisting the Twins' nucleus had been developed before his arrival as GM by an executive named George Brophy. MacPhail never denied that fact. What he did not do was stand pat and hope the core of Kirby Puckett, Kent Hrbek, Tom Brunansky, Gary Gaetti, Greg Gagne, and Frank Viola would develop a winning hand on their own.

"The best trade was getting Jeff Reardon prior to the 1987 season," MacPhail said in 1995. "The Twins hadn't had a season over .500 in 10 years. They did have a nucleus of good talent. I felt, if we could get a closer, everyone around him is going to get better. Once that trade was made ... he [Reardon] was the type of person who generated a lot of confidence around him, and the whole personality and way the organization was looked upon would change. It was the dynamics."

Perhaps the best personality sketch of MacPhail's Minnesota style came from Terry Ryan, the man who succeeded him as GM and has rebuilt the Twins while ensuring their farm system stood among the game's best.

"He hired well, and let people do their job," Ryan said. "He was very religious in making a decision. He had instincts for the game. You always admired the way he went through the rules. He prepared well. He never was a braggart. He was not afraid. He was never afraid of a huge signing. He was not afraid to sign a player for a huge amount [Kirby Puckett], even though it's not right for a market this size.

"I think he's a baseball guy, not a corporate guy."

MacPhail would prove to be a man of his word who believed strongly in team chemistry; believed that all parts had to fit properly. Twins announcer Dan Gladden attested to that fact when he came to the Twins in a trade with the Giants.

"I negotiated a two-year deal with Andy," Gladden recalled. "One thing I had in my contract when I came over is, I had a single room on the road—whereas the Twins players never had a single room. He had to honor my contract in the trade and that started the ball rolling. Other teams in the league were doing that. Andy was very fair. He didn't want a lot of garnishes in the contract. That was fine, too. I'd say he was very friendly. His personality was very approachable. You didn't have to be careful not to offend him or some of his beliefs. He allowed you to be yourself.

"He had a good idea about chemistry in the clubhouse," Gladden continued. "You didn't need all these marquee players. You needed players who could play collectively as a team. Gary Gaetti went down the next year, and we were looking for a third baseman to replace him. He was looking at Chris Brown from the Giants. He was asking not what kind of player he was, but how he would fit in the clubhouse. I didn't think Chris Brown at that time would have worked in the clubhouse. That's what MacPhail, building clubs, was looking for."

As a Twin, MacPhail clearly articulated a vision for quality, disciplined player development. His scouts signed the likes of Chuck Knoblauch, Torii Hunter, Jason Varitek, A.J. Pierzynski, LaTroy Hawkins, Corey Koskie, and other big leaguers. The development continued in the farm system, and his managers and coaches knew exactly where he stood.

"Andy was the boss," said Twins manager Ron Gardenhire, first a minor-league manager, then third-base coach in MacPhail's regime. "When he was in the room, he was the boss. You listened. He had a plan, and he stuck to his plans. When he would come to the minors, he was always very serious about getting things done. He always wanted to find out if there was something we could do in the minor leagues that could help us get better. When you're that detailed in your work, as Andy has been, it's going to work. He pays attention to an organization's working from the lower minor leagues all the way up. He had the belief you build from the ground up. You draft and develop players. You have to have a good development team.

"Andy was all about winning."

These kind of endorsements obviously filtered to Jim Dowdle, the No. 2 man in Tribune Company, when he cast about in the summer of 1994 looking to hire a baseball man to run the Cubs without micromanaging from company headquarters. Such meddling had been a serious problem for seven years, starting when investment banker-type John Madigan ambushed baseball guy Dallas Green. But when MacPhail got his offer from Chicago and asked for his release from a Twins contract that had two years remaining, he had to do it with conditions, which would turn out to hamper MacPhail in Chicago.

The Paradoxes of Andy MacPhail

First, he had to pledge to Twins owner Carl Pohlad that he would not make a lateral move, to a general manager's job, for five years. That promise he kept, not assuming the GM role in title until July 2000. But more critical in the end was MacPhail's own vow not to snare his Twins development people to trek the 400 miles to Chicago, where their talents were sorely needed on a farm system that had collapsed after Green's and Gordon Goldsberry's departures. He needed first-rate, experienced development people to jumpstart the system. Instead, he retained the ineffective [with the Cubs] Al Goldis as scouting director, while neophyte GM Ed Lynch hired Jim Hendry as farm director although Hendry had just three years' pro baseball experience. Hendry's strength was recruiting and developing a top college baseball program at Creighton, but now he was cast as an administrator.

"I promised them I wouldn't," MacPhail said of luring the Twins' development execs to Chicago. "I was under contract [to the Twins]. I promised I wouldn't raid his organization. Our people here are good.

"Name one Twins person who has left that organization. When the [five-year] time period came up, subsequently, we asked permission to talk to Twins people—one fairly recently. They've chosen not to come. One person, Wayne Krivsky, went to the Reds [as GM]. They are treated well, a loyal group: [scouting director] Mike Radcliffe, [pro scouting coordinator Vern] Followell, [special assistant Larry] Corrigan. Terry [Ryan] does as good a job as anyone in the game."

Ryan was not interested in coming to Chicago. MacPhail recommended him to step up to the GM's job.

Obviously, the promotion to president was the biggest career feather in MacPhail's hat. He would be the third-generation MacPhail to have served as a team president, this time with virtual owner's power. The money was sweet [a reported $1 million per season plus the typical corporate trimmings], and the hours were better than in Minnesota. One aggravation to family life in Minnesota, MacPhail once recalled, was having to work most of the typical nine-to-five shift with office and other duties, and then having to stay for the night game at the Metrodome. As Cubs president, he had close to banker's hours with only the 18 night games at Wrigley Field scattered about the home schedule. He could go home to Lark and their two sons in suburban Winnetka and blend in to affluent north-suburban life without the celebrity profile of so many of his peers.

Another question asked around Wrigley Field for years regarded where MacPhail's authority ended and his GM's began. On September 16, 2006, at Wrigley Field, he insisted he was a delegator of authority.

"As it relates to the job, two things guide the way I approach my responsibilities," MacPhail explained. "I don't like dilettantes that stick their foot in, stick their foot out, get half-involved. To me, you're only in or only out.

"Relating to any department, you have to let people do their jobs so they're all the way in. You've got to give them a reasonable amount of autonomy for them to do the best for their department on an everyday basis. I feel very strongly that I have to provide checks and balances against what it is they propose. You have to ask the right questions, assure yourself the proper amount of homework was done, something that's not harum-scarum, seat-of-the-pants-type thing. That's kind of the role I've approached in this job—the overall responsibility of operations of the franchise."

Yet, while he ostensibly trained Lynch as GM and allowed him to make the trades and explain to the media his logic (or lack thereof), the extent of MacPhail's handling of some GM duties or decision-making was in question for years. It made no sense for baseball man MacPhail to give up the wheeling and dealing at age 41, after less than a decade in baseball's flesh market. One baseball executive with inside knowledge of the front office said Lynch was, in function, the assistant GM, getting the players MacPhail wanted, while the latter fulfilled his no-sideways-move pact with Carl Pohlad. He added Jim Hendry had more autonomy than Lynch did. The best information was that Lynch had to run trades by MacPhail before receiving the final go-ahead.

I couldn't totally disagree with that analysis. After I heard of clubhouse unrest in July 1996, over Lynch's lack of moves to improve the Cubs with the trade deadline looming, I was admitted to MacPhail's office to get his and Lynch's reaction. The pair was discussing minor-league call-ups. Since when did the president of the ball club immerse himself in such front-office minutia?

MacPhail publicly second-guessed Lynch on only one deal—apparently the Jon Garland-for-Matt Karchner trade with the White Sox in July 1998, swapping the Cubs' best pitching prospect for a wobbly reliever. He said he had wished he had put a stop to the deal. MacPhail also second-guessed both himself and Lynch on not pursuing pitcher Kevin Brown after his less-than-stellar 1995 season with the Orioles. In retrospect, MacPhail told me on the final day of the 1996 season, the Cubs should have gone after Brown. MacPhail and Lynch seemed too satisfied with the 1995 rotation of Jaime Navarro, Frank Castillo, Steve Trachsel, Jim Bullinger, and Kevin Foster to import a potential ace. Of course, Brown shined with the Florida Marlins while those starters—aside from Trachsel—backslid and ultimately drifted out of the Cubs organization.

No matter who was pulling the strings, MacPhail had the power of the purse, and he opened it very carefully during Lynch's GM tenure. The executive who did not mind tendering the top contract in the game in Minnesota allowed Lynch only to pursue bargain-basement free agents in his first two seasons in 1995-96, ostensibly because MacPhail desired to pay down the debts of the strike.

The Cubs were being run as a middle-market franchise. MacPhail needed to go one direction or the other, but not in between—either strip down the franchise and start over, or stock up on short-term free agents who could vault the team into contention while the farm system was revived. He did neither. The Cubs had absorbed too many "broadsides," in MacPhail's words, to go the Atlanta, Minnesota, and Cleveland routes of building from scratch. MacPhail and his trainee GM hoped the Cubs could one year overachieve, and catch lightning in a bottle. Choosing an in-between, "slow, steady and unspectacular" course—acquiring the likes of Navarro, a pre-power Luis Gonzalez, Dave Magadan, and Doug Jones—would only condemn the Cubs to break-even baseball.

And that always provides a recipe for getting worse.

MacPhail simply acted defensively or passively, never comparing his franchise in market size or scope to the Yankees, Red Sox, or Los Angeles teams the way other baseball execs did.

"The two New York teams, two Los Angeles teams, and the Cubs," said one baseball honcho. "I think that's fair. They should be in that [top] strata. After they won the World Series, the White Sox are at the next level, but used to be probably two clicks behind."

Entangled In Ivy

Although he believed a series of Cubs World Series titles would be good for baseball, he still did not equate his team with the Yankees or Red Sox—even though former top Cubs pro scout Keith Champion compared the fishbowl atmosphere of Wrigley Field to ESPN's two favorite Eastern Seaboard teams.

"We certainly have a remarkable fan base that has stuck with us through thick and thin, but there's been a lot more thin than thick," MacPhail said. "We have not accomplished what other franchises have accomplished."

At different junctures in the game, he gave no justification for not ranking in the top three in payroll and player development. One view of MacPhail was that he linked the Cubs' overall revenue with what their spending should total. If they were 10th in revenue, then they'd be a commensurate ranking in payroll and player development funding.

It's doubtful the Cubs slipped as far as No. 23 in revenue in 1997. But five notches from the bottom of then-28-team Major League Baseball was where the Cubs ranked in payroll. Two years later, when I asked MacPhail where his franchise ranked in player-development spending, he responded around No. 13 of 30 teams—squarely middle of the pack. The idle-time joke developed in the press box that someone from atop Tribune Tower would have to prod MacPhail to increase his spending for that blessed event to take place.

The day when the Cubs would be in the top third in baseball would never take place under MacPhail. In 2005, he said the Cubs' player-development expenditures were "probably in the top 20 to 25 percent ... somewhere between No. 5 and 8."

On September 16, 2006, the Cubs inched up the ladder, but not to the very elite core, in payroll, as MacPhail revealed in the private-box interview.

"We've done better than most," he said of the team's revenues. "Our payroll reflects it. Payroll was around $104 million at the end of the year. That ranks fifth or sixth in the game, if not fourth. Unfortunately, the two highest paid players were on the disabled list last year, [Kerry] Wood and Nomar [Garciaparra]. This year, it was Wood and [Derrek] Lee. Too much of the payroll was on the sidelines."

He also tried to debunk the concept that the Cubs did not spend freely in the previous off-season.

The Paradoxes of Andy MacPhail

"The most money devoted to one player in the off-season was Derrek Lee," he said of the first baseman's new mega-deal. "People didn't think we had an active off-season. It doesn't get any notoriety—[Scott] Eyre, [Bobby] Howry, [Jacque] Jones. The highest signing was Derrek Lee, we got to him before he got to be a free agent."

I found myself fortunate to have garnered any degree of candor from MacPhail over his 12 years at the helm. Preferring his low-profile stance, he often tried to funnel his message only through the aforementioned smaller-than-usual traveling corps of beat writers. Only three Chicago-area newspapers—the *Tribune, Sun-Times* and *Daily Herald*—staffed the team wire to wire. Even in an era of shrunken travel budgets and cuts in baseball coverage, the trio of scribes was the smallest proportionally for a market Chicago's size. Even MLB.com, the on-line service partially owned by Major League Baseball, did not send Chicago-based staffer Carrie Muskat to all road games.

During an October 1999 interview for my previous inside-the-Cubs book, *The Million To One Team*, MacPhail confirmed his media-relations strategy that one baseball executive later said was "old fashioned, out of the 1950s." While suggesting that I was writing the book for a profit motive, he added that his "obligation was to the beat writers," as if these scribes worked on a volunteer, altruistic basis.

The statement was made during a tense time for MacPhail and me, coinciding with the back-to-back 95-plus loss seasons in 1999 and 2000 and the drafting of beanball pitcher Ben Christensen despite a public outcry. The previous spring, he thought I accused him and Ed Lynch of "hiding" from the fans during the start of the massive Cubs downslide. I replied that I never used such a word in the newspaper story, and retrieved a tear sheet to prove it. More than a year later, when Lynch stepped down as GM and was succeeded by MacPhail, in the press conference, I asked Andy, "Many say you have not had a plan. Now that you're GM, what is your plan?"

Already bristling at the first query, MacPhail verbally dismissed me when I tried a follow-up question several minutes later.

I wasn't the only one to feel MacPhail's verbal lash. *Chicago Tribune* Cubs writer Paul Sullivan, the most independent of the beat men and women, upset the president with some of his coverage in the late 1990s. At one point in 1999, Sullivan went on WGN-TV during a rain delay at

Entangled In Ivy

Wrigley Field to finger MacPhail and Lynch as prime culprits in that season's monster collapse. After Sullivan returned to the Cubs from a three-year switch to the White Sox, he was seen working his way down to MacPhail's front-row seat at Mesa's HoHoKam Park in spring training to talk peace. The détente apparently held until May 2006, when MacPhail angrily reacted to a Sullivan misquote of outfielder Jacque Jones. He called Sullivan and Dan McGrath, the *Tribune's* associate managing editor for sports, into his Wrigley Field office for a beef session. Apparently, MacPhail expanded his complaints from the Jones quote to a scathing review of Sullivan's Cubs writing career. Such a meeting did not reflect well on MacPhail, but also proved that the corporate-cousin *Tribune* was not in the team's pocket as popularly portrayed.

Perhaps Sullivan's and my experiences revealed the Larry MacPhail genes bubbling up like a dormant volcano in his grandson. More often, MacPhail was on the helpful side in dispensing information. In 2001, MacPhail the GM revealed that Don Baylor had a personal fund just short of $200,000 to pay for consultants, scouts, or training methods. I can never criticize MacPhail for stonewalling. We even had a gentlemen's agreement of sorts, where I could call his home up to twice a year to confirm major breaking stories on evening deadlines if the GM could not be reached. One time, he even took a call from my daughter, Laura, seeking information for a high school senior class project on baseball.

MacPhail seemed to loosen up when he assumed the GM duties. Not so coincidentally, Dennis FitzSimons replaced the retiring Jim Dowdle as Tribune Company Cubs overseer at the start of 2000. FitzSimons, a baseball fan who grew up in Queens and recalled his first game at Ebbets Field, was from the entertainment end of the corporation, and appeared to have a more liberal spending philosophy than Dowdle. His former positions included general sales manager and GM of WGN-TV, so FitzSimons knew all too well the effect of a winning team on ratings and advertising rates. After the 2000 season, he accompanied MacPhail and Jim Hendry on a recruiting trip to offer pitcher Mike Hampton a $100-million contract. Hampton, who signed with the Rockies, later praised the professionalism of the Cubs management trio. FitzSimons also played diplomat a few months later, early in 2001, in visiting Sammy Sosa in Miami in an attempt to settle his open-ended contract.

The Paradoxes of Andy MacPhail

MacPhail's moves as GM had vaulted the Cubs into contention in 2001, and they held on to first place until mid-August before fading. The 88-74 record was a slight deflation from the early-August high point of 19 games over .500, compared to 2003's mad dash in September to the same number of wins but a divisional title as well.

Looking back from 2006, MacPhail thought the Cubs had finally turned a corner in 2001, eliminating the nosedives in performance that marked Lynch's era. But it would turn out to be a false dawn. There would be two more seasons of 94 or more defeats under MacPhail before the curtain was closed on him for the final time.

"I came in '95, we finished a little over .500," he said. "In 1999-2000, we were bad. I thought we had the capability starting in '01 to get to the level where we would not have these dips. Clearly, it's been a matter of [players'] durability these last couple of seasons. Durability was a big issue. In 2002, we had [Mark] Prior and [Carlos] Zambrano, some guys coming on. I don't know why we were as bad as we were in '02. We rectified that in '03. Since that time, you should not have had those dips. Had we stayed healthy, I don't think we would have had those dips. I'm not saying we'd have postseason teams all those years, but you wouldn't have had 94 [or more] losses."

Standing in the visitor's dugout at Turner Field during the 2003 NLDS, I recalled asking MacPhail if he desired to model the Cubs after the Braves organization, which was then celebrating 13 consecutive divisional titles, with signs marking the achievement festooned all over the outfield walls. He did not hesitate in craving a copycat blueprint. Three years later, he basically admitted the Cubs had fallen short of creating a "Cubs Way," similar to the "Braves Way."

"Each franchise tries to put their brand or their philosophy, and it doesn't have to be an overwhelming strategy," he said. "There is a subtle different strategy. Oakland has to take a strike before they have to swing away. We had to put a premium on speed in Minnesota on turf. Here, we put emphasis on pitching. Where we've struggled, I've told this to our guys, what really is a hallmark of a really good organization as opposed to just an average organization is, do they really know what they have in their system? To me, we're not as good at that as we need to be."

Years back, MacPhail outlined a goal of becoming a pitching-oriented organization. But it partially backfired in two ways. The Cubs developed pitching, to be sure, often for other teams through their trade tactics. Moreover, the pitching was groomed at the apparent expense of another homegrown commodity.

"We put an emphasis on pitching throughout our system," MacPhail explained. "One of our problems was pitching we thought we had, but we never completely got. Either it never developed the way we thought, we traded it off too young, or it got hurt. But if you go back and look at pitching today, since we came here from '95, no organization has developed as much major-league pitching as we did. We've done a poor job developing position players."

Interestingly, being a pitching-oriented organization was the only response MacPhail could give me in the summer of 2005 when I asked him to define a "Cubs Way," if one even existed. Growing one's own pitching, however, is a standard goal of all 30 teams. The franchises that break out from the pack have an abiding philosophy about developing hitters' discipline at the plate and emphasizing character in players that they acquire.

MacPhail would depart without a definable "Cubs Way." No one really knew what the organization stood for. In his private box, MacPhail offered up his valedictory speech, even if I did not realize it at the time.

"Clearly, there are two immense frustrations I have," he said. "First, we haven't been to a World Series yet, and we've had plenty of time—plenty of time and plenty of resources. We were positioned to win, we should have won, and we didn't do it. Equally, if not more frustrating, is we've had no consistency and really can't sustain any momentum—'01 to '02, '03 to '04. We put resources on the table. We have to get consistent performance out of players and get a group that's more durable than we've had here recently."

MacPhail was a man out of his time in several ways. Had he shown the aggressiveness and vision in September 1994 instead of September 2006, they might have pulled back the curtain surrounding him to unveil a statue in tribute to the man who brought a World Series back to Wrigley Field.

Instead, unlike the MacPhail family royal image, he visibly displayed emotion as he departed his farewell press conference, leaving the Cubs with the same riddles and questions he had been charged to answer a dozen years earlier.

six

DUSTY'S INNER SANCTUM

CONSIDERING THE MOOD of the times, Dusty Baker and his employers seemed to be headed in opposite directions in the noontime hour of July 19, 2006. Dressed fashionably in shorts and a tropical-themed shirt, Baker strode into Wrigley Field's administrative entrance off Clark and Addison as if nothing weighed on him at all. He was not yet a dead man walking, and he strode into the old ballpark as if this day was Game 7 of the World Series, not just another day to mark off the calendar of a lost season.

Baker spied me waiting. "Are you ready?" he asked. "Sure," I replied, "but I've got to wait for my handler." I could have walked with Baker to his office, but protocol and procedures required that a team media relations official escort me. Her arrival would still be minutes away.

Baker walked in, and shortly afterward, a gaggle of top Cubs brass exited the same way. Former team president Andy MacPhail was accompanied by business chief Mark McGuire, baseball operations director Scott Nelson, and two other chaps. "What are you here for?" I was asked. "I'm here to interview all five of you guys. Who's first?" I replied. MacPhail playfully grabbed farm director Oneiri Fleita and moved him in my direction. But in a second, they were gone to their lunch date.

Finally, I was led through the empty clubhouse—players were still at least an hour away from arriving for the 7 p.m. night game—and then up the stairs and around the corner into Baker's office. The manager had already donned his uniform pants and a windbreaker. I had been in this room countless times, going back to 1989 and a few postgame sessions with Don Zimmer. I practically encamped once a home stand during Jim Riggleman's managerial tenure. But the march of time and the steady tightening of access dictated media could simply not walk into Baker's private redoubt. Dan McGrath, the *Chicago Tribune's* associate managing editor of sports, had been seen scurrying into Baker's office on a number of occasions after the manager's postgame press conference. But McGrath, who had covered Baker as a schoolboy athlete, had three decades in with the man. The old saw applied: Relationships are everything. Baker did not want media in his office, but it was nothing specifically against them.

"Hey, I throw my friends out of the office," he said.

No other manager had decorated the cinder-block office, which featured a small adjoining bathroom and shower, as elaborately as Baker. He had to be influenced by the celebrity-worship office décor of Tommy Lasorda, his old Dodgers manager who maintained a photo gallery of every show-biz connection. But for Baker, the layout was the rhythm of his life in and out of baseball. Photos of his wife and son, Darren, hung prominently on the wall behind his desk. Higher up was a photo of his father, Johnnie B. Baker, Sr. The younger Baker was 57, but he still considered Dad the strong head of the family.

All over the other walls, Baker had photo reminders of his baseball journeys—photos of him with Henry Aaron and Willie Mays, a vintage shot of Baker the Dodgers outfielder with Harry Caray, then his musical idols like John Lee Hooker. A CD player was affixed to the wall next to the photos, while a stocked bookshelf stood to the other side of his desk.

Baker's access in Chicago always had been managed carefully. Yet, surprisingly, few of my colleagues had bothered to try to bust down those barriers and enter the head of a man who enjoyed an eclectic baseball career. Group interviews before and after games seemed to suit most scribes and microphone jockeys. Although Baker could be approached next to the cage during batting practice, few took advantage of such openings. The group or pack mentality of Cubs coverage prevailed, though. In the winter of 2005-06, Bruce Miles, Cubs beat writer for the suburban *Daily Herald*, authored a critical piece about Baker's reluctance

Dusty's Inner Sanctum

to "reach out" to local media. I had always believed individual media members (ala McGrath) had to reach out to managers and coaches—not the other way around.

Baker would not enjoy a repeat of his San Francisco Giants managing days in media relations. The Wrigley Field office was too small to accommodate the horde of cameras that accompanied pregame briefings. He started out in a scrum in the Cubs dugout. By 2005, he addressed reporters in the tiny, stifling interview room, which doubled as the Cubs' "weather room" with a computer tapped into radar. He was now big time, big market compared to the Bay Area.

There would be scarce opportunities to get to know the real Baker as he had been chronicled back in the Bay Area.

"Many media members took quickly to Dusty and his hip style," recalled *Chicago Tribune* White Sox beat writer Mark Gonzales, who covered Baker while formerly working at the *San Jose Mercury News*. "Jazz and blues music [would play in the manager's office] in the background as he would compare Willie McGee to Joe Cocker while inhaling a large bowl of oatmeal or a Styrofoam plate of pancakes. I really missed Dusty's morning sessions because he could always bring up something that was non-baseball related. He could tease some writers if he suspected they stayed out late the night before. He's a well-rounded man who loves managing but has a life besides baseball."

Gonzales said Baker rarely, if ever, blackballed a media person covering him.

"He jumped all over Joe Roderick [of the *Contra Costa Times*] in 1994 after Joe wrote a story that accurately reported that Salomon Torres left the team," Gonzales said. "Joe got the information by interviewing players on a charter flight to Cincinnati, which was a no-no but no one told him about this. Dusty aired Joe out behind closed doors but never held a grudge against him. There was some tension in later years between Dusty and Henry Schulman of the *San Francisco Chronicle*, but Henry did a good job of covering the team and did a great job of summing up Dusty's managing and personality skills in a 2005 interview with Teddy Greenstein [of the *Chicago Tribune*].

"I only found it tough to cover Dusty in games in Los Angeles because his former Dodgers teammates were his first priority. He would welcome the likes of Ron Cey, Rudy Law, Doug Rau [in Houston], and

Entangled In Ivy

Steve Yeager, while beat writers would have to wait sometimes until an hour before the game to talk to him. Sometimes, it felt like we were an aching tooth to him anytime we were in LA."

Baker would never enjoy anything resembling a cozy relationship with Chicago media. He would never be a Jim Riggleman, enthusiastically welcoming those who covered him. The Bay Area-style give-and-take scenes were only available in spring training in Baker's Mesa HoHoKam office, which featured a blender for his eclectic fruit concoctions. Otherwise, he could be a distant figure if a newshound did not employ some ingenuity and persistence.

So three years' worth of nibbling around the edges at the batting cage and informal chats in the dugout after Baker's pregame talk, while the beat writers usually congregated in a group on the field, finally paid off in the office chat. Amazingly, Baker never held any lasting grudges against me over some tough—or maybe in his view, disrespectful—questioning over the years. Most of the time, Baker deflected the impact of such queries, answering through verbal misdirection, homilies, public relations prattle, or even throwing the question back in the reporter's lap. He possessed a silver tongue.

"You know why they call you Rev. Johnnie B. Baker? Because many preacher men are fast talkers, slick guys," I told Baker by the cage one morning.

"Well, this is a slick town," he replied.

When Baker old chum Wendell Kim committed the mother of all third-base coaching boners in sending slow-footed catcher Damian Miller into a sure out at home in a 2003 game against the White Sox, the manager defended the decision as being aggressive. Similar answers came forth until one day in 2004, after the Cubs had repeatedly stumbled and bumbled on the base-paths. "Do you think this team needs a remedial course in base-running?" I asked Baker in the group session before a night game.

He objected to the word "remedial," visualizing, perhaps, the cone-capped dunce sitting in the corner. During the game, both Aramis Ramirez and Corey Patterson committed base-path blunders in the same inning. The next morning, I was about to open my mouth in the group session when Baker pre-empted me. "You're not going to ask that remedial stuff again, are you?" he fired away.

Dusty's Inner Sanctum

After a brief pause, never a great ad-libber, I verbally blurted out: "What do you want me to call it, Little League?"

"Now you're out of line," was his shocked comeback. Reporter George Ofman of all-sports WSCR-AM fed that tape back to the station, and the exchange was played for three consecutive days.

Maybe the aggressive stance struck a chord in Baker, as did my fondness for baseball history, which many other sportswriters and players seemed to abhor. I began to sidle up to Baker behind the cage for assorted comments and small talk. Only a couple of months after the "remedial base-running" dustup, in August 2004, I approached Baker to get one comment about the growing dilemma of dropping Sammy Sosa from cleanup to sixth in the batting order. That hit the hot button. Baker pulled me aside, farther away from the cage, and gave me 10 minutes of "A" material. In the same location 10 months later, Baker admitted that he would not be upset if his contract wasn't extended prior to the 2006 season.

All these encounters with Baker were short-form. Requests to do an elongated interview in the office had never gone anywhere until mid-summer 2006. Baker said he didn't like how short bursts of his consciousness, or "excerpts," were misconstrued or twisted. Long-form, unabridged chats were better suited for what he had to say. I finally got the go-ahead as the Cubs stumbled badly early summer. A momentary thought crossed my mind that Baker was saying hello when it was time to say good-bye.

He disabused me of that notion when he began chatting on the office couch next to me. Talk of his dismissal filled the newspapers and airwaves, yet Baker acted as if he had an undistracted tenure ahead of him. He always looks at his glass as half-full. A few weeks after our chat, on August 4, 2006, with the Cubs 45-63, 14 games out of first and about 10 games off the wild-card pace, he refused to pack in the season. He was asked if he believed the Cubs were in the wild-card hunt. "We still got action," he said, recycling a Baker phrase more commonly used for a rally in a game.

Two weeks previously, I asked if the Cubs' interminable losing ways were like a tiger that couldn't be tamed.

"I think so," he said. "Nobody ever thought Boston could be tamed. Everything can be tamed. Just because everything has been gobbled up here, you don't quit throwing stuff at it. Sooner or later, you're going to throw stuff and throw stuff, and he won't be able to gobble 'em up. Then you'll be able to tame him and ride him."

So was Baker the guy who could tame the tiger?

"I hope so. That's why I came here," he said. "I still believe that's why I was sent here. I still believe that. If not, I would have left before if I didn't think I was the guy to do it. I could have [walked away]. A lot of people might have been happy, a lot of people might have thought I was forced out. I still believe the way I believe when I first got here. It's tough and gotten tougher the last couple of years with injuries and personnel changes—but you deal with it."

Baker had inferior facilities with which to try to elevate the Cubs. Again, he preferred not to whine.

"It's tougher if you get injuries," he said. "Our training facility is smaller than most. Most teams have two cages—one for the visitors. Everybody knows it's difficult, but that's the beauty and the challenge of it all. The challenge of it all is to overcome whatever it is and bring a winner here. That's why I came here; that's why I remain here. I rise to challenges. I know what I believe.

"Are you going to get tired of me someday? Maybe. But at this point right now, I got a job to do, and I go out there every day and do the best job I can do with the team I have."

After general manager Jim Hendry's ardent courtship of his services in the fall of 2002, Baker's hiring was almost universally lauded in Chicago. Tendered a $14-million, four-year contract, Baker, the "player's manager," was perceived as a man who could lure top-flight talent to the Cubs. Logically, it was assumed that he'd be Hendry's right-hand man in evaluating talent. But when holes in the evaluation process began cropping up in 2005, questions about Baker's part also were asked. After all, Tony La Russa is perceived to have a major say in the acquisition of talent for the Cardinals, the Cubs' archrival and a seemingly perennial contender. I cited La Russa as a member of the "brain trust" or "kitchen cabinet" of his organization when I asked Baker about his Cubs duties. Since Hendry was lacking front-office help, too—such as an assistant general manager and a senior baseball advisor—I inquired whether his boss possessed enough help to properly evaluate talent.

Dusty's Inner Sanctum

"I don't know that," Baker explained. "I didn't know that in San Francisco. I didn't know half the scouts there. Rarely do you get together as a group; and when you do, you still don't know half the people there. I have enough stuff to take care of here down here, in the shop so to speak. I'm the shop foreman down here. Jim has enough to take care of up there and down here. I am an advisor and consultant [to Hendry], but I don't know all the players out there for trades. I don't know the players in the American League. If I know the talent, I'd recommend this guy and that guy and that guy. Sometimes you can't get *that* guy. It's easier for people to come here because people want to come play for teams that I'm on. I've heard that many times. I'm not the one making that up.

"There's no way I know everybody in the American League. I know most of the players I see in the National League. You can't tell watching somebody one or two games."

Even though former team president Andy MacPhail had periodically stated a conservative management philosophy, Baker refused to involve himself in affairs out of his perceived jurisdiction, and couldn't say whether those philosophies had hindered the job he'd done or the Cubs' progress.

"That's not my department," he said. "What goes on upstairs is not my department. I don't micromanage; I don't run the whole organization. I'm an advisor to Jim if I know the subject matter; I run the clubhouse; I run the field; I run the team downstairs. That's my job."

Baker was, by no means, the perfect manager. For a literate, well-rounded man beyond baseball, he was surprisingly set in his ways of handling personnel on the field. Baker could not easily change his routines, lineups, and game strategies—the latter of which were never perceived as a strong point. If he had confidence in a veteran player, he'd be slow to remove him from the lineup, even long after the vet fell into a slump. Yet, throughout his Cubs tenure, circumstances conspired to disrupt any fruits born by his positive attitude. Somehow, his laid-back West Coast style did not sit well with most Cubs fans and skeptical media once the team's fortunes nosedived—whether it was Game 6 and 7 of the 2003 National League Championship Series, in the final week of the 2004 season, much of 2005 and all of 2006.

However, as the gears of his mind turned on his office couch, Baker again looked at the bright side. A religious man, he kissed his crucifix in the dugout when good things happened. Baker believed he had a calling to come to rescue the Cubs, although he protested he was mere mortal man: "I'm Dusty, not the Messiah."

"Ever since I've been here," he said, "most things that have happened adversely, my name seems to come up one way or another—whether I've had anything to do with it or not. But most of the time, stuff is thrown at the strong; stuff is thrown at those who believe more than those who don't believe. People try to bring those who believe down to not believe. I refuse to let it happen no matter what people feel."

Baker was defensive on one point—his $14 million, four-year contract. He simply did not like his paycheck brought up in conjunction with his work.

"The one thing I get tired of hearing, the one thing they always bring up, is my salary," he said. "I never hear anybody else's salary. I never hear Tony La Russa's salary; I never heard Bobby Cox's salary. There must be something out there. ... I don't want to call it envy. How long did it take for me to get to this point? Fifteen years. I started at $45,000 as a [Giants] coach. And when I started as [Giants] manager, I was at $200,000."

With the tiger chomping at him repeatedly, Baker needed all the faith that he could muster. One day around the cage, Baker he said he had to deal with "10 times the bullshit" he expected when he first came to Chicago. Jim Hendry and others had cautioned Baker that he would take some shots. Fans who held up signs "In Dusty We Trusty" in 2003 started turning on him when the 2004 Cubs began to underachieve in what was supposed to be a slam-dunk march to the World Series. Somehow, he brought out the worst in people. Both Baker and reliever LaTroy Hawkins received racial hate mail. Having experienced firsthand the horrors of hatred directed at teammate Henry Aaron during his 1973-74 drive to overtake Babe Ruth's home-run record, Baker surprisingly tried to turn the other cheek. Both he and Hawkins asked me not to discuss the written diatribes. Baker's reasoning? "You can't change their minds, and you'd only make it worse by publicizing them." The same haters set right-fielder Jacque Jones in their sites when he got off to a slow start at the plate, in the field, and on the base-paths in the 2006 season.

The critics even jumped Baker for the presence of young son Darren, who first gained fame over his near-collision at home plate during the 2002 World Series. Darren had the run of the ballpark when he visited on school vacation and occasional long weekends. Sometimes he'd climb into his father's lap during press conferences. Cynics suggested Baker used his son as a prop to deflect tough questions. Baker did not take offense at such logic, but explained that as a prostate cancer survivor in his mid-50s he wanted to spend as much time as possible with his child. Actually, Darren was engaging. One time, Paul Sullivan of the *Chicago Tribune* dropped a $5 bill under the dugout bench. Only a pint-sized human could retrieve the fin. Baker and the writers jokingly debated a fair finders' fee for Darren as he scrambled under the seat.

Amazingly, as less vitriolic types called for Baker's hide, basing their attack on his merit (or lack thereof)—not his race—in 2006, he believed that a decent chunk of the Cubs constituency supported him.

"There's also quite a few people out there who believe the way I believe," he said in his office. "As much as you hear some people against you, there's probably an equal amount of people who are for you, and know what the truth is, and what's real. People who want you up on the cross are usually more vocal and louder than people who don't. That's baseball. I love what I'm doing. I love my job."

The greatest charge against Baker—the prime reason he was nailed to the baseball cross—was the perceived overworking of Kerry Wood and Mark Prior before both fireballers broke down due to injuries from 2004 through 2006. Along with Carlos Zambrano and Matt Clement, Baker had four starters in 2003-04 who ran up extremely high pitch counts. Just reciting raw numbers, Baker appeared to abuse the starters. But he took his biggest false rap on this issue. In reality, Wood and Prior burned themselves out.

"I think he gets a lot of unfair knocks about a lot of things, but that [pitcher handling] especially," Dick Pole, Baker's bench coach with the Cubs and Greg Maddux's original big-league guru, said in 2005. "I read how he abuses his pitchers and lets them go so many pitches."

Wood, Prior, Zambrano, and Clement often ran up their counts in five to seven innings. Wood completed just four games in the 2003 regular season, while Prior went the distance only three times. In one 2003 start, Prior struck out 16 Brewers in eight innings. He had enough. Baker took him out and put in closer Joe Borowski, who promptly served up a game-winning, two-run homer by Geoff Jenkins onto Sheffield

Avenue. Even with those modest complete-game numbers, Baker was fingered as promoting burnout.

But the only way Baker could have "protected" the quartet was to have pulled them after five innings, six at the most. He found himself in a damned-if-you-do, damned-if-you-don't situation. If Baker protected the starters, he'd burn out his bullpen quickly by daily summoning them in the middle innings. If he let them go nine innings, he'd have been roasted alive for allowing them to throw 130 to perhaps 150 pitches.

A combination of the lack of fine control, almost other-worldly stuff that caused defensive hitters to foul off a scores of pitches in each at-bat, batters taking pitches to try to tire out the starters, and the sheer number of pitches required to amass healthy strikeout totals added to the pitch counts in short order. The Cubs foursome, if anything, was victim to its own collective talent.

Zambrano ran up more pitches faster than either of his better-known teammates in 2003-04. He had 12 games in which he threw 110 or more pitches in a five-to-eight-inning outing in 2003, then 19 more in 2004. On June 26, 2004, Zambrano threw 128 pitches against the White Sox in six innings. He also threw 122 pitches against the Athletics in 6 ⅔ innings on June 20; 123 against the White Sox in 6 ⅓ innings on July 2; 125 against the Astros in 5 ⅔ innings on August 28; and 124 against the Reds in 6 ⅓ innings on September 27. The only negative from Zambrano came after a May 8, 2005, start against the Phillies. Baker let Zambrano throw a complete game with 136 pitches. Before his next start, Zambrano said his arm felt like "concrete." But he was not injured and made all his starts the rest of the season.

Wood's heaviest workload was a whopping 141 pitches—but in only seven innings, against the Cardinals on May 10, 2003. During '03, Wood had 19 appearances of five-to-eight innings' duration in which he threw 110 or more pitches. That dropped to eight in 2004 due to a triceps injury that caused Wood to miss two months.

"Do you blame the manager or Woody?" Clement asked. "Do you blame Woody for throwing 100 mph on his 115th pitch? How awesome was Woody's arm?" Clement added that the dugout would have been up in arms, figuratively, had one of the starters been cruising, even dominating, at the 110-pitch mark and Baker arbitrarily pulled him.

Dusty's Inner Sanctum

Larry Rothschild, Baker's pitching coach during his entire tenure, confirmed Clement's analysis in 2005.

"They'll throw a lot of pitches early on, then settle in and throw very well in the fifth, sixth, and seventh," Rothschild said of the Prior-Wood-Zambrano troika when healthy. "They'll be at 115 pitches after six innings, but they're throwing the ball very well. The dilemma is, do you take them out when they're throwing the best in the course of the game? It's happened in 80 percent of their good starts."

Baker was particularly hounded for riding Prior hard down the stretch in 2003. The right-hander's regular-season high-pitch number was 133—in just 6 ⅔ innings—against the Pirates on September 27. Prior also threw 133 in his next start, a complete-game victory over the Braves in the NL Division Series. Prior had 11 games in which he went five to eight innings and threw at least 110 pitches.

Only on Prior could anyone possibly second-guess Baker, said Clement. His reasoning was that Wood had more experience as a five-year veteran, while Zambrano, physically more strapping than his rotation mates, proved he could handle such a heavy load without harm.

"I'm not saying he overused him," Clement said of Prior. "But he was under 25, had such great stuff, and you had to treat him with kid gloves. I would have been cautious."

With his background as an aggressive hitter called "Scald" and a hitting coach, Baker had the stereotype of a ham-handed approach to handling his starters. But in a dugout conversation in 2005, Baker said he had developed a system over the years. If an average pitcher goes through two men-on-base jams earlier, the third time won't be the charm; Baker will consider pulling him.

"But Zambrano and Prior can handle three, four, five stressful situations where the average guy doesn't," he said.

"You know, if you're in the sixth or seventh, and you've walked a couple of guys, given up three or four runs, or had some tough innings, you're close," Wood said in 2005. "But when you've gotten 20 of 22 guys out going into the eighth inning, it's a little easier."

Baker also said he never uses a one-size-fits-all approach to rationing their workload. In San Francisco, he believed Livan Hernandez and Russ Ortiz were capable of going "135 to 140 pitches." In contrast, lefty Kirk

Rueter "would go 85 to 90 pitches, and he'd lose it so quickly you'd have to get him out of there."

Wood was in full agreement with Baker's limits.

"If it's been smooth, you haven't had to pitch out of jams and have a rhythm, you can throw 125 that day," he said. "There's times where I said I could continue to go and they [Baker and Rothschild] both said no. There were more of those times than where I said I had enough and they wanted me to go back out there."

Baker did not develop the pitcher stress test by guesswork. He said he learned from ol' master Tommy John during his Dodgers playing days.

"When I was playing, I was always talking to pitchers, always trying to learn how they think to be a better hitter," he said. "I talked to Red Adams [longtime Dodgers pitching coach], but who I really talked to the most was Tommy John. He told me, 'If a guy's a seven-inning pitcher and gets into trouble in the third or fourth, he turns into a six-inning pitcher.'"

Baker even reached up to baseball Valhalla for counsel.

"I always talked to Sandy Koufax, every chance I got," he said of 1979-vintage meetings with the southpaw immortal, then the Dodgers' roving pitching instructor.

Even after he handled brickbats thrown at his record with the pitchers, Baker got no breaks in dealing with his personal area of expertise—hitting. The Cubs had too much power for their own good in 2004, and not enough two years later. But the common theme through Baker's tenure—and in fact extending all the way back to the 1980s—was lack of patience in the lineup. The 2006 Cubs ranked last in runs scored and walks taken in the National League. Two years earlier, lack of walks negated the value of four 30-homer producers, and came back to haunt Baker in the season's final week, when the power was turned off and the Cubs had no other way to scratch out runs as their playoff chances drained away.

The Cubs were virtually the anti-*Moneyball* team—the antithesis of Athletics GM Billy Beane's philosophy of extreme patience at the plate, of taking pitches 'til it hurt. Conversations were forced onto that topic in Baker's office in 2006. He did not dodge the issue, though, as he did in some postgame sessions, where those questioning his hitters' lack of patience were answered with statements about hitting aggressively. Baker

Dusty's Inner Sanctum

seemed to preach a middle ground between *Moneyball* and whacking away at the first or second pitch.

"Everybody doesn't have the same eye up there, that's No. 1," he said. "No. 2: You've got to pick a certain pitcher to have that philosophy against—because if you pick a pitcher who is throwing strikes, you're down 0-and-1 from the very beginning. No. 3, you've got to have guys who aren't prone to the strikeout in order to get deep in the count. If you've got guys prone to the strikeout, the deeper they get in the count, the better chance they have to strike out. Every time you strike out, you have no chance to do anything."

"I had Chili Davis ask me years ago, 'How do you walk?' Everybody doesn't know how to walk. You walk, basically, by being selective, by zoning in or out—depending on what the guy's repertoire of pitches is—and the ability to foul off pitches that aren't good pitches to put into play. Just going up there taking isn't the answer.

"I saw Minnesota versus [Mark] Buehrle, and they were swinging at the first pitch because they were first-pitch strikes. Now, if Buehrle was a guy like [Tom] Glavine, throwing first-pitch balls that were near-strikes, then it would be a totally different story. You've got to have the right pitcher, the right person, the right batter up there, and the right philosophy. The philosophy changes per pitcher."

The prime example was control-challenged Rockies pitcher Jason Jennings' victory over the Cubs on May 26, 2005. Jennings threw just 86 pitches in seven-plus innings as the Cubs were retired consistently on the first or second pitch. I had never seen Baker more upset over his hitters' approach after that game. He revealed that he had asked Todd Walker and Neifi Perez to take more pitches against Jennings. Dipping into his memory bank, if Jennings had issued so many walks previously, why didn't the Cubs work the count?

"The thing about it, he had changed his approach that day," Baker said 14 months later. "Before, he was nibbling. Last time we saw him on film, he was nibbling. That day, he was coming at guys, but he was coming at guys with near-strikes. Sometimes they're on; sometimes you're off. There's no one definitive way or answer. I'm not a big Billy [Beane]-Ball guy. I know you need walks. Walks put pitchers in the stretch and advance runners. I understand [extra runners]. Early in the year, Juan Pierre was trying to walk. Every time, he was 0-and-2 because everyone knew he was taking the first pitch. Juan Pierre had to make an adjustment to start swinging at some balls early in the count, then the second go-around, they would start nibbling, figuring he was swinging. He wasn't taking anymore. That's where there's a game inside the game. Sometimes the pitcher doesn't have good control."

Baker believes a lineup can be more patient—but not to the extreme of the Athletics.

"The A's haven't won big," he said. "They got to the playoffs, basically, by trying to walk with no speed and depending on homers to try to win close games. Most of the games they lose in the playoffs are close games. To me, I like a full game. If I could have some guys who have speed, some contact guys … mix in three power hitters … mix in some guys who have the ability to walk."

The Cubs once had that lineup—their 1984 NL East title team. The "Daily Double" of Bob Dernier and Ryne Sandberg set the table and combined for 77 stolen bases. No. 3 hitter Gary Matthews, a close Baker friend, was almost a second leadoff man with an NL-leading 103 walks. Keith Moreland, Leon Durham, Ron Cey, and Jody Davis then handled RBI duties. Six players had 80 or more RBIs. The lack of institutional memory of team management about the '84 Cubs probably hurts the team two decades-plus later.

"No, I was not really aware [of the '84 Cubs' statistics]," Baker said. "I was aware of them, but I didn't think of them as the perfect lineup for this ballpark. You were here; I was in San Francisco at that time; and I wasn't really keeping up with the Cubs at that time. The teams that I was on—in L.A.—we had pitching, bullpen, right-left; [Davey] Lopes' and [Bill] Russell's speed at the top; Reggie Smith walking 100 times in the middle; Steve Garvey, Ron Cey, and myself, Rick Monday. We had three center fielders: Reggie Smith, myself, Monday. Also, we had Ken Landreaux. That's the kind of team that could beat you 2-1—fundamentally sound. We could bunt when necessary, hit and run when necessary, or hit the ball out of the ballpark. We could beat you 10-9 or 2-1.

"In order to have a perfect team, it takes a while to build. It's going to take a lot of finances in modern times. And you have to have it integrated between some minor-league call-ups, some players who were here before, some free agents. You have to call on a number of resources.

Dusty's Inner Sanctum

It's hard to bring it all up out of yours [farm system] because nobody has that many. It's hard also to get other free agents because you don't how they were trained to play baseball. Certain organizations are more fundamentally sound than others. You get kids out of Minnesota, most of the time they run the bases good, and they're fundamentally sound. You get guys out of other organizations, they might be slug-and-hit organizations, like it was when I was with the Braves."

Two weeks after the office chat, Baker supervised the switch of rookie shortstop Ronny Cedeno to second to accommodate slick-fielding shortstop Cesar Izturis' arrival from the Dodgers via the Greg Maddux trade. Such a move was a Baker rarity. He never liked to move a player to another position midseason, protesting that the "ball will always find you." For an old hitter, he was an adherent to putting the best defensive team on the field as possible at the sacrifice of hitting.

"Where I had reservations is where guys hadn't played there before," he said.

Baker's line in the sand hurt the Cubs in July 2004, after Aramis Ramirez had been lost for two weeks due to a groin injury. The manager opted to put favorite utility player Ramon Martinez at third and good-field, no-stick Rey Ordonez at short. The entire left side of the infield was impotent at the plate. Meanwhile, certified No. 2 hitter Mark Grudzielanek had to sit when Todd Walker played second. Grudzielanek had formerly been a good-fielding shortstop and even played third in his rookie year with the Montreal Expos in 1995. He said he was willing to shift to third to get his and Walker's bats in the lineup at the same time, given a couple of days of workouts at the position. However, Grudzielanek added, no one asked him to move.

Nobody asked Baker to make a preposterous position shift ala Leo Durocher, who shifted third baseman Ron Santo to left and second baseman Glenn Beckert to center for cameo appearances. But the Cubs needed both hitting and on-base percentage. Grudzielanek knew his way around the left side of the infield, but Baker believed he had gotten used to the mechanics of playing second for a long time.

"It was his throwing," he said. "I was worried about him making the longer throw from shortstop instead of across his body at second."

Forget about his strategy and hitting-coach background. The main attraction of Baker when Jim Hendry hired him was his "players' manager" talents. He would keep a clubhouse on an even keel emotionally. He somehow kept quarreling personalities like Barry Bonds and Jeff Kent—at one point at each other's throats—productive and focused.

"Dusty's greatest attribute as a manager is that he treats the players fairly," Matt Clement said. "He doesn't sell the players out."

Player complaints about Baker were few and far between during his Cubs tenure. Reliever Scott Williamson had to backtrack when he publicly stated that he was not one of Baker's "boys" after becoming disenchanted with how he was used in mid-summer 2006. He was soon traded to San Diego. To be sure, Baker had his favorites, those who stayed in the lineup after they stopped producing. One player who was rumored to be on the outs with the manager, though, thought fondly of him. Infielder Jerry Hairston Jr., underutilized during his one and a half seasons as a Cub, asked me to relay greetings to Baker after he was traded to the Rangers. There would be little miscommunication as in the Baylor days. When Clement was dropped from the rotation with a month to go in the 2004 season, he did not find out directly from Baker.

"I went into Dusty's office to ask what was going on," Clement said. "He apologized and said it wasn't supposed to come out that way."

The flaw in accurately determining his team's mood may have come in the same Baker style that keeps media and other hangers-on from his office. He generally stayed in and around his office when the Cubs were not taking batting practice. He usually did not flit about the clubhouse or trainer's room, kibitzing Ozzie Guillen-style. He seemed to want players to police themselves.

Not every player was capable of such self-discipline. Left fielder Moises Alou had been a habitually late clubhouse arrival with all his previous teams—Montreal, Florida, and Houston. He continued his tardy ways through three different Cubs managers—Baker, Bruce Kimm, and Baylor. When a 4 p.m. time for players to be dressed was written on a clubhouse easel board, Alou often sauntered in as late as 4:20 p.m.

"No. 1, I never saw that," Baker said of Alou arriving late. "My office is up here. 'Mo' don't walk in this door here. You're probably down there in the main clubhouse. You're proper to ask this. You have to remember. I tell my players, especially my real good players, 'It's okay to bend the rules, just don't break 'em.' I was a pretty good player myself, and

Dusty's Inner Sanctum

[Tommy] Lasorda told us the same thing. 'Mo' was 'fashionably' late, according to you. Now, when 'Mo' goes out there to play, who's a better player than 'Mo'? On certain things, you allow your stars and key players to bend the rules, but not break them. Not on the field—there's only one way to play the game."

Trouble was, third baseman Aramis Ramirez broke the rules of team play on the field. The television cameras did not lie. They caught Ramirez loping out of the batter's box on extra-base hits repeatedly since he was traded to the Cubs in 2003. The corker came in a 2006 game in Milwaukee, when Ramirez moved in slow motion on a triple that banged off the right-field wall. Ramirez had to turn on the jets when he realized the ball was still in play. Right-fielder Geoff Jenkins made a quick recovery and threw a bullet to nail Ramirez at third. Had he been running hard all the way, Ramirez probably would have had a triple.

Baker finally acknowledged afterward Ramirez had not been running hard. Yet, in his office, he claimed Ramirez was putting out more than he had with the Pirates, his old team.

"Aramis is running and hustling a whole lot more now than he was when we first got him," Baker said. "He knows it, and he's conscious of it. But sometimes, when you're doing something for so long and people let you get away with it for so long, it becomes second nature. That was a rap before he even got here. We have a fine box, a kangaroo court box down there, and every time this happens, there's a fine."

So was Ramirez summoned to the very same seat in which I perched to receive a lecture from Baker? Other players, too?

"Enough times," he said. "It's nobody's business who sits in this seat in my office. That's how you lose other players [to rip players in front of teammates]. Some guys operate that way; I don't operate that way. Go down there and ask them. They don't want to come up in my office. Go ask Rod Beck; go ask anybody I had on my teams. If you come in my office, they'll say, 'Oh man, they've got to go to the principal's office.'

"Most times, if you come in this office, it's something I've got to discuss with you baseball-wise on the good side, or a personal problem, or it's something you've screwed up on the baseball field out there, which I don't really tolerate. I'm not going to hoop and holler and yell out there in the dugout, and unnecessarily chastise everybody for the reasons of one guy. It also happened to me a few times. 'Why don't you call me in instead of talking around the subject and singling me out in front of the whole team?'"

To cut down on such on- and off-the-field behavior, perhaps the Cubs had to do a better job scouting character—the sixth tool, as defined by the Atlanta Braves, the model stable, disciplined, fundamentally sound organization. But, in Baker's mind, the type of player who could thrive in Atlanta is not the same as the one who could handle Chicago.

"Everybody's not the same," Baker said. "The thing about the Braves is Atlanta's a whole lot different than Chicago. There's a whole lot different pressures in Atlanta than there is in Chicago. It's hard to compare Atlanta with Chicago—different towns, different needs, different hungers for the teams. There's so much history here. Atlanta doesn't have the history we have here. They don't have the 100 years since the last time this happened, that happened. When you talk Chicago Cubs with anybody who knows the Cubs, they're going to mention 15, 20 key dates in time. When you talk with somebody from Atlanta, they're going to mention one or two. It's a totally different character."

So then how did Baker define "character" as a sixth tool?

"No. 1, it's hard to find five tools," he said. "That's very difficult. I think there's about 10 of those in the game, basically. Character is that person with that desire to win with his game being at the top of his list. A lot of times you don't know until a guy is there already. The Braves have made mistakes, too. They'll fool you in the beginning. What you see on the other side of the field is totally different from what you get on your side of the field.

"You think, 'Man, I thought this guy was tough.' Then you get him on your side, and every time he slides or does whatever he does, he comes up hurt. Or another guy you thought was soft, you get him on your side, you find out this guy's hard—this guy's a player.

"You're looking for ballplayers—not just a hitter, not just a fielder, not just a runner. You're looking for a ballplayer that has the capabilities to take advantage of every edge that he can take advantage of whether it's an extra base, whether it's an overthrow, whether he cuts a ball off, the little things. I think we get so caught up in the numbers, the stats, we lose track of the little things that aren't even in the stats. Advancing runners, giving yourself up, these are things that are noticed and kept track of, but very rarely are."

Dusty's Inner Sanctum

The clock was ticking on two fronts. Baker would usher me out of his office in a couple of minutes. And his time as a manager was rumored to be down to a game or two. Time to ask an obvious, direct question. I mentioned Andy MacPhail's 1994 statement: "It's a failing of the front office when you fire a manager." Would Baker believe that if he and the Cubs had to part in the near future?

He answered without either hesitation or seeming trepidation.

"No," Baker said. "I'm not going to blame the front office. If anything, you think about things. 'Why didn't it work?' Then you look at it realistically. You don't like it. I've never been in that situation, but I'm not going to blame anybody.

"Sometimes it's circumstance. Sometimes somebody has to be the scapegoat. Sometimes you can do as well as you can and do everything right, and it still doesn't work. I know in my heart there's no way in heck we'd be in this situation if all the circumstances hadn't happened over the course of this year from the time we went to spring training. If it happens, life goes on. They'll get another manager. The clock keeps ticking. Life goes on. You'll have to find something else to do. You'll be down for a little while. Then, you'll have to pick yourself right up, and no matter what, dust yourself off and keep right on steppin'."

The next day, Jim Hendry announced Baker would remain as Cubs manager the rest of the 2006 season. The man who supposedly loved his veterans was breaking in a kiddie corps of starting pitchers and key position players. He would enjoy only a stay of execution. By season's end, Baker seemed resigned to his fate. On October 2, 2006—less than four years after Hendry ardently courted him as the man who would jump-start the Cubs—Dusty was told he would not be offered a new contract.

Baker offered a few words of thanks before he exited stage right. Like Don Baylor before him, his true feelings on his Cubs experience would be held close for the time being. The mellow fellow now yielded to the fiery guy, Lou Piniella. The merry-go-round in the manager's office continued with no end in clear sight.

seven

THE MISSING-MAN FORMATION

THE SURROUNDING Wrigleyville area was a weekday-off day, quiet at this early September noon hour. The kids had gone back to school, their parents correspondingly trudged back to work, and many fewer of both groups thus planned to go to the night game with the Pittsburgh Pirates seven hours later.

Thus Bar Louie, a popular hangout for the Cubs front-office crowd on the east side of Clark Street, one-half block south of Wrigley Field, had similarly slow business when Jim Hendry strode to a back table, ordered a diet soda and a salad, and began chatting about how he goes about his business as Cubs general manager. As always, he produced his cell phone—Hendry's third "ear"—to be ready for action.

Over the next 90 minutes, the cell would ring just four times, all but one call on ball-club business. That's a light load for Hendry, who had traded slugger Phil Nevin to the Minnesota Twins on the same phone days earlier while standing in the parking lot of son John's youth football practice field in suburban Park Ridge. He said he once made three business calls on Christmas Day.

The cell stayed off seven years earlier when Hendry met me at Ron Santo's old restaurant in Park Ridge, where he discussed how he was attempting to rejuvenate the Cubs' long-moribund farm system; how he preached winning to the minor-leaguers he then supervised; how the general manager's job—at the time held by Ed Lynch—was considered one of the most attractive in the majors.

While in a good mood, Hendry was by no means at his jibe-filled best. Many pregame sessions by the Cubs dugout featured the GM roasting sportswriters for their choices of apparel, as if the wash-and-wear Hendry was one to talk. He could be as rumpled as those covering him. If anyone suggested he was corporate-ized as a stuffy Tribune Co. loyalist, they were way off-target. On hot days, Hendry's shirt could field growing perspiration stains even though he had grown up in near-tropical Dunedin, Florida. He would not be a clone of Don Grenesko, the former Cubs president and Tribune Co. suit who'd wear a crisp, long-sleeved dress shirt and tie firmly clasped at the neck on sultry Wrigley Field afternoons without showing a bead of sweat. It was as if Grenesko had his sweat glands removed to assist in cold-blooded management of the team. In contrast, sightings of a tie-wearing Hendry were uncommon. He usually wore blousy, open-necked, short-sleeved cotton shirts.

That seven-year gap between chats in an eatery might have seemed like 20 with all that had gone down with the Cubs, baseball, and the outside world ever since. One thing was certain. The atmosphere at Bar Louie's and the surrounding digs was far from funereal, but it still was nothing like Hendry had ever experienced in 15 years in pro baseball. The Cubs were spiraling down with no parachute to one of their worst seasons in the past 40 years. They may have fielded the largest payroll—$94 million—ever for a last-place team.

Manager Dusty Baker got the lion's share of zingers for the 2006 debacle. But Hendry drew plenty of fire on his own, only three years after making enough good moves—and perhaps leaving out one or more key transactions—to put the Cubs within five outs of the World Series. Most of the criticism focused on a second straight winter of roster construction that hardly measured up to the standards of Hendry's first two years as general manager.

A crucial subtext was present. The reasons why Hendry should suddenly misfire, not complete the job, and leave the roster with obvious holes drew attention to the story behind the story.

While unloading a no-longer-welcome Sammy Sosa consumed his off-season, Hendry opened the 2005 season with capable backup Todd Hollandsworth as the starting left fielder. He managed to come up with

The Missing-Man Formation

an aging Jeromy Burnitz to replace Sosa in right field. In addition, with LaTroy Hawkins obviously ill-suited as a closer and Joe Borowski questionable to return to his 2003 effectiveness, the Cubs were left vulnerable in the ninth inning. Middle relief was also shaky going into the season and got worse as the months wore on.

The roster setup for 2006 was even worse. Glendon Rusch and Jerome Williams were over-evaluated as rotation replacements for the oft-injured Kerry Wood and Mark Prior, whose recovery abilities were also over-evaluated. Although Hendry got a decent left-handed bat for right field in ex-Minnesota Twin Jacque Jones, his scouts did not adequately pick up Jones' severe throwing problems. Hendry rated Jones as a No. 6 hitter, but he left a hole for a run producer behind Derrek Lee and Aramis Ramirez at No. 5, forcing Jones to bat uncomfortably higher in the order. The shortstop's job was handed to Ronny Cedeno with no competition, and Cedeno stumbled badly two months into the season.

Behind the scenes, among discerning media and baseball people, the question was being asked: did Hendry, as aggressive as he was, have enough help in the front office to make enough moves at the right time and properly evaluate talent? And closely related was the speculation that Hendry's front-office "brain trust" was not up to standards of the more successful big-league franchises.

There had long been chatter that the Cubs had the fewest scouts in the game, but the math disproved that claim. They had no less—and in some cases likely had more—at the big-league level than most other franchises.

However, the sheer numbers and front-office roster did display one inescapable fact. Hendry lacked perhaps one extra baseball man—and maybe two—who could serve as a supplementary talent evaluator. He already possessed enough numbers crunchers and contract processors in the office. But he appeared to need extra help who could offer the proverbial second opinion and ensure all other teams' front offices would be covered in complementing his own relationships with general managers. That's a big field to cover—29 other teams. The job of reaching out with the baseball tentacles seemed too big for one man.

Lacking on the Cubs' office roster was an assistant general manager's position, a common job with most other franchises. Interestingly, both Hendry and then-boss, former Cubs president Andy MacPhail, held assistant general managers positions in their careers—Hendry with the Cubs in 2000-02 and MacPhail with the Astros from 1982-85. While Twins general manager in the late 1980s and early 1990s, MacPhail employed Bob Gebhard as his assistant general manager, a position that has remained on the Minnesota front-office payroll ever since.

Further, the Cubs lacked No. 2 executives, usually labeled with an "assistant" title, to farm director Oneri Fleita and scouting chief Tim Wilken. Such positions were standard with other teams. MacPhail even held assistant farm director and assistant scouting director posts when he first broke into the game with the critically understaffed Cubs in the late 1970s. Fleita, a Cuban-American and former player for Hendry at Creighton University, also doubled as Latin American operations director, another position usually staffed with another individual with big-market, high-revenue teams.

The Cubs even worked a man short for five years in the burgeoning Pacific Rim scouting beat, which had produced an increasing flow of Japanese, Korean, and even Taiwanese players to other teams in the new millennium. Leon Lee, Derrek Lee's father, worked as Pacific Rim coordinator for four years before his 2001 departure. The Cubs did not fill his position, preferring to outsource the work to a consulting firm. Finally, after the 2006 season, native Canadian Steve Wilson, a left-handed pitcher on the 1989 Cubs NL East champions, was named Pacific Rim scout.

The bottom line on all of this had come about 14 months earlier in a Sunday morning conversation with MacPhail up in the Wrigley Field press-box lunchroom. Curious about the seeming problems with talent evaluation compared to the then-surging cross-town White Sox, I asked the then-head of Cubdom why the supposedly less-affluent South Siders had more front-office staff in both baseball operations and marketing than the Cubs.

"We're somewhat encumbered physically by the [lack of] space we have," MacPhail said initially, referring to Wrigley Field's tight quarters. The 2007 construction of a new building on the west side of the ballpark, which would have contained expanded office space, has been delayed.

MacPhail then said something astounding:

"The other part is, I would rather be one man too short than one man too heavy. People would like to be engaged, want to have areas that they're responsible to, and they're happier in some activity than having too many people with too few tasks, people fighting over who's doing what."

Desiring to run an understaffed front office and stating it publicly was truly surprising. I ran that statement—and the one about the squeeze on space at Wrigley Field—by an executive with another team, one that you could call fully staffed. He scratched his head as he spoke on condition of anonymity.

"I still don't understand that," he said of the "one man too short" concept. "I'm missing [on the idea] I'd rather be understaffed than overstaffed; for me, I'd rather be overstaffed then get rid of the people who aren't pulling their weight. You look at the other 29 clubs, after the GM, you usually see three guys: an assistant GM, a director of player personnel [scouting], and a farm director. Each [of the latter two positions] usually has someone behind them. Lack of space? The Cubs have some modern offices in Mesa [at spring-training headquarters]. And a big building [Tribune Tower] on Michigan Avenue has some offices."

I had backtracked—and had confirmed by Cubs sources—how the front-office staff had been cut from its Dallas Green-era peak, quickly reduced as soon as Tribune Company suits John Madigan, Don Grenesko, and Stanton Cook had seized control of the team following Green's ouster in late 1987. An assistant general manager's position was on staff for just four seasons ever since. And the farm system, in rapid decline once the late Gordon Goldsberry was sacked in 1988, did not have a No. 2 administrator in all the ensuing years. MacPhail merely continued a trend started a half-decade before his arrival as president in 1994.

The Cubs front office overall has been run very lean. Vice president's titles were handed out—to the general manager, business operations chief Mark McGuire, since-promoted marketing maven John McDonough, and more recently Mike Lufrano, community-relations chief and general counsel—as infrequently as player numbers were retired and run up the Wrigley Field flagpoles. The supposedly cash-strapped Milwaukee Brewers, in contrast, had some 10 vice presidents on their roster under owner-acting commissioner Bud Selig in the mid-1990s.

When he came over to run the Cubs, MacPhail discontinued the front-office structure he presided over as Twins general manager. Bob

Gebhard served as MacPhail's vice president of player personnel—"the same as an assistant GM," he said—for five years with the Twins before moving on to become the Colorado Rockies' first GM in 1992.

"We worked very closely together," said Gebhard, now an Arizona Diamondbacks scout. "He would contact clubs, and I would contact clubs. We shared ideas about players who would be available, who would help us. We talked it over. I maybe went out and saw that player or one of our scouts saw him. Andy was great to work for. He listened to everybody's opinion. I did as much background information possible on every player. The final decision was certainly his, but I was another source of gathering information for Andy."

A too-nosy author was not the only one asking about the lack of an assistant general manager to back up Hendry. Gary Hughes, the GM's own mentor and, along with Fleita, his top confidant, was inquisitive at one point after he came aboard in 2002 as special assistant to Hendry, charged with scouting both leagues in the western third of the country.

"What happened is, I asked him why he didn't have one [an assistant GM]," said Hughes, legendary in scouting circles and Falstaffian in stature. "Jim said he had Randy Bush [a special assistant hired in early 2005] and me."

And that's exactly what Hendry told me as his cell phone chimed on and off and a pair of salads was consumed.

"I don't look at that as a negative," he said. "I have plenty of staffing in the major-league scouting area, plenty of staffing in the amateur scouting area. We added Randy Bush. If you told me I could have added Randy Bush and Gary Hughes with the position he's in—or someone in the office to help me make phone calls—I would have taken Randy Bush and Gary Hughes any day."

But the definition of an assistant general manager goes beyond crunching numbers, shuffling reports and handling less-critical contracts. Just listen to Astros GM Tim Purpura, an Oak Lawn, Illinois, native who was the assistant GM behind predecessor Gerry Hunsicker, one of the most aggressive and creative traders of the late 1990s and turn of the millennium.

"The way baseball operations work: you divide up the teams, and there's certain teams you're assigned to, to keep in touch with during the course of the season," Purpura said. "The GM makes the deal. You do the footwork, the background work, get the feel for what's going on. Even with scouts, they'll get inaccurate information, so you try to whittle down what's real from what's not.

"There's no doubt about it. Whether it's contracts, rules, watching the waiver wire, complying, there are big pieces of that assistant GM's job. When you step into that GM's job, things go fast; you got so much going on that you don't have the time to spend on the details. You become more of a big-picture guy."

Purpura's model of an assistant GM is a talent evaluator and relationship guy. ESPN baseball analyst Steve Phillips had the same blueprint when he served as Mets GM; Phillips' assistant was allowed to talk to other clubs.

Hendry was scout-based, putting a lot of emphasis on coverage by Hughes, Keith Champion (center of the country, but replaced by Paul Weaver in fall 2006), and Ken Kravec (east), with assistance from Bush. Former GM Ed Lynch also is listed as an assistant to Hendry, but he's usually limited to scouting games out of Phoenix and working spring training.

"Not to be disparaging to the other assistant GMs, I feel I have those kinds of people but with different assignments," Hendry said, his cell phone silent for a spell. "Gary Hughes is at the ballpark every day. He's a relationship guy. He calls me when he talks to Billy Beane in the stands at Oakland. He's giving me the same information as someone on the office with a different title would have, and maybe better. Kenny [Kravec] has a long history. He can go sit in the pressroom with John Schuerholz in Atlanta, and we're going to do the same thing as if I had an assistant GM talk to [Braves assistant GM] Frank Wren on the phone. They hear rumors at the park, and I take that rumor and call that other GM. It happens all the time."

Hendry's management style has filtered down to his closest front-office confidants. Fleita works without a formal assistant as he doubles up with two jobs. He figured he was the only executive in baseball who is both minor-league and Latin-American director, and his bailiwick stretches thousands of miles—from Boise to Caracas.

"This is the only way I've ever worked," Fleita said one day in October 2006 from the Cubs' Mesa offices, where he was monitoring the fall league. Fleita had started work at 4:30 a.m.

Entangled In Ivy

"This was what I was hired to do," he said. "I was never one to ask. If asked to do something, I get it done. I've always done two jobs for the Cubs. I am the only person I'm aware of who does the farm system and Latin America. I work a lot of hours. Would it [an assistant farm director] help? I don't know."

Meanwhile, Wilken, based in the Tampa area, works without a formal Chicago-based scouting assistant. Instead, he anointed Sam Hughes—Gary Hughes' son, who's following in his scouting footsteps— a national cross-checker to oversee the other regional super-scouts.

Fleita and Wilken do converge with Hendry in early November, when his player acquisition process actually starts in the annual organization meetings.

"We left the organizational meetings [in late 2005] totally ready to attack [Scott] Eyre and [Bobby] Howry," he said. "All the big-league staff sits in on those meetings. I have separate meetings with big-league staff. That's where you ask: 'Who knows Howry and Eyre? Do we want this guy?'"

Once games begin in spring training, Hendry leans on his special assistant scouts.

"Say it's from the Orioles," he said. "Ken Kravec has the 10 East Coast teams that are fully his. Keith Champion has the 10 in the middle. Gary has the 10 farthest west. Randy Bush is our new full-time guy who will be an outstanding employee. If it's a Baltimore player, the first thing I'll do is pull up the reports. We may have the last five years of reports. We'll have Kenny's stuff, who will see that club at least three different series during the year. Ten clubs apiece is not an [assignment] overload.

"That's how it starts," Hendry further explained. "Then we'll see who else on that scouting report has seen him. I'll read the report, call Kenny to talk about the player to see how I'm reading the verbiage of his report and the numbers how he projects them. I want to hear that dialogue. I can't just read it on paper and say I'm going to make the trade. You call and see if any other scouts have seen him on the match-ups. You call Gary and Keith, and say, 'You saw Minnesota and Baltimore. How did so and so play against the club [you're covering]?' It's cross-referencing.

"If it's a Latin guy, [Oneri] Fleita might have someone in the Dominican who knows the guy, knows the makeup, the character, coached him in winter ball. Somebody always knows somebody. You explore that. Or a manager I knew, let's say Lee Mazzilli had him, but Lee's not there anymore. I knew Lee well enough to ask. You have to—that's your job. You just don't read the stats, read the written scouting report by Ken Kravec and say, 'Let's go get George Castle.' With the money at stake and the contracts you're inheriting, you have to do those background checks."

After four decades of talent evaluation, Hughes is just getting to know the younger GMs who have filtered into power the past few years. For the more familiar faces, Hughes knows when to stop and start on trade talks.

"He (Hendry) and I know how far I can go," he said. "I know my place. I might be talking to someone and he'll ask, 'What do you think about the money part?' I'll tell him that's out of my league (and talks need to be switched to Hendry). It might be a brief conversation or one where more can get accomplished."

Hughes' definition of a good scout: "You have to have good judgment, No. 1. You need to have enough nerve to make your opinion known. You can't be afraid to fail. He'll [the GM] will call it to your attention that you got it wrong."

For his office backup, Hendry said he has delegated assistant GM duties to Scott Nelson, director of baseball operations and a 24-year front-office veteran; and Chuck Wasserstrom, the director of baseball information after a 16-year stint in the media relations department. Hughes said both are in essence assistant general managers, but with different titles. However, most teams do employ Nelson and Wasserstrom types along with an assistant GM and the full complement of big-league scouts.

"I think you need both," Gebhard said of fielding a complement of an assistant GM and stats-and-contracts specialists in the front office. "The person in the office, if he's qualified, can go out and see players himself, which is similar to what I did over there [Minnesota]. Front offices are put together two different ways. One is, if the general manager is a rules guy, then he may want a baseball guy as a right-hand man as we were in Minnesota. Some general managers are more the evaluator-type, baseball-player development-scouting, and they may want a rules guy to help him."

Entangled In Ivy

Hendry apparently trends toward the latter model, working with Nelson and Wasserstrom, both Chicago-area natives who grew up as Cubs fans.

"If you look at it real deeply, Scott and Chuck have a lot of different duties for me," Hendry said. "Chuck and Scott probably do more work than their job titles and descriptions say. I'm getting the information I need. I'm getting the statistical analysis from those guys. I'm getting the contract information from those guys. Scott works every day on the bulletin—reports on the waiver guys. I have all the information on future free agents, future arbitration guys. Scott does a lot of the background work on the arbitration cases.

"Scott is very good in the office on the budget stuff when Andy's not around—contract help, legwork for arbitration cases. I probably increased his load. He's very good when [daily major-league] bulletin comes. If there are three guys on waivers from the American League, I have their reports attached to the back of the bulletin within a half hour after the bulletin comes out. Scott's got every transaction, people who are available; he's got our scouting reports from the last three-four years. If it comes out before 3 p.m., I have everything before 5. I have 48 hours to make waiver claims. Managing the 40-man roster is more consuming than you think. He's involved with Mark O'Neal on the training reports, both the major and minor leagues."

Wasserstrom originally switched from former mediarelations chief Sharon Pannozzo's longtime top aide to a position analyzing statistics.

"Chuck does more than that," Hendry said. "He's involved with Fleita's guys, all the computer stuff, all the information to our scouts on the road, the six-year free agents and arbitration guys, potential free agents. He helps compile the data sent into me. Chuck has a pulse on all the national publicity, the clips, he breaks it down with me. He's very well-connected from his media background."

In 2006, Nelson and Wasserstrom were assisted by intern Jake Ciarrachi, son of Dave Ciarrachi, the owner of the Rockford, Illinois, team in the independent Frontier League and a 40-year bleachers fan. "You'd love to add a guy like Jake [full-time]," Hendry said. "I don't feel like we're missing anything at the higher levels. There's not a part of me that gets in my car and drives home and says, 'God, if I had a little more help, I would do better.' I don't have that excuse."

The Missing-Man Formation

Hendry also goes it alone when contact with other teams is concerned. In 2005, former president and CEO MacPhail said he desired that only his GM, not a subordinate, contact his counterparts throughout baseball. Again, that was a contrast from MacPhail's former methods of operation with Gebhard back in Minnesota.

"I would agree with Andy," Hendry said a month before his boss' resignation. "I'm the right guy for the way Andy wants to do it. I'm a phone guy. I do my deals with the other GMs. There's no BS. We get right to it when [he] talks about a trade. He's not trying to be up there while you're down here."

Yet, while Hendry believed that he had two capable office-based aides in Nelson and Wasserstrom, the one or more talent-judging confidants who could personally give him a second or third opinion on talent were missing from his "kitchen cabinet." An assistant GM often comprises part of that brain trust—so do other baseball operations executives or senior executives. Hendry believed that MacPhail served the latter role, even while the former president centered on the business side of the operation in his final seasons. MacPhail was not in tune with the nitty-gritty of talent evaluation as he was during his Twins GM days, or perhaps even his early Cubs presidency's tenure. Speculation asserts that Hendry had, under MacPhail, more latitude and wiggle room to operate than Ed Lynch—MacPhail's first, and novice, general manager.

"How many teams have a president across the hall who won two World Series as a GM?" Hendry asked before MacPhail had stepped down. "Who's got a president of a club who has the GM and baseball background Andy does? Andy doesn't meddle in the stuff that he thinks the GM should do. But if I get stuck on something, I don't have go any further than across the hall. I don't have to call the commissioner's office to get a ruling on something or get a suggestion. He's terrific. We were applauded for some of the creative deals we did, structuring the contract. Certainly, I got some advice from him how to structure some things, rules interpretations. If I need some financial clearance above the budget, he's right across the hall. He's not hard to find."

After MacPhail's departure, Hendry would have to lean on Nelson even more for rules interpretation—another task heaped on the front-office veteran.

Entangled In Ivy

Hughes said he confers via phone with Hendry at least once a day from wherever he's scouting out West. Yet the phone, like e-mails or instant messaging, does not take the place of personal give-and-take in which a set-in-stone opinion often can be softened when other facts or analysis is presented. Often, a strong manager is part of the kitchen cabinet. The most successful franchises of the past generation featured a manager with as strong a personality and conviction as the general manager. Hendry and Baker did not work together prior to 2002. While Baker said Hendry informed him of most moves, nothing gave off the impression the manager shaped the roster. Baker had said he advised Hendry if he knew the player.

"I never acquired a player in the winter or when we're in the race without talking to him," Hendry said of Baker. "I did not feel the need to tell him about [trading] Neifi Perez when we're downsizing [in August 2006]. I didn't call Dusty the night before to tell him, 'Neifi's getting traded,' because I didn't know. It happened in a two-hour window. I had to get Neifi out of the dugout [to inform him at game time]. I've never not involved Dusty in the big-league acquisitions in the off-season. He was very helpful, he knew [Scott] Eyre very well."

Baker apparently had persuaded Hendry not to plunge into deals for third baseman Joe Randa and Jeromy Burnitz at mid-season 2003. His counsel: Wait a little while longer and even better players would be available. Hendry snared third baseman Aramis Ramirez and centerfielder Kenny Lofton in the same deal on July 23. Lofton came with Baker's recommendation after he managed him the previous year in San Francisco.

"I went after Burnitz in '03," Hendry said. "I thought I'd do the deal with [Mets interim GM Jim Duquette], but they thought their deal with the Dodgers was better. He went to the Dodgers, and a week later we got Lofton and Ramirez."

Hendry also said he talked to Dick Pole, Baker's bench coach, when he was contemplating dealing for catcher Michael Barrett after the 2003 season. Pole had coached on the Expos while Barrett played in Montreal.

Baker described himself as the "shop foreman" working under Hendry. The best and longest-lasting managers are much more than that. The strongest manager-GM relationships are uncomfortably close in geography to the Cubs. First, Whitey Herzog in the 1980s, then Tony La

The Missing-Man Formation

Russa starting in 1996 wielded tremendous power over their St. Louis Cardinals rosters. Herzog even started as GM in 1980, then turned over the daily grunt work to lesser executives while he ruled the Cardinals from the dugout. It can be said with certainty that the intense La Russa is the alpha male of the Cardinals today. And it helps he has known GM Walt Jocketty for two decades—since their days together with the Oakland Athletics.

"Walt makes it clear, he wants the input of the guys in uniform," La Russa explained. "So he always includes the coaches and the manager, what do we need, identifying potential guys to acquire, and then we give our opinion. We evaluate the names that come up. He puts our comments together with those of our scouts and his own observations, and then he makes a decision.

"Everybody has their own perspective. Scouts look at tools and see a guy play some. Guys in uniform watch the actual competition against your club, form an opinion about not just tools, but how much he competes, how much he cares about the outcome, so they can relay an accurate picture to the GM. You make a decision about the guy you want to acquire and get all the perspectives."

La Russa, by now, expects to have a major say in roster construction.

"Three [managerial] situations I've been in—Roland Hemond [White Sox], Sandy Alderson [Athletics], and Walt Jocketty—operated by soliciting as much information and then made a decision," he said.

Jocketty, who has found ways to keep the Cardinals atop the National League Central since the millennium, involves front-office aides (assistant GM) Jerry Walker and Bruce Manno, along with former White Sox GM Ron Schueler. He'll even work his own clubhouse.

"Sometimes, I'll ask a player if he's played with a guy before," Jocketty said, "what kind of a guy he is … some of our veteran guys I feel comfortable talking to. Make sure you get a guy who can fit in to your club, not only talent, but also strong character."

Former Cubs manager Jim Riggleman, who has seen how different front offices operate before he became St. Louis' director of minor-league instruction, describes Jocketty has being "mild mannered … he doesn't have knee-jerk reactions. He has great thought processes. He uses his [people] resources well, including Tony as a kitchen cabinet. When you're La Russa, Bobby Cox, Joe Torre, you're naturally going to have your opinion respected. Tony loves the Cardinals, and he wants the legacy of the Cardinals to be carried on. He respects the history."

Torre's name always comes up when successful front offices are mentioned. Over the last decade, the quasi-dynastic Yankees featured a brain trust headed by GM Brian Cashman, advised by manager Joe Torre, and Gene Michael, top super-scout and a former Cubs manager. Detroit general manager Dave Dombrowski built a competitive team in Montreal, then stocked a world champion with the Florida Marlins in 1997 before reviving the Tigers in 2006. He casts a wide circle for his brain trust.

"You try to do as much homework as you can on any move you make," Dombrowski said. "You're not just talking about ability, but also makeup of an indivdual. You make a lot of phone calls in that regard. You usually have a second opinion if it's a big trade. You go back to your free-agent scouts if they were in a position to see the player as a young player. You talk to your manager and his big-league coaching staff. At times, it could be a dozen to 20 people. If we're talking specifically about a trade, vice president of player personnel Scott Reid and assistant GM Al Aliva are involved, and then we'll talk to a scout or two that have seen the player at the major-league level."

Another manager-GM brain trust that seemed to work for a while was Bob Brenly and Joe Garagiola Jr. with the Arizona Diamondbacks.

"Absolutely, Joe never made a move without my prior knowledge," Brenly said from his latter-day vantage point as Cubs television analyst. "If there were some questions, and we differed on a guy's value with the ball club, I would take it up with my coaching staff: 'What do you think of this guy?' I would even call coaches and players I was familiar with on other teams, who were familiar with the guy we were talking about. There's a lot more than the numbers when you talk about adding a player to the mix of the team and possibly altering the chemistry of that ball club. I was part of the decision-making process. It was always a team effort."

Franchises change front-office styles according to the executive in power. Paul Hagen, national baseball writer of the *Philadelphia Daily News*, recalled how Ed Wade kept a relatively small group of people in his court as Phillies GM. But successor Pat Gillick was different in his first year in 2006.

The Missing-Man Formation

"He likes to hear more voices," Hagen said of Gillick. "Lee Thomas [Wade's predecessor] liked to hear a lot of voices. It comes down to personal choice."

Dombrowski won't limit contact with other teams to just one subordinate. Avila can contact other teams in the preliminary stages of personnel moves with permission of the boss. So does Reid, a former Cubs scout.

"If he's doing that, he's doing it because he has good relationships with those other teams, or I might be working with something else," Dombrowski said. "Scott Reid and I worked together a long time; he worked with other people for a long time; and he'll pick up the phone and do that, too."

The give and take also curbs the tendency to make hasty or rash moves or misevaluate a player. Those second and third opinions, delivered in person, can make a GM take another look and avoid a potentially bad move.

"You don't want to have 'yes men' around you," the Astros' Purpura said. "You want people around you who will give you honest feedback of how you're viewing certain ballplayers. You want to get an objective view rather than a subjective. I challenge our guys all the time to give me their thoughts and not hold back."

The game's best GMs don't let their egos get in the way of quality advice, even if that advice dissuades them from sticking to their original feeling on a move.

"Guys have talked me off a guy," the Cardinals' Jocketty said. "I respect their opinions. Mike Squires sees the American League; Jerry Walker sees the National League. If they don't like a guy for some reason, we'll look in a different direction."

"Sure, that's why you keep digging all the time," the Tigers' Dombrowski said. "There've been times I've had someone in mind I've been thinking of acquiring. But then you get more information. All of a sudden, you back off on that move. That's happened to me throughout my career."

Bob Brenly recalled "several times" that he talked Joe Garagiola Jr. out of a move for the Diamondbacks.

Entangled In Ivy

"There was one particular player Joe tried to sell me on several times," Brenly said. "Based on my experiences with this particular player, I didn't think he was a good fit with our team."

The primer for flawed evaluation of a player—and perhaps the absence of that second or third look—was displayed with the Cubs in 2006. Although Jacque Jones finished with home-run and RBI numbers that satisfied the Cubs, he might not have been signed as a free agent had Hendry received a true picture of what developed into some of the worst throwing ever seen from right field at Wrigley Field. This is where the office-based second or third opinion would enter the picture, following up on Tim Purpura's idea of separating what's real from what's not on scouting reports.

After a few Jones throws were unintentionally grounded 75 feet from his right-field position or were air-mailed for the box seats, I asked a couple of former Minnesota Twins teammates about him. First was Ron Coomer—also an ex-Cub—who played with Jones at the start of his career in 1999 and 2000. Coomer said Jones threw erratically, "like a slider," and ball would meet Mother Earth quickly. Later, I queried Doug Mientkiewicz, a Twins teammate of Jones of even longer standing. The honest and voluble Mientkiewicz, now with Kansas City, also reported Jones' throwing woes. But then he mimicked a hard swing. "That's why they signed him—25 homers," he said. Late in the year, another player said Cleveland Indians mid-June scouting reports on Jones' arm said it had a case of the "yips."

As a lesser problem, Jones displayed strange base-running decisions early on, being doubled off second base three times in two weeks on line drives to Cubs' opponents' left fielders. The Twins always had preached aggressive base-running, but Jones' mad dashes off second busted all fundamentals standards. As the season progressed, the drunken-sailor tactics died down, but Jones' throws seemed to possess minds of their own.

As we continued chatting at Bar Louie, I relayed the comments by Coomer and Mientkiewicz. Why didn't the Cubs' scouts pick up on the wanderlust of Jones' throws? What did they say about him?

"The throwing problems weren't consistent," Hendry said. "He had them, then he lost them, then he had them again. He didn't have them all the time. He had a little stretch where he had problems at home."

The Missing-Man Formation

What would have thrown the red flag with the scouts?

"If it was happening all the time and he never threw anybody out at home plate. Nobody ever wrote about it when he was signed. Did anybody write about his throwing problem all winter?"

Keith Champion had the primary coverage of Jones in Minnesota.

"Champion saw him 10 games, Mark Servais saw him six, seven," Hendry said. His other special assistants also watched Jones in different ballparks. "Gary [Hughes], Randy [Bush], and Kenny [Kravec] probably saw him four to five," he added. "Five different people saw him 25 to 30 games, and not at the same game. Stan Zielinski saw him when he played the White Sox."

Back on May 27, Hendry had this take on the scouting of Jones:

"We not only scouted Jacque heavily last year, but we have a very healthy relationship with the Twins," he said. "Not just with Andy [MacPhail], but with Randy Bush, who gets tremendous inside information. Twins coaches said that Jacque's base-running mistakes were really out of character, that he was a solid base-runner for seven years. He was not a prolific base-stealer, but a solid major-league base-runner. He played that way against the White Sox. People saw him play 17-18 games a year, and it never happened before. When you play seven, eight years in the big leagues, it's not as if you have to be reminded by your coaches every day not to get doubled up on a line drive to left field. That's not an explanation I'd blame the coaches for. There's no history of him being a bad base-runner. So it wasn't like he ran the bases poorly in spring training."

While Hendry worked to fine-tune the sagging evaluation process, he also had an even more important task at hand than bringing a World Series to Wrigley Field. During the downer seasons of 2005 and 2006, he entered a new role as a single father. A difficult divorce with his ex-wife, Andrea, resulted in Hendry sharing custody of grade-school children John and Lauren. The dual roles of doing the right thing by his kids and working a backbreaking job involving odd hours and travel were challenging. Hendry bought another house six blocks away from the former marital home in northwest suburban Park Ridge so the kids would be in the same school and park districts while they lived with him.

Hendry grew up in a close family in Florida, and said he wouldn't do it any other way with his own children. He was often spotted tossing a ball in the air to John in left field after games. Both children spend a lot of time at the ballpark and even commandeered the microphone in the interview room one day in 2005 after postgame chats had finished.

"I don't think I would ever want to be of the opinion that I work harder than anybody else," Hendry said as we walked out of Bar Louie's and back to Wrigley Field. "That's for someone else to write. Whatever I've done work-wise the last couple of years hasn't worked up to my standards. I look at it as, 'I better work a little harder this off-season because we certainly don't want to go through this again.'

"I do the best I can with them," he said of the kids. "They're at the age where they're starting to understand how busy I am. They know when I get to their events and their ballgames after work, it is an effort to do it. They appreciate it. I'm certainly never going to be neglectful to them. I don't portray myself as working any harder than 29 other guys in the industry. All I want them to know is you're supposed to get up every day and work hard. When I can be with them, I will. I'm in a good relationship now that's been good for me."

Since 2005, Hendry has been dating a Louisiana woman named Vicky, who worked with his older brother John. He said Vicky is good with his children. MacPhail understood Hendry's family situation. Front office stalwart Patti Kargakis, who has worked in the player-development department since the mid-1980s days of the admired Gordon Goldsberry, sometimes picks John and Lauren up from school and takes them to Wrigley Field for a night game. Another front-office employee accompanied the children on a plane to spring training in 2005.

"They're great kids, they've been through a tough couple of years, but they're doing well," Hendry said. "They understand I'm doing the best I can. I would hate to think I ever walk through the door and didn't give it my best shot because I had other issues, personally. That's not an excuse either. I'm trying to do the best I can for the Cubs and the best I can for my kids—and that's the way it is."

eight

THE WRIGLEY CHARACTER

THE BOYS were a bit edgy in the clubhouse.

In the second week of July 2003, the Cubs had endured an 11-20 slump that dropped them to the .500 mark at 47-47, three games behind the Houston Astros. But the backslide did not deter most of the players emotionally, who possessed that special, winning feeling.

"We're ready to win," said first baseman Eric Karros. Intrigued, I sat down with Karros and several teammates at one of the long card tables in the Cubs clubhouse and discussed the state of the team, mixed with a healthy dollop of Cubs history. Media aren't really supposed to sit anywhere in the locker room, let alone at the tables in Wrigley Field's space-challenged private sanctuary.

"What are you, one of the coaches?" chimed in the *Chicago Tribune's* Paul Sullivan, noticing my seated position. "Invited guest," I replied. The discussion broached what the Cubs needed to win the division, and we debated how aggressively general manager Jim Hendry should pursue reinforcements via deals before the trading deadline at the end of the month. "What about you, Woody?" I asked Kerry Wood as he passed.

"I just pitch," he responded as he continued to his locker.

I reported the conversation, with no names, as "restlessness is spreading through the Cubs clubhouse as players are growing impatient for general manager Jim Hendry to make deals" in the next morning's *Times of Northwest Indiana*. Seven years earlier, I had reported similar irritation from Mark Grace, Brian McRae, and even manager Jim Riggleman [again, no names in the paper] about then-GM Ed Lynch's inactive approach to improve a similarly break-even team.

Karros and Co. wanted Hendry to surrender minor-league prospects from the Cubs' then-well-rated farm system for veterans. In the course of the chitchat, many expressed doubt over Hee Seop Choi, a rookie slugger platooning with Karros, and some thought his swing was not yet up to big-league caliber. Subsequent seasons would prove this analysis correct. Experienced help was needed.

The players in the informal clubhouse roundtable were suspicious of parent Tribune Company's commitment to win, believing the corporation only desired to pack Wrigley Field. They questioned why Baker was the only big-ticket hire in the off-season, with Hendry passing on first baseman Jim Thome, who grew up a Cubs fan in Peoria. Many noted that the salary committed to acquiring free-agent relievers Mike Remlinger and Dave Veres and starter Shawn Estes was not so large.

Hendry would not respond to players' pleas for deals unless they approached him directly. "I'm in that clubhouse every day, and I'm available," he said.

But Baker liked the spirited in-house discussion about trades. "Hell, yeah," he said when asked if the players were right to lobby for deals.

Within two weeks, Hendry would satisfy the players' yearning for additional help. He acquired third baseman Aramis Ramirez and center fielder Kenny Lofton from the cash-strapped Pittsburgh Pirates, giving the Cubs a much-needed RBI bat and a leadoff man—a position that gave the team fits for years—who also could fill in for injured centerfielder Corey Patterson. Soon afterward, Hendry dipped into the Pirates' talent well for first baseman Randall Simon to platoon with Karros, pushing aside the perennially hyped Choi for what would become the last time in his short Cubs big-league career. The only needs overlooked were extra bullpen arms, a factor that proved fatal during the 2003 National League Championship Series.

The players' grousing sounded, at first glance, like typical clubhouse politics. Yet, what it truly symbolized was legitimate, winning chemistry, good attitude, and the strength of character needed to win in Wrigley Field—elements too often lacking in Cubs history. Like the will o' the wisp, they were here one moment, gone the next, without word on when

The Wrigley Character

they would return, without any articulated plan on how to create their comeback.

Definitions of baseball "chemistry" wander all over the map. The game's house is divided on whether winning breeds chemistry, or good chemistry is required to promote winning.

"We can debate that all day," said former Cubs pitcher Steve Trachsel, who won 15 games for the Mets in 2006. "You have to have chemistry in the clubhouse that will carry over onto the field—and then you have to win. Al Leiter and I used to argue about that from a pitching standpoint. Do you have to have confidence to win, or does winning give you confidence? We each took opposite sides."

But there can be no doubt about the concept of character, closely related to chemistry. Obviously, no team wants an epidemic of bad character in the clubhouse.

"You always want character guys, anybody who tells you different is BS-ing you," Hendry said in 2006. "It seems like, if you're winning, people are writing about good chemistry you have, a good clubhouse. Chemistry in the clubhouse is hard to define. I can't say there's a guy you wouldn't have over in your back yard for a barbecue. We might have the best guys we've had, and we're not winning."

But, more often, winning and good character are joined together. Baseball and the disciplined preparation required do not wander tangentially. There's only one way to play the game—with hustle, dedication, and concentration. Shortcuts rarely work. Those who elect not to run out batted balls, repeatedly make mental mistakes on the basepaths and in the field, show up late to the clubhouse, and believe their talent will overwhelm additional preparation inevitably drag down the entire team effort.

In the end, the cumulative effect of such behavior has been a key element in Cubs failures. Others teams seem to possess an excess of character and know how to go out and find it. Like the lack of a hitting philosophy that promotes patience and discipline, the Cubs have fallen short on scouting what some baseball insiders have called the "sixth tool"—character. Strong character logically begets strong team chemistry.

Whenever the Cubs have surged forward from their more typical National League netherworld perch, they often have possessed a clubhouse full of both characters and character.

Entangled In Ivy

The 1984 and 1989 NL East title winners were givens in these categories. In 1998, Rod Beck, Terry Mulholland, Mickey Morandini, Kevin Tapani, and others gave the Cubs a gritty persona for an overachieving wild-card team. Jokesters and softball-player types dotted the 2001 roster that kept the Cubs in first place through mid-August.

The 2003 Cubs had as much good chemistry and character as raw talent. The intestinal fortitude overcame the decline and absences of Sammy Sosa due to his corked-bat episode and several injuries, along with an underproductive offense for much of the season and shaky setup relief pitching throughout the entire year.

Karros was not at all out of line in his prodding of Hendry, via a reporter, to do more. After all, Hendry himself considered Karros a key chemistry component.

"We obviously were trying to get rid of [Todd] Hundley," Hendry said of his frantic effort after the 2002 season. "You tell me how many great things you heard coming out of L.A. about Eric Karros. Not that many. We made the deal; hey, it was best for Todd. Eric Karros was one of the best human beings in that clubhouse I've ever met. If I had one thing to do over again when we didn't win in September '04, [it was acting on] Eric Karros getting released from Oakland that August. I would have signed Eric Karros on September 1 even if he never got an at-bat in '04. That's how much I thought about Eric Karros. Sometimes you don't know for sure until you have that guy yourself. The guy who said Karros is a great guy is [Tommy] Lasorda. He was right."

Hendry also made the right judgment on Lofton, about whom baseball people still said negative things in late 2006 even as Lofton, at 39, was a key sparkplug for the Dodgers' National League West title. Dusty Baker had claimed he asked Hendry to hold off on trading for the likes of third baseman Joe Randa and outfielder Jeromy Burnitz so the Cubs could wait for even better players to soon become available— namely Lofton and Ramirez.

"Dusty made the right call on Kenny Lofton in my discussions with him," Hendry said. "Face it, a lot of people don't always say nice things about Kenny. Kenny was not only a real good player for a couple of months, but was outstanding [in the clubhouse]."

Indeed, Lofton played a leadership role in his nearly two and a half months as a Cub. He got into Sosa's face twice when the pampered-

The Wrigley Character

poodle slugger, indulged by all levels of the organization, put himself before the welfare of the team. Lofton also talked to Ramirez about not running hard on contact, a chronic problem throughout his Cubs career.

Lofton was often standoffish to media, but his persona was never warped in the manner of old Cleveland Indians locker-mate Albert Belle. He had his priorities straight, as when I pulled him aside 10 minutes after the team clinched the NL Central on September 27, 2003, amidst the maelstrom of bodies on the field. Lofton said the celebration of the moment was great, but it was only the beginning of a long playoff journey. There would be greater priorities soon enough.

"In '03, we just had some guys wanting to win," Lofton said from his 2006 vantage point. "There was a mix of guys out there with the same time, with the same goal, trying to win. We had good pitching; we had a good offensive and defensive club. It just didn't work out for us [in the NLCS], but we had a good attitude."

"He really made a big difference in that [pennant] push," 2003 second baseman Mark Grudzielanek said. "Absolutely [he knew how to win]. As a leadoff man, he pushed me down to No. 2, which took a lot of pressure off me. With the vets we had and leadership we had in that clubhouse, there were a lot of guys who wouldn't allow a lot of shit to go on there. With Kenny, he fit right in. Anytime you have a team with the clubhouse we had, if you're a decent guy and you go out to play, you'll get along just fine."

Grudzielanek said Lofton was right to challenge Sosa, whose 2003 political portfolio included calling commissioner Bud Selig from the Cubs clubhouse with an apology immediately after being caught with the corked bat.

"To see certain things and especially when things don't go about the way you want to see them," Grudzielanek said, "and we're all trying for the No. 1 goal. When you have that little glitch in the engine, whatever it may be that you want to fix, you're going to say something. He [Lofton] was going to be the kind of guy who's going to say something, to make sure we don't need this. Sometimes on a losing team you're not going to say anything. You had a lot of leadership on that team."

Lofton, Karros, Grudzielanek, fellow starters Estes and Matt Clement, closer Joe Borowski, reliever Mike Remlinger, and catchers Damian Miller and Paul Bako were among the main character men who

133

contributed to the chemistry of the '03 Cubs. But when the team reconvened in Mesa for spring training before the following season, many of the key parts—such as Lofton, Karros, Miller, and Estes—were gone. Greg Maddux was an ultimate character guy coming in, but the net effect was subtraction by subtraction. The same clubhouse feeling of '03 no longer existed.

"It all started because you got rid of five to seven players for '04 when we felt we had a great opportunity here—a piece here, a piece there," Grudzielanek said. "I'm a firm believer that you need a good clubhouse. In '03, we had one of the best clubhouses I had ever been in in my 12 years of experience. I'm a big fan of making changes and doing things. When they didn't do anything for the playoff run for a reliever, and then they go out and trade guys the following year from a great group of guys, it was a problem."

Forecast by *Sports Illustrated* to win the 2004 World Series, that season's Cubs somehow started off on a bad foot with media and fans, and things only got worse as the season wore on.

Due to the crush of media in the post-2003 euphoria, television cameras were banned from the clubhouse pregame. Five lounge chairs were set up in the north end of the clubhouse, clogging an already too-tight area. Reporters were prohibited from standing in that area of the locker room unless they had a specific interview with a player.

"The recliners were a place to be comfortable and be able to watch TV," 2004 reliever Kent Mercker said. "Contrary to what people believe, we were not here to watch TV; we're here to play baseball and win. You have a lot of free time between the time you get here and go on the field, so you need to relax. It was not there to keep the media from anything. If you want to talk to me, go to the dugout. To even mention the recliners was ridiculous. That puts an image in there that these guys sit around, recline back, don't care. What if they were cement seats?"

The recliners disappeared going into the 2006 season, replaced with just a card table. "It just was too cramped," said Cubs clubhouse manager Tom Hellmann.

Meanwhile, newly acquired reliever LaTroy Hawkins announced he would no longer speak to media at the end of a June 2004 press conference that anointed him closer when Borowski was hurt. Other complaints were lodged against media coverage throughout the season.

The Wrigley Character

Outfielder Moises Alou criticized umpires and became riled at television announcers Chip Caray and Steve Stone and their alleged short shrift of the lineup when doling out credit for any Cubs success. Caray and Stone became a running sideshow starting in late August after Mercker called the press box to complain that Caray was giving too much credit that afternoon to Astros pitcher Roy Oswalt.

The slumping Sosa refused to entertain any thoughts of being dropped from the cleanup position as well, and Baker warily acceded to his wishes for weeks on end. By midseason—as the Cardinals surged far out in front in the NL Central and the wild card became the only viable playoff option—the Cubs turned from the plucky heroes of 2003 into a thoroughly unlikable team, one of the least appealing in modern team annals. They were termed "whiners."

"We ain't no whiners," Baker said on September 11, 2004. "The thing I hate the worst is whining. I don't allow whining in my house. You get nothing for whining.

"All I know is I've never seen this much coverage of non-baseball stuff since I've been in baseball—not even close. I could almost wrap 10 years' worth of stuff into this one year, really. Last year, it was exhilarating and thrilling that we were winning in the first place. Now, this year it's, 'How come we're not in first place?'"

Interestingly, Mercker, whose own good clubhouse character reputation took a knock over his involvement in the Caray-Stone affair, insisted the '04 Cubs were a tight-knit bunch. "Best attitude of any team I was on," he said. "I read where there was no team chemistry; that there were players who didn't get along with other players; that Alou got mad at umps; that Dusty couldn't control his players. Baker wants you to stick up for yourself. Everyone got along. Never been on a team where more guys got together for dinner, we had 12, 13, 14 guys get together. That's team chemistry.

"I didn't know it was an unlikable team. I have theories, but there are certain members of the Chicago media who want to say things. You don't have to have any credibility. I know none of the players thought it."

Grudzielanek had a slightly different view and used the "w" word—whining.

"The Cubbies, they haven't won in a long time," he said. "In '03, we weren't supposed to win. After that year, after that performance we gave, we were supposed to be better the following year. The pressure of that really contributed to a lot of problems, and a lot of things if it didn't go away. You heard whining; you heard this, you heard that."

Some character issues that hadn't been crucial in previous years bubbled to the surface like never before in 2004. Sammy Sosa, of course, finally melted down as the result of his trademark self-centeredness ("This is my house," he'd call Wrigley Field), which, along with the constant pampering by the entire organization, alienated him from teammates. That he initially balked at being dropped in the batting order at midseason and departed unexcused during the first inning of the season's finale at Wrigley Field were all that had to be said about Sosa's character flaws.

Mercker was one Sosa teammate who did not have serious problems with his behavior. "I was there one year, I have nothing bad to say about Sammy," he said. "I heard people who'd been around him more than one year—they had issues with him. If he wanted to stay in his own hotel, ride his own bus, have his own locker, who cares? If he's playing right field and driving in runs, that's fine."

Moises Alou also had personal holes that were masked by his team-leading run production in 2004. Amazingly, Dusty Baker was unaware Alou sometimes wandered into the clubhouse 20 minutes after the mandated players-be-dressed time. Both Baker and Alou's teammates excused his tardiness and other seemingly languid methods of preparation by citing the outfielder's on-field production and life-of-the-clubhouse persona. Left unsaid was Alou's poor situational hitting and baserunning, which could have improved with a better pregame routine.

"He's a professional player," Grudzielanek said of Alou. "When he was on the field, he gave everything he had. You can't take anything away from him. I consider him a good friend. He had his routine, had his schedule. If it was all right with everyone else, he came in there for treatment. At my age, I don't necessarily come on time. I stay off my feet and do things to get ready. Rest, for a guy like that, is something he needed to make a nice run."

Still another character case was center fielder Corey Patterson. Each step forward for the prodigy was canceled by a sometimes-immediate step backward before he washed out of the organization after the 2005 season. Yet, his retrogression was more mental and emotional than physical. After spending part of winter ball working on his bunting with then-Cubs coach Sandy Alomar in 2000-01, Patterson was not with the Cubs all the way through the '01 campaign. He was demoted to Triple-A Iowa when veteran Michael Tucker was acquired to log most of the time in center. However when asked, whether he had more to learn in the minors during one of his stints with the parent club, Patterson responded, "No," that playing at Iowa no longer had any value, that he would learn in the majors. When he uttered that statement, he was just 21 years old.

"You can call that false pride," Cubs scouting director Tim Wilken said of Patterson's statement. "He hasn't opened up the blinders [at that point of his career]."

Three years later, I asked Patterson about the concept of patience and drawing walks, which would make him even more dangerous on the basepaths considering his blinding speed. His response: pitchers aren't going to walk a player they know is going to be running; thus, they were going to throw him strikes, and he'd be swinging away. Patterson's skewed thinking obscured the fact that it's the hitter's responsibility to get on base by any means, and that no pitcher in his right mind would serve up fat pitches for fear of walking a speedster.

Patterson seemed to have perfect baseball character when I first interviewed him in 1999 in Lansing, Michigan. Modest and unassuming, he seemed to use two words where three were more appropriate. However, continual hype focused on his expected ascendancy to superstar status in Chicago and could have changed him. An innate stubbornness also surfaced, as, continually, Patterson was instructed to employ more plate discipline, to little effect. It's apparent, as in any walk of life, good character can be altered through the years.

The onus then falls upon the talent evaluators at both the pro and amateur levels to perform the extra research that uncovers legitimate character, translating into an alert, motivated major leaguer. That requires the skills of a private detective at times, certainly the willingness to see beyond the superficial.

"You have to use a combination [of techniques]," Hendry said. "In my spot, you have to make the call. On the flipside, you can have people who are coaches and managers who had that player four or five years ago, but their opinion on that player doesn't count. It doesn't mean he'll play for you now as he did back then. It's human nature for people in the dugout to want to reacquire someone who played well for them and not reacquire someone who didn't play well. If it's not this year's information, you want from field people what kind of character we got, what kind of guy he is."

Hendry expects Tim Wilken, who stocked the Blue Jays system with talent in the 1990s, to rejuvenate a somewhat sagging Cubs talent draft pipeline. Wilken sees numbers and time as two obstacles impeding scouts as they try to determine character in prospects. Each area scout is monitoring up to 100 players as potential draft fodder.

Timing is also crucial. In addition to watching the player's demeanor while interacting with his teammates, the ins and outs of character are determined best through home visits. Yet, with 30 teams scrambling for players, a prime prospect can become overwhelmed in the months just before the draft. If a scout can get into the home the previous autumn, he has a better opportunity to get a good read on the prospect.

"It's probably a sixth sense for a scout," Wilken said. "You can misread a lot of people. They can be two-faced. Someone can be seeking attention, seeking to be liked. I emphasize to the scouts later in the rounds—given their chances aren't as good as the higher picks—make sure as best you can to know their mental makeup for when they're meshing together [in the minor leagues] with the higher-level prospects."

At the major-league level, scouts have to be the ultimate people persons if they truly want to go behind the scenes to judge character accurately.

"We stress to the scouts to get to know the staff members with the opposing clubs," said San Diego Padres general manager Kevin Towers. "Talk to them, take them to dinner, try to gather as much information as possible from a friend or someone you might know. You have to dig."

A handful of players are easy to analyze. One was Cubs team leader Derrek Lee.

"We have enough information about him from the [former] Marlins people who worked here, myself, and his father [Leon Lee, a former Cubs scout]," Hendry said. "Those are easy things. You do the best you can, but you're not always right. People change."

Witnessing how the Cubs clubhouse was melting down steadily in the late summer of 2004, I chanced into a meeting with veteran scout Gene Watson while covering a Sox-Phillies game at U.S. Cellular Field.

The Wrigley Character

Watson, formerly a Braves scouting mainstay, mentioned the concept of character as the "sixth tool" that Atlanta believed was just as important as the five physical tools.

"Bobby Cox has a 25-man system," Watson said. "You either fall in line with this system or don't survive."

That stream of consciousness led right to Cox—the centerpiece of much of the Braves' success from 1991 to 2005—to get a more complete explanation of how Atlanta discovered players with character and further developed that quality. The result was not only consistent winning (before a 2006 backslide), but the absence of malcontents and the constant of the Braves clubhouse ranking as one of the game's best. Media loved working the Atlanta locker room. There were no Albert Belle characters.

"I don't think it's much different than anyone else's organization, to be honest with you," Cox said in 2006. "We had a good run with good drafting through the years. There're a lot of rules in the minor leagues. Paul Snyder started it, and Dave Moore took over. They treat them like men, but they have tight reins on them—a lot of discipline. We want them to play the game as it should be played, but they work on fundamentals. We do make as many fundamental mistakes as probably other teams. They do work awfully hard on them. We kind of do everything the same way top to bottom with all of our fundamentals. If you're going to play it that way up here, you better be trained to do it that way. In that respect, it's real good.

"You want to sign the best players you can, but you certainly look for makeup and character. It's a huge part of it. You better look at that issue. Of course, when you make trades, you try to do the same thing, too. You want to do the best for the organization. There's no short, quick fixes, things like that."

Mimicking the Braves, then surpassing them as each season of the 21st Century progressed were the Minnesota Twins. Once earmarked for contraction, the Twins are now one of the gold standards of player development, just as disciplined and motivated as the Braves.

"You look at guys who fit, every ball club wants that, fit the mold, run balls out, something we have a lot of respect for," Twins manager Ron Gardenhire said. "Guys like Kirby Puckett always did it—he was the best I saw. That is the mold, but that's not always the way it is. Make sure people you bring in understand that from the get-go. Our guys do know character. When they scout from other teams, we get reports on what kind of person they are. If we don't know, we'll find out, by asking people on other teams."

Of a similar mind-set is Cardinals manager Tony La Russa, who is even more succinct in defining character, of which there was no shortage through most of his tenure in St. Louis.

"What goes on in a guy's head and heart is as important as his talent," La Russa said. "You take a talented guy who doesn't care and isn't going to commit to doing it every day, and he can't help you win. We look at how hard a guy competes—does he compete for the right reasons?"

Some of that same devotion to character propelled the Detroit Tigers into the 2006 World Series, only three years after they lost an American League-record 119 games. Obviously, Tigers president-GM Dave Dombrowski is a budding expert at directing the quest for the right type of players, after building up a contender in Montreal and a 1997 World Series champion with the Marlins.

"Character is very, very important," Dombrowski said. "We put a lot of emphasis on that. Be careful how you define it, careful how you do your homework. We want someone to play hard for us, have a winning attitude, want them to represent the organization in the correct fashion. Players come from all kinds of backgrounds, so what's acceptable in one culture is not acceptable in another. You have to be careful in your research. You want people who will do little things to win ballgames and follow guidance in your organization.

"You have to make sure that it's accurate information, that someone's not giving you information you want to hear and not just trying to move a particular player. You have to be aware of what you're being told. If you have the right resources, you try to do the digging in the clubhouse, if you can."

Of course, on-field production sometimes trumps character questions when scouts' reports are analyzed. The late-night-loving Moises Alou reported late to his team's clubhouses, even for night games, long before he arrived at Wrigley Field—but he always had a job in baseball because of semi-consistent numbers of 30 homers, 100 RBIs, and a .300 average.

The Wrigley Character

"You're going to get numbers out of him," said one veteran scout. "The numbers will translate into a good contract, not necessarily a good chemistry guy. His reputation was a kind of malingerer—J.D. Drew, Jeff Kent, Gary Sheffield, the same thing."

But what if the scout was asked to make the call on Alou?

"I would still have probably recommended him," he said.

A longtime talent evaluator, Gene Watson said that, while scouts "do the best you can to dig up off-the-field habits," in many cases talent-hungry organizations decide to overlook personal foibles. "You say, 'I understand this is a risk for us to acquire this guy,'" he said, "'but his ability level is very valuable to us,'"

What would Padres GM Towers think of a player who often arrives tardy?

"Ability is the biggest thing," he said, "but the last thing you want to do is bring a guy with poor work habits who doesn't handle himself in a professional manner into your clubhouse. That guy can turn your clubhouse upside down. That's why you have to be there early as a scout for batting practice. Who are the leaders? Who are the followers?"

Baker said Alou was a veteran allowed to bend the rules, not break them.

Watson understood the logic. "It depends on what the manager expects. A lot of guys believe that as long as you show up on time to stretch, be out on the field, participate in batting practice, and know it's time to play, that's all that's important. I've acquired guys who had great ability—off the field it's a frat party."

Hendry's last word on Alou also was positive.

"You can't be critical of Moises; he's had a great career wherever he's been," he said. "He's played through injuries. To me, he's a high-character guy. It's awfully hard for someone in any of our positions to define someone's character as good or bad."

But the character issue deepens when the Cubs aura and the Wrigley Field environment are considered. Alou and so many others recruited or traded to the Cubs had to deal with playing and training conditions absent anywhere else in the majors.

Until 2005, the Cubs were limited to just 18 night games per season at home, and none on Fridays. The heavy daytime schedule has now been fingered as a potential detriment to the Cubs' efforts to win, as it affects the body clock over the six-month-long season with the constant switching from a predominantly night-game schedule on the road to consistent afternoon contests at Wrigley Field. The small clubhouse, cozy trainers and weight rooms, and a batting cage inaccessible during games are drawbacks missing in newer ballparks. Above all is the constant mention of lovable losers, curses, hexes, and billy goats—also features absent with 29 other teams—all in a fishbowl atmosphere of fans and media that the Cubs' own officials compare to that of the New York Yankees and Boston Red Sox. Few players can easily handle the working conditions of the Chicago Cubs; and it can be particularly tough on players making the transition from small-market teams.

Oddly enough, the Cubs' top pro scouts had an opinion at odds in 2006 with then-team president Andy MacPhail. "Do players lose focus here with the distractions?" MacPhail said. "Some of that smacks as excuses. That doesn't explain why we have had so many bad seasons. Maybe it's a factor, but it's too easy a way out. It's more [an issue of] talent and durability. Sometimes we just haven't had the talent."

But the scouts spotted a trend:

"In a nutshell, you really got to look at the situation with the Cubs, Yankees, Red Sox," said Keith Champion, former special assistant to Jim Hendry. "The media in those markets is really tremendous compared to [small] markets, where there is not a lot of atmosphere."

Players also need a strong constitution to succeed in Wrigley Field.

"When you come to Wrigley, it's a special thing. But if you're afraid, you're not going to succeed," said Gary Hughes. Not only did he have the most experience with four decades in scouting, but Hughes was Hendry's mentor and top advisor as well, even participating in the new manager interviews immediately after the 2006 season. "What you're looking for is a guy who's strong, quote, unquote—mentally strong."

Champion and Hughes are not off in left field with their analysis. Their opinions are cross-referenced by the Twins' Gardenhire.

"At Minnesota, there are only a few media," he said. "Chicago's not like that—same as New York and L.A. There are a lot of people. You're going to get it. I'm sure it is a little bit different going there, seeing all these things said about them. It probably knocks their socks off a little bit, and they have to step back. It's not easy. Going from Minnesota to a big market is not the easiest thing to do, because Minnesota's pretty laid back when it comes to that.

"There are going to be some players who can block things out. Other players are high-strung, and they are going to have a harder time. LaTroy [Hawkins] is high-strung; he's an emotional player. LaTroy's arguments aren't about himself; he's defending teammates and the manager. That's where he gets into arguments. Jacque [Jones] is the same way. That's the core we come from—a family defending themselves against outside forces. When you shoot at one of our family members, guys will come back at you.

"That's the great unknown, you never know what you're going to get with a player in handling the pressures of playing in a big city. You can research as much as you want to. Yet, eventually, it will get down to putting the guys on the field. Baseball, on the field, is the easy part—guys can do that. It's all the surrounding stuff that eats you up. Whether he can get through the distractions, that's the issue."

Hawkins, a prize free-agent signing by GM Jim Hendry, was eaten up by media coverage, which was magnified five times when he was thrust into the closer's job in mid-season 2004, a position for which he was emotionally ill-suited. After an almost daily chorus of boos and media criticism, Hendry had to trade Hawkins to the Giants for his own good in 2005, just two months into his second Cubs campaign.

Others endured a culture shock coming to the Cubs. Gary Hughes cited examples of two players he shepherded in the Montreal system, relievers Mel Rojas and Antonio Alfonseca. Both had played in cavernous stadiums in Montreal and Miami, respectively, in front of small crowds.

"The first thing to adjust to is playing in front of a full house every game," Hughes said. "If things are going well, it's an easy place to play. I think the crowd picks you up. But in Montreal, in front of 4,000 people, you've got to be self-motivated. With 4,000 people, it's 'If they don't care, why should I?' But you still have to give a good performance out there."

Rojas, signed to a free-agent contract with much fanfare for 1997, immediately melted down as the closer and did not even last the season as a Cub.

"Mel was a great person, and he was extremely successful in situations in Montreal," Hughes said. "Things got magnified here. After a couple of bad outings, people got on him in Chicago."

Entangled In Ivy

Alfonseca became progressively worse as Cubs closer in 2002 after coming over in a trade from the Marlins that cost Chicago Dontrelle Willis.

"He had a tough time succeeding," Hughes said of Alfonseca. "He came here in good shape, then maybe he didn't stay in good shape. He was used to working in anonymity [in Florida], now he's in Chicago. Maybe it was the intimacy at our place compared to Dolphin Stadium."

No player can afford to have stage fright.

"As a winning player, you have to be willing to fail on the field in front of 40,000 and however many millions on TV," said former Cub Steve Trachsel. "If you're willing to fail on the field, you will have success."

So failure can breed even more of the same if the player can't handle life in the fishbowl. Homegrown Cubs centerfielder Corey Patterson—compared to Lou Brock by Dusty Baker—wore out his welcome, too. Hendry had to help him get out of Dodge, too. Once reestablished in Baltimore in 2006, where he was again a teammate of Hawkins, Patterson called the Orioles' atmosphere more "laid-back" than Wrigley Field. That picture of Camden Yards synched with Keith Champion's view of careers salvaged when they departed the Chicago fishbowl.

"All you have to do is look at people who struggled at Wrigley Field," he said. "You look at guys who struggled at Wrigley Field, they've gone on to survive elsewhere." He counted Patterson, Hawkins, and Alfonseca in this group.

Hawkins, Patterson, and Jacque Jones also had to deal with the far, ugly extremes of their Cubs experience. Just as manager Dusty Baker did, they too received racial hate mail. The despicable messages did not stop with the mail, though, and bled over to Jones' cell phone in 2006. Upset by late-night calls from buddies Hawkins and Jones, who confided about the racism they had never experienced in Minnesota, Twins centerfielder Torii Hunter contractually placed the Cubs among the five teams to which he could not be traded in 2006. The hate mail was the worst byproduct of the Cubs' failure to reach the World Series in 2003 and their subsequent failures. Players should not have to deal with society's worst.

Even the most logical signing—a homecoming—can turn out disastrous if a combination of a player's personal life and bad health meet in a perfect storm. Such was the case with catcher Todd Hundley. The idea seemed so romantic in late 2000—bringing Hundley, holder of the record of most homers in a season by a catcher (41 with the Mets), back to the franchise where his father, Randy, was a folk hero in the late 1960s.

But the apparent dream turned nightmare when Hundley slumped, could not even hit his weight, and left the Cubs to undergo a mysterious rehab process. Manager Don Baylor had to be careful catching Hundley on hot, humid days, because he got dehydrated—a strange symptom for a supposedly in-shape pro athlete working all his life in warm weather. Hundley had a cornucopia of personal problems and potential conflict with his teetotaling, taskmaster father. He ended up being booed even louder than Hawkins or Patterson, and finally broke down one day in 2002 to give it back to the fans via a vulgar gesture.

"He had [personal] problems in high school [at Fremd in suburban Palatine]," said a veteran scout. "He got dehydrated due to his physical condition. I would have thought the Cubs had an idea there were physical things going on."

Hendry, then in training for his GM's job, explained the Cubs' logic in signing Hundley.

"We needed a catcher at the time," he said. "They're hard to find. They're not available. He looked like a good fit. He played reasonably well the year before. You were down to paying Charles Johnson $35 million or paying Todd Hundley $22 million. Everybody felt good about it the day we signed him. Many issues occurred along the way, and he had some very serious health issues, too. He hurt his back worse than it had ever been hurt. In fairness to Todd, he didn't fail because he didn't try. It got away from him a little bit. We weren't the only club willing to give Todd Hundley a three-year deal."

Even after a player gets through all the potential negatives, he ends up with more on his plate as a Cub in Wrigley Field than almost any other big leaguer. The Friendly Confines, sitting in world-class Chicago, is one of the Midwest's top tourist attractions. Players' families get caught up in the history and atmosphere.

"A distraction here is, Chicago is a fabulous town that everyone wants to come to," Steve Trachsel said. "When you come to play here, you have friends and family that don't want to visit you if you play in Cincinnati, but they want to come and visit you in Chicago. You can block that out and focus on the game, but that becomes part of your preparation."

Entangled In Ivy

"If the family wants you succeed, they will realize you're not a tour guide while you're in town," former Cubs manager Jim Riggleman said. "You have a routine; you're working. We had meetings about all that. Players were nodding their heads."

So what makes up the ideal personality to survive, and thrive, in Wrigley Field? Riggleman, now director of instruction for the archrival St. Louis Cardinals, points to the one player who performed longest since the careers of Billy Williams and Ron Santo ebbed in the mid-1970s.

"A Mark Grace-type guy," he said of the 13-year first baseman, quipster, baseball politician, companion of actresses, near-chain smoker, and present-day Diamondbacks announcer. "Someone who doesn't take himself too seriously. You need talent first; but if you have that kind of talent, you also have a looseness about it that maintains confidence when you're struggling. If fans get on you, you tell them you'll get 'em tomorrow. Mark was good with media, good with the fans. You need someone who's not wound too tight."

So what does Grace himself think?

"Baseball's supposed to be fun," he said. "I had fun every hour I was on that baseball field. I always looked at myself, and I looked at players who were so wrapped up in whether they had a good game or a bad game. They would take the game home with them. I just learned that's a great way to have a short career, to lack the ability to let things go, getting too high on the good times and too low on the bad times.

"Bottom line, I knew what my job was—to be the best first baseman for the Chicago Cubs that I could possibly be. I wasn't in charge of who would pitch. I wasn't in charge of the decision-making. For 13 years, they had me play first base; and I wanted to reward them every single day I went out there."

A perfect character, Grace was not. He was an earthy type, even guttural, to say the least. Many women and saloons knew his enthusiastic presence during his Cubs reign. When asked how he could be out every night while playing the heavy daytime schedule, Grace replied, with a straight face, that he started early after game's end and finished early. Whatever his curfew, he was in the clubhouse on time and ready to play each day.

Another Mark, with a surname of DeRosa, possessed a similar good attitude toward Wrigley Field before he ever played his first game as a

The Wrigley Character

Cub. And the concept of character ranked highly with infielder DeRosa, the first off-season free agent the Cubs signed for 2007, and those who knew him.

"Greg Maddux had good things to say about him," Hendry said. "He's a high-character guy."

DeRosa's self-description backs up such analysis: "I enjoy hitting No. 2, moving guys over, playing 'small ball,'" he said. "I'd like to provide some leadership, be a character guy."

No matter what the personality, or whether he's played in a market big or small, only one element is common to players with solid character. And that's probably best demonstrated by Cubs lefty Rich Hill's September 2006 response to the potential distractions of Wrigley Field and its quirky syndrome like none other in sports.

"We've won all through the minor leagues," Hill said of his young teammates, called up en masse due to injuries in 2006. "Why wouldn't we win here, too?"

nine

D-LEE'S TEAM

I WAS ALWAYS PARTIAL to Andre Dawson, but you had to get to know the guy first. Some might get the wrong idea when you first noticed him, and you'd logically want to keep a distance.

Dawson's face was locked into a clench as a Cub in the late 1980s. His stare could freeze you at 100 yards. "Intimidating," Dawson said of the impression some drew, but outside appearances ended up deceiving. "The Hawk" explained he merely was taking his job seriously and thus his facial muscles and gaze reflected that. Get to know him, and Dawson—who should be in the Hall of Fame but isn't—could laugh as easily as the next man. Dawson also used two words where three normally would do. Yet, he wasted none of his verbiage and made nearly every word count. You would get more profound, thoughtful streams of consciousness out of Dawson than most other major leaguers who'd gab away, dispensing notebook filler like empty calories.

While winning the National League Most Valuable Player award in 1987—posting one of the greatest offensive seasons in Cubs history—Dawson easily became the team's leader and focal point, but by no means was he a vocal leader. However, the combination of production and persona made him the center of the clubhouse, a man who commanded respect through his mere presence. And having dedicated himself to a rigorous pregame preparation program, arriving early to get in shape so he could play through a dozen surgeries on his knees, Dawson became the gold standard by which I measured devotion to excellence in all those who followed. Ditto with legendary clubhouse boss Yosh Kawano, who branded Dawson the best man he ever had in the locker room over his more than half-century on the job.

Few could measure up. Many big names failed, even embarrassing themselves and the pinstriped uniform they donned. Sammy Sosa was a Cub for 13 seasons, but despite all his glittering numbers, he never touched Dawson as an emotional focal point.

Then Derrek Lee came to the Cubs in 2004.

Within a year, Lee was the worthy successor to Dawson. Starting as the fourth wheel in the middle of the lineup after Sosa, Moises Alou, and Aramis Ramirez, Lee worked his way to the forefront after Sosa and Alou departed. An amazing season, in which he belted 46 homers, flirted with .400 early on, and finished at .335 to win the National League batting title, making him the Cubs' go-to guy—a status felt negatively in the won-lost column after Lee's wrist was broken just a month into the 2006 season on a play at first in Los Angeles. More importantly, though, his quiet, dignified demeanor, a throwback to Dawson, made the Cubs Lee's team—no questions asked.

He even smiled.

It couldn't be any other way. Not only did Lee come from a baseball family in which his father and uncle played professionally, but during his six seasons in Florida, he also crossed paths with Dawson, who works as a Marlins special assistant.

"I kind of admired how he carried himself," Dawson said before scurrying to work with Marlins outfielders before a home game at Dolphin Stadium. "He was soft-spoken and quiet. I see some of the qualities in him that I expected in myself. I'm not surprised at the route he's gone. He enjoys the game, knows how to have fun. He's not consumed with success or failure. Still, he's got to lead by example, and he'll do it through his makeup, character, attitude, and all-around performance. He's going out to win."

Always a good listener like Dawson, such philosophies, along with good baseball breeding, rubbed off on Lee, forming one of the best personal packages to grace the Cubs' clubhouse in recent memory.

As he sat on the steps leading into the Wrigley Field home locker room one midsummer day in 2006, trying to strengthen the wrist that wrecked his and the Cubs' season, I suggested to Lee that he possessed those Dawson-like qualities.

"Having comparisons to Andre Dawson is a huge compliment because I'm a big fan of his," Lee said. "Getting to know him, I think he's a great person. You learned stuff being around a guy like Andre Dawson. He still works out, probably harder than any of the players do. You can see his work ethic, and it just shows something."

Pundits had been proclaiming the Cubs to be Derrek Lee's team for a while at this juncture. But when ace Carlos Zambrano acknowledged Lee was the team leader, that he would love one day to talk to players in the same manner as Lee—where his words had clout—confirmed all the analysis.

Lee is eloquent in a restrained way. He won't shout or bluster. He has no need to, like Dawson. Their physical presence alone—Lee is 6-foot-5, big-guard lean muscle—is enough to command attention.

"I accept that," he said of the team-leader role. "It's a funny thing to say it's your team. I see what you mean about [being the] focal point. I'm the one who has to answer the questions after the game. I'm completely accepting of that. Later on in your career, there are times that you have to accept more responsibilities. I feel right now is my time.

"The only way you command respect is backing up what you say. If you're going to get on someone, you better be doing it yourself. I just try to go out and play the game the right way. Lead by example. I don't jump on guys a lot. I do speak to guys. I think there are a few guys on the team that take that role. Older guys did that when I was young. Show the right way to go about it."

Dawson concurred the quieter approach is better. "Players are very sensitive," he said. "I like the approach of not really getting in a guy's face. You talk *to* people instead of talking *at* them."

Aramis Ramirez, the man who bats behind Derrek Lee in the Cubs' order, believes Lee's personality lends itself to leadership.

"You don't become a leader by screaming at people and all that stuff," he said. "You just go out there and do your job, and play the way it was supposed to be played. You scream at people, and they're not going to respect you."

Another player with a similar personality to Lee's is former Cubs second baseman Mark Grudzielanek, now on the Royals. He calls the comparison to Dawson "a good analogy."

Entangled In Ivy

"There's times when he'll stand up and talk, but not too often," Grudzielanek said. "He's a quiet soul who goes about his business. He has that fire and that leadership to go out on an everyday basis. You need a few [more vocal] around him for certain meetings to speak out. When you have to take guys aside, he's not one of those to do it. But for the presence that you have on the team and on the field, he probably one of the best you can have.

"He's the type of guy who can handle it. He's not the type of guy who's going to blow up his head and be too cool for everybody. He's a very-level headed and grounded individual."

Although several vocal types are always welcome, the lower-decibel style does work in setting examples for team leadership.

"That's the important thing, the respect. When you do talk and you are serious, they listen," Grudzielanek said. "The guys who are out there yelling and barking all the time, people will blow them off. It will go in one ear and out the other. When I call the kids aside, they know I'm serious."

Dawson was only one of a long line of veterans who influenced Lee as he came through the ranks. He cited Tony Gwynn, Greg Vaughn, and the late Ken Caminiti with the Padres, his first team. Gary Sheffield and Bobby Bonilla were examples when he first came to the Marlins.

Then everyone's best Cubs teammate, Greg Maddux, arrived back in town at the same time as Lee in 2004.

"You learn from Maddux, the second he walks in, the way he goes about his business," Lee said. "Every fifth day, he was ready. That speaks volumes about a teammate."

Maddux also was a non-voluble chap, but, like Dawson, profound when he put forth his strict ration of words. Apparently, the example-by-doing works better in the long run than the example-by-chattering.

"You show up every day to work, ready to play," Lee said of gaining respect of teammates. "I'm not a real vocal guy; I'm a quiet guy."

Yet, Lee is his own man in his vocal restraint. He's no chip off the old block.

"My dad would speak to anyone all day long," he said. "All my life, I've been a quiet guy. Not really my mother's [personality], either—she's outgoing. I got the opposite end."

That restraint extends to Lee's feelings about his stature in society.

D-Lee's Team

"I don't understand why, because I hit a baseball well or catch it well, that makes me better than a doctor who performs surgery or teachers who teach class." he said. "Everyone has something they do well. Mine is baseball. I might get more attention for it; but to me, I'm the same as anyone else, so there's no reason to get a big head or ego."

With the contract of his dreams, tens of millions of dollars due to him for his blue-collar work ethic, Lee also claims he has built-in insurance against personal arrogance.

"I try to treat everyone the same," he said. "We're all human beings; we're all the same. I really don't comprehend getting a big head when you're a baseball player. We all know money means virtually nothing when judging the value of a person. We're all human beings, and I think everyone deserves to be treated the same unless they treat you otherwise.

"It [money] doesn't change you. Don't get me wrong, I know my daughter's taken care of, her kids are taken care of; and probably their kids are taken care of. In that sense, it's a great feeling—you can help your family and friends out. But as far as changing who you are, it doesn't change you; unless you allow it, maybe. It's hard to explain."

Okay, put it another way: How does Derrek Lee define earning his substantial paycheck on a typical day?

"That's a great question," he responded. "We make a diving play, the team wins; we might have gone 0-for-4, but we felt like we helped the team win. That's a good day for us. But the fans say, 'He went 0-for-4.' When you focus on it [winning], that's when you do well individually."

Lee was part of a special era of second- and even third-generation players who took advantage of the game squarely in their genes. Lee's father, Leon, was a longtime minor-leaguer who gained greater fame as a Japanese pro-baseball star. He had 268 homers and batted .308 for the Lotte Orions, Yokohama Taijo Whales, and Yakult Swallows. Leon Lee broke into Japanese baseball in tandem with his older brother, Leron, formerly a journeyman outfielder in the major leagues, who had played for the Cardinals, Padres, Indians, and Dodgers.

Lee followed his father through his entire decade-long career in Japan. He spent third and fourth grade attending classes at an international school. In other years, Lee summered with his father. Although he's not fluent in Japanese, he can understand key words and phrases.

"I loved it," he said of his time in Japan. "It's very Americanized. You can go to McDonald's; you can go out to get pizza. It opens your eyes [to another culture]. It's kind of arrogant to think it's your way or the highway."

The elder Lee's connections with Japan ended up paving the way for his son to come to the Cubs. Post-career status as a baseball TV commentator and publisher of a baseball magazine in Japan gave him an entrée to become the Cubs' first full-time Pacific Rim scout in 1998.

"I established a reputation for off-the-field activities," Leon Lee said in 2000. "I worked with disabled kids and orphans. They said I had a Japanese heart, but you are never really accepted as Japanese. I learned Japanese. I made up my mind that I would be there. My interpreter started teaching me some Japanese songs. I actually went on TV, sung Japanese songs, and made a record. I was on TV in a singing contest. I had a sing-off with a Japanese singer. I got 100, he got a 98. ... The people appreciated it that here's a guy making an effort to acclimate himself to Japanese culture."

Leon Lee also made contacts in nearby South Korea. His big prize was first baseman Hee Seop Choi, signed off the Korean national team in 1998 for $1 million. After the 2003 season, the Cubs turned Choi into Derrek Lee, completing the circle started by the latter's father.

Lee practically fell into the Cubs' laps. Trying to purge some salary after their 2003 World Series championship, the Marlins had a deal to dispatch Lee to the Baltimore Orioles, but the trade fell through. The Marlins then turned around and quickly made a deal on November 25, 2003, with Jim Hendry, who had longtime Florida connections. After several years of big minor-league numbers, Choi's stock had fallen a bit during the 2003 season, when he produced stats that were punctuated by a concussion from an on-field collision with Kerry Wood.

At the time of the deal, Lee already had become the player the Cubs had projected with Choi. The cavernous dimensions of Pro Player Stadium (now Dolphin Stadium) had dampened his power numbers. Lee had been a top power prospect in the Padres' minor-league chain, posting a 34-homer, 104-RBI season in Class AA in 1996—three years after he had been the team's first-round draft pick after turning down a basketball scholarship to the University of North Carolina. However, Lee only got a chance to play 22 games with San Diego. He was dispatched to the Marlins in a 1997 trade for Kevin Brown.

After struggling in 1998-99, Lee slugged 76 homers from 2000-02. Then, he boosted his output to 31 homers in the wild-card playoff run in 2003. Quietly, he also developed a reputation as a nimble first baseman despite his 6-foot-5 frame. He won his first Rawlings Gold Glove Award in '03.

Lee was at his most infamous—as a Cubs opponent—in Games 6 and 7 of the star-crossed 2003 National League Championship Series. His two-run double tied the game 3-3 in the eighth inning of Game 6 off a tiring Mark Prior. The next night, Lee collected a single to give the Marlins a 6-5 lead that they would not relinquish.

The enemy soon was a friend, though, as Lee moved on to a radically new baseball lifestyle. He first had to endure a period of adjustment, particularly to the Wrigley Field environment and scheduling. A notoriously slow starter, Lee's bat was cold in the chilly Chicago weather, an absolute contrast from hot and humid Miami. Worse yet was his body clock, finding assimilation to the heavy schedule of home day games difficult. Even though he was a homebody, Lee simply could not put himself down for the night until 1:30 or 2 a.m., even though he had to be at Clark and Addison within eight hours to prepare for batting practice.

Typical of Lee's personality, he never complained about the early wakeups—unlike prominent teammates such as Moises Alou. In keeping with the personal discipline that governs his life, he also went about finding a way to adjust.

"There's nothing to complain about," Lee said. "You know, coming to Wrigley Field, that you're going to be playing day games. All you can do is make the adjustment. Now, I love the day games; I love playing here at Wrigley. You just have to go to bed early. I'm probably in bed before midnight every night. Even on the road, I'm up early. I like it. I feel like I have a fuller day."

Lee simply followed the lead of Cubs Hall of Famer Billy Williams, who was able to play 1,117 consecutive games through seven seasons of what was then an all-daytime schedule at Wrigley Field.

Entangled In Ivy

"[Lee] coming over here after playing all night games [in Florida], I saw this," Williams said. "I said he'd have a better year [in 2005]. Playing day games is worse than night games. You've got to get to bed."

As he adjusted to his new team and schedule, Lee's bat heated up. It helped he was the fourth run producer after Alou, Sammy Sosa, and Aramis Ramirez. He did not endure the typical pressure that affects Wrigley Field newcomers. In June 2004, he batted .385 with 20 extra-base hits and 19 RBIs. Included were 10- and 12-consecutive plate appearances in which he reached base. He twice had five hits in a game.

Lee, like Williams, also was an iron man. He waved off suggestions that he needed rest, playing in 161 games. The everyday style may have cost him at season's end, just when the Cubs went into the tank over the season's final week and coughed up a 1.5-game lead in the National League wild-card race. After a 10-game hitting streak that concluded September 20, his RBI bat was cold in the season's fatal, final home stand. He finished at .278 with 39 doubles, 32 homers, and 98 RBIs.

Much of his production before the slump served as a forecast for his 2005 dream season, in which he combined power and average like few others in modern baseball.

Dawson compared Lee to a player from his own playing days—Dave Parker. But Parker was a left-handed hitter, giving him a step or two advantage running to first to beat out a few extra hits and tack on points. Jack McKeon, his old Marlins manager, knew Lee was close to fulfilling his potential. In a more hitter-friendly ballpark, McKeon predicted Lee could hit 50 homers. He didn't realize at the time how close he'd come to that vaunted power number.

Reversing his career trend, Lee came out smoking in April 2005. He had one of the most productive months in Cubs history with a .419 average and 28 RBIs. He continued the blistering pace through June, batting .407 while running his totals to 23 homers and 65 RBIs by month's end. Thus, Lee was enveloped in a swirl of Triple Crown talk.

Lee at first thought such projections were premature. However, when informed Williams had a chance at the Triple Crown in his batting title season of 1972, he let down his guard.

"I don't think it's a bad thought [to] try to win it," he said then. "Why not? That means you're having a great season. The only thing you can do that's in your control is go up there and have a great at-bat. You can't control the RBIs because if no one's on base, you won't get it. You can't control the home runs because, if someone hits more, you don't win. All you can control is keeping that focus so you don't give away that at-bat."

Lee also had an intelligent approach to his craft. The best hitters never tried to uppercut at power-friendly Wrigley Field. Maintaining the same, level swing would produce home runs as a byproduct of good hitting mechanics.

"I try to hit the ball hard every time," he said back in late spring of 2005. "It's the same swing. Home runs are the byproduct of getting extension—hit the ball in the right spot and it goes in the air. Home runs are almost a mistake. You try to hit a line drive hard and, if it gets in the air, fine."

No matter how he was fated to finish, Lee had become one of baseball's most dominant hitters. At the plate was where he could burst out of his personal restraint, where he could believe he was the boss, in total control while displaying just enough arrogance to fuel his production.

Sitting on the clubhouse stairs in the quiet of his 2006 disablement, Lee could put a finger on his emotions of wielding his lethal bat.

"That's when your ego does come in," he said. "When you're still in the box, and you're playing well; you just feel like you're the best player on the field, and you're going to do something good. You feel like you're better than the pitcher. You still respect that pitcher, but you feel you're going to win that battle there. It's a confidence in yourself, that you're going to get your job done. That's what half this game is about."

It's a controlled ego trip, though. Lee has never forgotten that baseball is still a game of failure.

"That's the nature of this game," he said. "It will humble you quick. Day to day, you can be feeling great and go 0-for-5. You just have to understand that and keep the same level approach every day. This game is about fighting your insecurities. You go 0-for-4, things can start creeping in your head real quick."

As 2005 wore on, and the Cubs began floundering, Lee could not quite maintain his early season pace. He hit .284 in August and .291 in September.

Entangled In Ivy

Yet, by any measuring stick, he had one of the best offensive seasons in Cubs history while favorably being compared to Cardinals superstar Albert Pujols as baseball's best first baseman.

"He was as good as Albert then," Ramirez said. "The only difference is, Pujols has done it every year since he came into the league. D-Lee has been around, but he can be [as good]."

Lee won the NL batting title at .335, while also leading the majors in average. Lee also led the NL in hits (199), doubles (50), total bases (393), extra-base hits (99), and slugging percentage (.662).

His 46 homers set a record for Cubs first basemen and was the eighth-highest season total in team history. He did not go more than two consecutive games without a hit. The .335 average was third highest for a right-handed hitting Cub in 75 years, after Bill Madlock's .354 and .339 marks that captured successive NL batting titles in 1975 and 1976. Pitchers respected Lee, too, issuing him 23 intentional walks over the season's course. He scored 120 runs.

For good measure, the acrobatic Lee won his second Rawlings Gold Glove award at first.

And yet, Lee had to exercise the utmost patience to validate his own ability. The broken wrist delayed his quest to repeat the 2005 heroics.

"It was a great season," he said, "but, for myself, I need to do it again. I've had one good season. Like Sammy [Sosa] did it for five, six years. Billy Williams did that every year. I want to repeat that and continue to repeat that until I'm satisfied. You're always trying to get better. Honestly, it's hard to have a better numerical season than [2005]. But I feel like— to have an MVP-dominant season—that is what I want to do again."

The sheer excellence of Lee's season made him the first among equals on the Cubs.

"He's got that kind of personality. People look at him and expect him to carry the team," said Ramirez.

When Lee was effectively lost for the rest of the season on April 19, 2006, the damage to the lineup was as if two run-producing players had been wiped off the roster. To his teammates, he had been Jordan-esque in his impact on the lineup.

"It's not just for me; it was for everybody," Ramirez said. "Any time you miss a guy like that, it's like if you take Pujols out of the Cardinals' lineup. Everybody saw that they struggled when Pujols went down for two weeks. Not just the guys around him, but the whole team will struggle."

One man makes that much of a difference in a team game?

"That kind of a player will," Ramirez said. "In D-Lee's case, it does."

Ever modest, Lee begs to disagree.

"One player shouldn't make that much of a difference," he said. "Baseball's definitely a team game. You have to pitch well, play good defense, run the bases well; and you have to hit well. One guy doesn't make that much of a difference over a course of the season. I think there were other things going on with us this year rather than injuries."

Little has been publicized about Lee's off-the-field persona in his three Cubs seasons. He wouldn't have it any other way. He's consistent in and out of the ballpark in his low-key manner.

"I'm the same guy, quiet," he said of his life away from baseball. "I'm just a boring guy. We [wife Christina and daughter Jada Ryan] just like going for walks, maybe go see a movie, go to dinner—nothing flashy, just basic stuff.

"If I go out twice a season in Chicago, that's about right. I'd rather stay in, get my rest, watch a movie at home. Playing day games five days in a row, it's an adjustment. Now I love it. I feel I have a normal life."

The Lees had a big family outing on August 17, 2006. They were part of the gallery at the PGA Championship at Medinah, watching Tiger Woods, Phil Mickelson, and crew pass by.

"We keep it simple," Lee said. "In the off-season, we always stay in Sacramento. That's where all my family is, where [my daughter's] grandparents are."

Oddly enough, the voluble personality absent from Lee has resurfaced in preschooler Jada.

"My wife and I were talking about it," he said. "My daughter can be ornery sometimes with adults, be disrespectful. You have to stop it quick. We feel we treat everyone with respect. That's my main value system—you treat everyone with respect. If you do that, I feel you'll be okay; but now's the time you have to squash it."

Jada's headstrong manner became the least of her parents' problems in September 2006. Out of nowhere came the announcement that Derrek had to take a short leave of absence just after he was in position to get a few weeks' playing time near season's end. Jada's vision was affected in one eye by a disease called Lebers Congenital Amaurosis, or LCA, which affects some 3,000 children in the United States. A misty-eyed Lee, his voice cracking, made the announcement to stunned media at Wrigley Field.

At the same time, he did not take the family crisis lying down. In conjunction with Boston Celtics co-owner Wyc Grousbeck—whose family was affected by LCA as well—Lee established the Project 3000 Foundation to speed research into the disease, which is as yet incurable in humans. Working with the University of Iowa's Dr. Ed Stone, who had examined Jada, Lee hoped Project 3000 would spur genetic research and provide better information in advance of the cure.

Baseball and pennant quests thus paled in comparison to his urgent, personal mission. However, even before he took on a new opponent in a genetic disease, Lee would disabuse the idea that he works in an environment in which he'd never win.

"I don't like the word 'luck,'" he said. "You play good baseball, and things go your way. You play bad baseball, and things don't go your way. If you're a great shooter, you'll get the bounces on the rim. If you're a bad shooter, you won't.

"Take that out of your mind-set. Make yourself accountable."

ten

SIX INNINGS OF LOUNGING, TWO MINUTES OF TERROR

ON A LATE-SPRING morning in 2005, newly anointed Cubs closer Ryan Dempster hoisted a hybrid bicycle down the stairs into the home clubhouse. When Dempster mounted the seat at the bottom of the stairs, heads instantly turned.

Somehow, Dempster peddled among mere centimeters of empty space the narrow clubhouse and avoided striking humans, card tables, laundry carts, even stray bats. He stopped at Kerry Wood's locker, which was conveniently located close to the off-limits sinks and mirrors, got off, and wheeled the bike through the sink-and-mirrors section before stowing it in the back equipment room.

The bike was Dempster's choice of transportation to dodge ballpark traffic from his in-season home just five blocks away. He'd be the logical Cub to pedal himself to Wrigley Field. A couple of relievers, starting with a chap named Ray Newman in 1971, had biked to the ballpark. A few years back, Houston Astros manager Larry Dierker used to rollerblade to Clark and Addison via the lakefront path from his downtown hotel. Some Cubs, most recently including Moises Alou and Kyle Farnsworth, commuted via motorcycles. Generally, though, those who don't opt for the gargantuan gas-hog black SUVs with tinted windows—the modern equivalent of a 1956 Cadillac—are considered the off-center types, which describes Dempster, the funniest, quickest-witted Cub of modern times, perfectly. He considers that off-centeredness an absolute requisite of maintaining his on-the-job sanity.

Oh, a few weeks later when the bike was heisted, Dempster was mad. Some twisted fan had stalked Dempster, followed him home, and stolen the bike from his back yard. That must have been baseball's version of a left-handed compliment. As the new closer, he was deemed important enough to be stalked.

It's a wonder anyone in baseball wants to be a closer, or yearns for any bullpen job, for that matter. Relief pitching could be the most thankless job this side of a field-goal kicker in all of sports. Some will say a quarterback endures the most pressure, out there exposed, all by himself. At least he's got a line to block for him and receivers to catch his passes. And the kicker has a long snapper along with special teams blockers for help. But the reliever is totally alone out there. He can throw one pitch that means defeat, disgrace, infamy, the loss of a pennant. He can't hide. He can serve up a grand-slam homer that snatches victory away so suddenly, almost violently. On the other hand, if a starter gives up four runs in the first, then settles down, a modest comeback by his teammates could still award him with a victory.

In the absolute worst-case scenario, ex-Cub Donnie Moore—haunted by serving up the Dave Henderson homer that denied the Los Angeles Angels entrée into the 1986 World Series—committed suicide in 1989. Fans harangued another former Cub, Mitch Williams, after Toronto's Joe Carter slugged the World Series-winning homer off him in 1993. Williams was never the same.

Minus such horror stories, garden-variety relief work requires a strong stomach, stout heart, and short memory. The life is usually six innings of inactivity, even lounging around in comradeship in the bullpen and soaking up a summer day or night, followed by two minutes of sheer terror when the phone rings to summon the reliever into a jam.

The reliever who survives takes his craft seriously, but an otherwise lighter disposition helps. Thus, Dempster suits the pressure-filled job in which he's rewarded the majority of times by saves and punished in a few instances with crushing, memorable defeats. In fact, Dempster is an amateur stand-up comic hailing from Canada—home of many famed quipsters. He is too fast for all his teammates and inquiring media, and would have held his own had he guest-starred back in the day with

Six Innings of Lounging, Two Minutes of Terror

Johnny Carson, the entertainment world's Babe Ruth of ad-libbers and quick wits.

"My wife [Jenny] gets mad at me sometimes because I'm always cracking jokes," Dempster said. "Sometimes, I don't take things too seriously, but laughter is the best medicine. If you're laughing, life is better. I remember my first joke. It was a 'knock-knock' joke. It started when I was two and a half. My mom and two younger brothers love to joke, quote movie lines, love to laugh."

With the Florida Marlins in 2001, Dempster talked a Boston comedy club owner, who had him on his fantasy team, into letting him do eight minutes of stand-up while in town to play the Red Sox on Father's Day. Dempster's father was in attendance.

"It's good to be in Boston," Dempster told the appreciative audience then. "I've noticed the Big Dig [interrupted by cheers], and I've seen the official state tree of Massachusetts—the three-foot orange cone."

He dreams of hosting *Saturday Night Live*, remembering his favorite era of Chris Farley, David Spade, Adam Sandler, and Mike Myers.

Even a book signing is fodder for one-liners. Dempster filled in for Kerry Wood at a signing for a children's book authored by the Cubs' wives on July 29, 2005. The crowd of hundreds in a Skokie, Illinois, Barnes & Noble wound around an upstairs banister and snaked down a staircase to where Dempster, teammate Jerry Hairston, and their wives were signing an average of three books per customer.

What happened to Wood and wife, Sarah, a major impetus behind the book? Wood later said he had to beg off because of injuries, his ongoing conversion to the bullpen, and a rehab trip to the minors. As Dempster and Jenny scribbled their autographs in assembly-line fashion during the signing, Dempster's eyes lit up with an improvised punchline:

"Kerry Wood's car was hit by a water buffalo, so he couldn't make it."

That Dempster takes absolute joy in baseball and his surroundings, having made it growing up in the left field of rural British Columbia, strengthens the humor. A few weeks before the book signing, after a Wrigley Field game, Ryan and Jenny Dempster and some friends took the couple's three Labs—two yellows and one black—for a romp on the diamond. The dogs were wrasslin' with one another at shortstop, where few canines had ever gone. The entire group wandered out to center field, where Dempster posed with the pooches for photos by the yellow "400" sign carved out of the ivy.

He was kind of sheepish the next day.

"They went to the bathroom on the field," he shrugged. Don't worry. No one would tattle. The comedian-pitcher had built up so much goodwill that befouling the sacred Tribune Company turf would be forgiven.

Probably one entertainment venue at a time is all that will be calling Dempster. Until he's summoned into 30 Rock for late-night Saturday duty, Dempster has to settle for being the life of the Cubs clubhouse, comic leader of the bullpen, and the team's ninth-inning man. Over his two-plus seasons, he had an interesting foil in serious southpaw Will Ohman, and they were joined by another left-handed complement, Scott Eyre, in 2006. Eyre is author of his own brand of humor and Dempster's fellow conspirator on several pranks.

All the seriousness was concentrated in the right-handers. Seeing service in 2005-06 was homegrown Michael Wuertz, who will remain grounded after fighting his way up the minor-league chain as a pitcher with the image of more determination than pure stuff. A big-ticket acquisition to accompany Eyre for 2006 was the quiet, businesslike Bobby Howry, a long-ago White Sox closer who survived shoulder surgery to develop into one of the game's best setup men.

Other relievers have come and gone during Dempster's tenure. LaTroy Hawkins, a popular teammate but uptight in his public persona, was literally booed out of Wrigley Field. Roberto Novoa was up and down from the minors—and up and down in the bullpen almost daily as ineffective and injured starters forced early phone calls to the 'pen. Yet, by 2006, the relievers were the closest-knit group on a Cubs roster that changed nearly as often.

And by far the loosest—Dempster, Ohman, and Eyre, within the confines of their bullpen world, practically kept the baseball tradition of pranks alive by themselves. Dempster is dead serious when he discusses the lack of levity in baseball clubhouse life. He is the true inheritor of the late Moe Drabowsky's spirit. One time, in the late 1950s, Drabowsky—who played the stock market—found the bullpen phone could get an outside line. Drabowsky dialed up his stockbroker and jabbered away, tying up the phone. Cubs manager Bob Scheffing tried calling the

Six Innings of Lounging, Two Minutes of Terror

bullpen to order a pitcher to warm up, but repeatedly got a busy signal. Eventually, a frantic Scheffing signaled the relievers with towels.

"I really don't think people have as much fun as they used to," Dempster said. "It almost seemed like, if we have fun and something goes wrong, the papers are writing 10 articles. 'They're joking around when they're losing games?' Or even if we do win, are they worried about playing a baseball game or having fun?

"Last time I checked, when we go out there and they say, 'Play ball,' it's a baseball game. Sure, it's a competition, a lot of people depend on us as a livelihood. At the same time, it's 162 games a year. That's tough. So what you gotta do, you gotta stay loose, you gotta have fun. Nobody does the hotfoot; nobody puts bubble gum on top of a hat because the guy might get embarrassed on TV. A guy makes millions, he's a celebrity— and we can't embarrass somebody? C'mon. ...

"Anytime anyone gets me with a good prank, I appreciate it. It's good humor. It's funny. It seems people's ego or feelings get hurt. Nowadays, instead of a guy going on the DL for a torn hammy, you're worried about him going on the DL for hurt feelings."

Pranks surely are an effective welcome to the clubhouse. The first one played on me was in spring training 1996 at HoHoKam Park in Mesa. I had left my notebook on a table for one minute to speak quickly to Cubs catcher Scott Servais. When I turned around, the notebook had vanished. I started pointing at infielder Jose Hernandez. "Don't look at me," he protested. Finally, Sammy Sosa nodded to me and pointed to the top of a water cooler, on which the notebook was comfortably resting.

Two years later, my radio microphone disappeared when I set it down temporarily on a Wrigley Field clubhouse table. I issued a plea to the players to return it. Minutes later, it reappeared, or at least the top part of the two-piece instrument did. The top was placed standing on a clubhouse table. Shortstop Jeff Blauser had accomplished his most useful act as a Cub by heisting the mike and taking it apart.

In the same year, Blauser and first baseman Mark Grace commandeered both the mike and the Marantz tape recorder in the Wrigley Field home dugout and proceeded to tape some vile, profane commentary about me, knowing smiles on their faces throughout. Fortunately, they were recording on a blank tape. Infielder Manny Alexander dumped ice water on me twice in 1998 when the Cubs clinched the wild-card berth in a playoff against the Giants. Five years later, after the Cubs clinched the NL Central, Moises Alou specifically sought me out and took aim with a bottle of cheap champagne. I had taken care to don a windbreaker beforehand.

You're pranked when you're one of the gang. Dempster taketh, and he giveth back, with compounded interest. Will Ohman was the object of one of the greatest pranks of modern baseball times during spring training 2005. "Far beyond [typical]," Ohman said. "It was very impressive. A lot of work went into it."

The prank began when, according to Dempster, "Someone messed around with Will's locker a little bit, did a few things. Because of my reputation as a practical joker, he asked a few people. Someone on the team asked if it was me. I told him to tell him I did it, but it wasn't me that did it.

"He decided he wanted to play a prank on me. He did it on a day that I was starting against the Royals in Surprise (Arizona). He super-glued the zipper on my pants closed, put eye black in my hat, and messed with all my shoes. I proceeded to give up eight runs that day."

Dempster's comic reputation has become well established. Fox Sports miked him during a *Saturday Game of the Week*. Dempster mimicked Harry Caray and Joe Buck live from the bullpen in mid-game. Two days before Ohman nailed him, MLB Productions called and wanted to film Dempster performing a prank.

"As soon as this happens, I called them on way back from Surprise and said, 'Yeah, you guys might need to come to the park tomorrow or the next day.'"

Dempster was diabolical in his planning.

"During stretch, I took his car keys out of his pocket," he said of Ohman. "He was out on the field. I knew he had no chance of being in the locker room. He had a 2003 Yukon Denali. I pulled it right out in front of the clubhouse door. I got a guy to bring a professional NASCAR-style jack and four blocks from an auto-body shop. The No. 1 important thing when you're doing a prank on somebody—involving hiding personal possessions—is you don't want to damage anything. That's not right, a good prank is a good prank without damaging anything.

"I jacked his car up on the blocks, took all four tires off and proceeded to hide these tires around HoHoKam Stadium, and then put the car right next to the concession stand near the clubhouse so all the fans could see it. Let's just say I was proud of the way it turned out."

The MLB Productions crew then went to film Ohman. He couldn't figure out why he was the subject of their cameras. He puffed his chest out.

"They were just waiting for his reaction," Dempster said. "He walked into the bullpen, and there was a nice big tire sitting out in the bullpen waiting for him. He missed the one in the shower, he missed the one in the coaches' room, he missed the one in the dugout bathroom. He finally saw the one in the bullpen. Someone said, 'Will, that looks like one of your tires.' You could see his head go back, and he walked out to the parking lot. He finally saw [his car] next to the clubhouse."

After Eyre's arrival, Dempster had a prankster associate ... or maybe a rival. One day as he was doing a live ESPN interview after a game, Dempster got the shaving-cream pie in the face. But he kept talking through the lather until the end of the interview. The obvious culprit was Eyre, and Dempster suggested that the lefty better have eyes in the back of his head for the inevitable payback. Only in August 2006 did Dempster reveal the whole episode was a setup with Eyre to make it look like a prank. Moe Howard, wherever he is now, would have been proud of the *Stoogesque* slapstick.

Dempster has looked for the light side of life ever since the homespun humor of his childhood in tiny Gibsons, British Columbia. His quick wit earned him a quick ejection from science class by his junior high teacher, Mr. Smethurst, as relayed to *Sports Illustrated* a few years back:

"He was trying to discuss the planets," Dempster recalled. "We kept calling it 'ur-ANUS,' and he kept calling it 'UR-anus.' I repeatedly asked him, 'How big is ur-ANUS?' Finally, he kicked me out."

Dempster is such a good team guy that, on the dare of his teammates, he stripped down—whether he got to Full Monty status is unclear—and quickly circulated inside a Lincoln Park watering hole where his teammates had gathered one beer-soaked night in the summer of 2004. "Just say, I served people at the bar wearing just an apron," Dempster said. However, he wasn't in a laughing mood the following spring training when columnist-provocateur Jay Mariotti suggested Dempster had streaked down a street in full view of all. As wild as Dempster can be, he knows he can't go R-rated in a G-rated atmosphere.

Entangled In Ivy

Cubs general manager Jim Hendry, who signed Dempster in a kind of gamble for 2004 as he was rehabbing from Tommy John surgery, figured Dempster had just the right temperament for the thankless job. As a rapid-fire ad-libber with a biting wit, Hendry makes fun of sportswriters' already dumpy apparel, so he knows a kindred soul when he sees one.

"Everybody's different, but in his situation, it probably really helps, especially in this role," Hendry said. "It's a role where you have to be a cool customer. You have to go out there and let it all hang out for an inning. And if it doesn't go well, you got to have the personality to let it go and get at it the next day."

Dempster's humor does have its limits, though. At some juncture, the fun must yield to game preparation. The life of a reliever is an ebb and flow of workouts, idle moments, camaraderie with fellow pitchers, and then the most stressful moments that games can manifest.

Generations of Cubs relievers, of course, have started out their workday shagging flies and running in the outfield, where they have received eyefuls as far back as the cusp of the 1970s. Frisky female bleacher fans have flashed their breasts at generations of passing pitchers, a practice that has diminished in a more security-conscious 21st Century. The pitchers have been interactive, but not in the way you'd think. On hot days, sometimes they'd turn groundskeepers hoses on sweaty fans. On 90-degree July 29, 2006, Dempster amply watered a Cardinals fan holding up a sign mocking the Cubs in the first row in left field.

Batting practice is the last time many fans see the relievers until mid-game or later. Unless they're low on the seniority list, they often start out their game routine in the clubhouse.

Scott Eyre, who gets down to the bullpen by the third inning, listens to the same "eight to 10" songs before the game. He showers for the second time that day "because I like to be clean." Thus, he makes sure to launder the same undershirt and cutoff fleece he wears daily. The exception is his hat, which is never changed. "It's pretty nasty," he said of caked-on dirt and sweat residue.

The relievers get a better scouting report on the hitters they'll later face from the centerfield television camera instead of the bullpen bench.

"I sit right here," Bobby Howry said of his locker. "I watch the game on TV. You can't see the strike zone; you can't see anything [from the

Six Innings of Lounging, Two Minutes of Terror

bullpen]. You gotta see what the ump's zone is. There's no point being down there the first three innings."

Will Ohman, whose locker is across from Howry's, also hangs around to start the game.

"I'm usually in the clubhouse the first four innings watching hitters on TV," he said. "When you're looking at a 40-inch TV instead of watching people from 250 feet away at a weird angle, you'll see [better] where hitters are stepping, where they are in the box."

None could see themselves as relaxed as all-time Cubs closer Lee Smith, whose in-game clubhouse naps were famous. Smith, of course, claimed he stuck around scouting the hitters on the smaller screen TV sets of the 1980s. Nodding off today is considered very bad form. Kyle Farnsworth, among other off-the-field histrionics of his Cubs bullpen career, got into trouble for stealing 40 winks in a 2002 game.

"For me, personally, it's tough to sit in here for six innings and then go out there and get loose," Howry said of the concept of clubhouse naps. "I wouldn't feel like I was into the game. Sleep in seventh, get dressed in eighth, pitch in ninth? I couldn't do that."

One obvious reason the pitchers filter one by one to the bullpen: they don't like to be cramped together on the bullpen bench through the entire game. "There's room for all, but we have to snuggle up a little bit," Howry said. "We've got a few chairs."

At least one pitcher has to start out the game in the 'pen if disaster strikes the starter through early bombardment or injury, but that early bird also has another responsibility.

"Everything I've been taught, the bullpen bag with snacks and fingernail clippers and all that stuff, the most junior guy in the 'pen takes it," Ohman said. "It's a backpack with sunflower seeds and antacids. Never let a guy with more service time than you beat you down to the bullpen."

Keeping in tune with the superstitious habits of major leaguers, Eyre always takes a diet soda down to the bullpen. "I don't drink it all, I maybe take a couple of sips," he said. "Having had ADHD, it's a focus point."

Most studious and serious of all the relievers seemed to be Wuertz.

"Starting in the fourth, you've got to start getting mentally prepared," he said. "It's more concentration than anything. I can talk and pay attention to the game at the same time."

Entangled In Ivy

However, sensory distractions—along with the arrival of Dempster the quipster—provide worthy competition for attention. Too much interaction with fans sitting behind them would disrupt their concentration. Still, the relievers don't forget who pays their salaries.

"Treat others the way you want to be treated," Wuertz said. "The majority of people are season-ticket holders, and you see them every day. It's easier to go about business when you see familiar faces every day."

The relievers can listen to the fans' conversations.

"'Hey, no cell phones,' we'll say," Eyre laughed.

Those fans who choose to razz the relievers don't know how deep they've jumped when they dive into Dempster. He'll always get in the last word and wins any battle of one-upmanship.

"When a fan heckles you, it's not that they don't like you. They just want to get a reaction out of you," he said. "You throw it back at them, give something back that they don't want back, and give it back with interest. You don't let them get in the last word."

"He's pretty good at throwing curveballs at hecklers, but in a funny way," Wuertz said. "It's pretty good stuff. He's definitely quick-witted."

Amateurs try to raise his hackles by calling him "Dumpster." Yet, as he once told *Sports Illustrated*, fans would have to do better than that: "I say to them, 'I've never heard that before in my life. So original. You should be writing screenplays.' Usually they get embarrassed and don't rag you again."

Dempster believes any verbal jousting is fair game so long as it's not personal—or profane. Although he enjoys triple-X humor as much as anyone; in public he models himself after Johnny Carson and Chevy Chase.

"Guys who could make you laugh without cursing," he said. "As long as it's clean and they're not dropping the F-bombs."

Classic movie lines have been a Dempster specialty since childhood in Canada, and he gives his teammates a free education in TinselTown. They learn the game by swimming with the shark—or, in this case, the closer.

"We rag on each other, have fun, and it keeps us loose," Dempster said. "The more relaxed you are, the better you're going to perform. If you're uptight, you're not going to perform."

Six Innings of Lounging, Two Minutes of Terror

While they're laughing with and at Dempster, the relievers face the temptation of adding on calories during the idle middle innings. Fans are constantly offering them snacks—and, yes, there are a few worthy successors to 1980s Astros reliever Charlie Kerfeldt, who scarfed down a vended hot dog live on TV from the Shea Stadium bullpen.

Eyre, the consummate left-hander, admits to have surreptitiously quaffed a malted milk courtesy of a fan, talking gulps by shielding his body from view of the dugout and television cameras—and later pitching in that game. Dempster has devoured peanuts—"they'd be considered like sunflower seeds"—passed down from the box seats. Someone tried to deliver a pizza to the bullpen, but the pitchers respectfully declined it. Beers always are offered to the same result. Another time, Dempster overdosed on gum. To amuse his bullpen mates, he stuffed 42 pieces in his mouth. The serious types like Howry and Wuertz abstain from sneaking a bite.

"You remember, you only got three hours on field, you better be prepared to hold off," Wuertz said.

In the spirit of baseball follies, the entire bullpen crew cannot deke opponent left fielders as happened to the Giants' Leon "Daddy Wags" Wagner back in 1958: The Cubs' Tony Taylor shot a liner into the bullpen, and it rolled under the bench. The relievers kept pointing behind the bench and Wagner fell for the ruse. By the time he figured out the baseball's true location, Taylor had circled the bases for an inside-the-park homer.

"There's some kind of flap now that prevents the ball from rolling in there," Howry said.

While the middle innings proceed, Howry is able to concentrate on the game while Dempster and Eyre are chattering away. Ohman now zeroes in on potential hitters he'd face within the next hour.

"I'll scout lefties extra hard for situations that could arise when I'm in there," he said. "How he swings the bat one day isn't how he swings the next day. He could have gotten in the cage following a game after some bad hacks. You play manager in your own head. A lefty coming up, I'd project what would I do if that happens; so, when the situation does arise, I don't have to worry about being unprepared. I've already played it through in my head as to what I can do."

Entangled In Ivy

Ohman thus knows when he'd likely come in; yet, according to Howry, he still jumps when the phone rings for the first time. "He's high-strung," Howry said.

Ohman has his routine, though, after the call has been received.

"It's time to work," said the lefty. "That's all. No butterflies. The only time it's ever really an adrenaline rush is if the phone call is of an immediate nature. You're in the middle of a count to one guy, a lefty's on deck, and they call down. You know, 'As soon as this guy is on, I'm on.' That's when adrenaline kicks in."

As a middle-inning man whose role isn't set like Dempster, Howry and Eyre, Wuertz can't be sure the phone is summoning him.

"It's an adrenaline rush when you don't know and your name gets called," he said. "If you don't hear that phone ring, you're in trouble. You always want to get into the game. That's the last leg of that whole process."

Eyre has his own warm-up routine when his name is called via the phone.

"I take my fleece off and pour water over my head," he said. "I'll throw 10-15 warm-up pitches—usually fastballs, several sliders, and then I'll finish with fastballs. You can get a good feel for your pitches here. The home [bullpen mound] is real good, same as the [game] mound."

None of the relievers can sweat bullets upon entry, though—even in the middle innings, no situation is stress-free.

Dempster, of course, remembers Mr. Smethurst here. "'Ur-ANUS' will pucker up if you let it get to you," he said. "That's the toughest thing. You get out here at Wrigley, the crowd's going nuts, and you're out there with a runner on second. A base hit scores the tying run. Sometimes you have to calm yourself down a bit, because you have that adrenaline going. The attitude comes not so much before the game or during, but afterward. You've got to let stuff go, good, bad, or ugly.

"I like the idea of coming into the game with the bases loaded and two out in the eighth," Dempster continued. "Don't get me wrong, I like the one-two-three innings. I don't mind it [no wiggle room for failure]. I thrive on that—it's fun to try to get three outs before the tying run crosses the plate, no matter how it's done. It's intense when you're out there, but you prepare and try to stay ready and stay focused to do the job. Some people are afraid of failure; some are afraid of success. How many times have you seen guys in the big leagues at this level content with being a very good player? Maybe they can be a great player. Maybe they're afraid of success. With success, you have expectations. I've always thrived on that."

The emotional rewards are enormous for any reliever who completes his high-wire act, especially after getting out of a jam with men on base. Here's how some members of the Cubs bullpen described such feelings:

Eyre: "You just aced a test you didn't study for, and the anticipation to see what the results are."

Wuertz, on surviving a bases-loaded jam: "The way I look at it, it's damage control. Limit it to one run. If you give up no runs, you feel like you've walked across water. You feel like you're floating through space, especially if it's a big game."

Ohman: "You've just done, in our profession, the ultimate thing. You went out there and stopped damage from occurring. I'm fired up. There's a relief because you're done. If I throw two fastballs down the middle, and two guys making diving stops, I'm not going to say, 'Ooh, yeah, all right—I got out of that,' but I'm not going to sit and dwell on it and say, 'I stink.'"

Howry's approach, like much of his personality, is more businesslike and matter-of-fact.

"I don't really get into it one way or another," he said. "I've had too many of them going the other way. I probably was a little high-strung in '04, coming back from surgery. I was away for almost a year. After the last couple of years, it's even keel. You realize: with just one pitch, you're done."

The exact opposite is the finality of the blown save and the blown game. The closer who fails simply can't hide. He has the long walk of defeat from the mound, often to a chorus of beer-soaked boos. A ravenous media in the locker room—the same media who chuckle with him after a save—besiege him. His teammates often run and hide.

However, if he's a pro, he will face the music afterward.

By necessity, Dempster had to leave his game at the ballpark, especially in an unnerving 2006 season. With a new son, Brady, added to the household, it was no time for dark moods after hours.

"I never take it home," Dempster said. "I might be a little upset when I come home, but it's no one's fault but mine. Why take it out on anyone else?"

Dempster did not like the situation, but he gamely faced the postgame inquisition on May 13, 2006, at Wrigley Field. While pitching against the Padres, he served up a three-run Mike Piazza homer that just made it into the left-field basket in the ninth, erasing a 3-1 Cubs lead and a sure Greg Maddux victory. The future Hall of Famer had allowed just an unearned run and four hits over 7 ⅓, throwing just 73 pitches. The 4-3 loss broke Dempster's string of 26 consecutive save opportunities, which stretched back to the previous July.

The locker room was empty as media filed in, save for a fuming Kerry Wood, sitting by his locker with a laser stare out into nowhere. Then Dempster appeared to analyze the disaster.

"It's not the first time Mike's ever hit a homer," he said. "Get the leadoff guy on there and I made a bad pitch to Giles. The slider backed up on me, and he hit it right in the basket."

He was no longer the automatic closer (33 saves in 35 opportunities) of 2005. He wasn't just plain lousy ala Antonio Alfonseca or Mel Rojas, or an older guy in decline like Rick Aguilera. Dempster, though, had several rough patches, and the shaky defense and poor execution of the 2006 season made matters worse for him.

"Everybody wants you to go out and blow [just] two saves a year," he said. "I'm still learning how to do this. I'm still learning how to deal with this. I never dealt with failure [as a closer in 2005]. The way I look at it, I've overcome a lot harder obstacles in my life than blowing a save. I know I'm good enough to go out there and get three outs.

"No matter what the setback or how poorly the Cubs would play, Dempster never let go of the ultimate high for a closer, in the ultimate baseball game.

"It's also pretty exciting when you do get the save, the opposite end of the spectrum," he said. "I can't wait for the day when I can do it in the playoffs and World Series, to go out there and save a game."

Dempster had survived such trials by fire before. He had been necessitated into the closer's role due to an injured Joe Borowski—the incumbent in 2003 and into 2004—and the repeated failures of replacement LaTroy Hawkins, who was miscast as a closer. He got his first

Six Innings of Lounging, Two Minutes of Terror

save opportunity just 21 months after undergoing Tommy John surgery on his elbow.

Dempster was pulled from the starting rotation and was thrust into the bullpen amid speculation during a May 11, 2005 game at Wrigley Field against the New York Mets—and Piazza, who was finishing his final year in the Big Apple. Brought in to protect a 3-2 lead in the ninth, Dempster walked Doug Mientkiewicz with one out and gave up a single to David Wright. The Cubs crowd, already agitated by Hawkins' failures, stirred uncomfortably. They cheered when Dempster struck out Victory Diaz, but then a different, and familiar, reaction came forth when Dempster gave up a game-tying single to pinch hitter Eric Valent. To add injury to insult, Piazza then rocketed a liner off Dempster's forearm. In pain, he scrambled to throw to first for the final out, then retreated to the trainer's room. Derrek Lee's homer in the bottom of the ninth gave Dempster a scavenged win, but he did not stick around to provide witty banter as usual. "I don't want to blow you guys off, but I got to go get X-rays," he announced as he exited the clubhouse stage left a few minutes later.

The Canadian was built tough, though, and the liner just raised a welt. He was back in closing, converting 14 in a row through the next two-plus months.

"It's gone well, but it was tough at first to make the adjustment," Dempster said. "If you have success at the start, it feeds off it."

After the Hawkins disaster and continuing problems with middle relief, manager Dusty Baker could worry a bit less in the ninth, at least until the insufferably stifling night of July 24 in St. Louis. Dempster was protecting a 4-3 lead in uneventful fashion with two outs in the ninth. Cardinals rookie pinch hitter Steve Seabol came up as the last hope. Dempster got two quick strikes on Seabol, then, suddenly, he got the idea to get Seabol fishing. Seabol took an outside pitch, then another. The third broke low and away for ball three. Finally, Dempster walked him. Dempster's own notoriously impatient teammates could have never coaxed a walk after being down 0-and-2.

The next day, he was asked what happened.

"I walked him," Dempster said, uncommonly without a trace of wit. "I threw four balls in a row."

There had to be more than that.

Entangled In Ivy

"It's the same, why do you go 3-and-0 and get the guy out?" he said. "I had to throw a strike. I didn't throw a strike. I thought he was going to be a little more aggressive, he wasn't, and he just laid off some pitches. In that case, lay off some fastballs. He was a new guy coming up, and I thought I'd take advantage of it. He put together a good at-bat, laid off those pitches. You just live and learn."

He learned, all right. Hector Luna, pinch running for Seabol, followed manager Tony La Russa's gamble to steal second, microseconds ahead of the tag. Old-school pepper pot David Eckstein then slapped a single to right to tie the game 4-4. The Cardinals had made something out of literally nothing against Dempster. The blown save wasn't fatal in the end—Neifi Perez sliced a drive down the right-field line for a grand-slam homer in the next inning to give the Cubs the win.

Nine days later, on August 2 in Philadelphia, Dempster repeated the Seabol at-bat in quadruplicate. Protecting a 2-0 lead, he walked four consecutive Phillies with one out to force in a run. With no more wiggle room, Dempster somehow righted himself to strike out David Bell, and then pinch hitter Tomas Perez to nail down his shakiest save.

"Wow," he said afterward, his light side still intact. "If I could put people on the edge of their seat any more back in Chicago ... I apologize. That was interesting to say the least. A character-builder, I guess; that's the best way to look at it."

Dempster had the right mentality to purge the negatives out of his system to media afterward. All the best Cubs closers vented that way. Rod Beck was unabashed. Joe Borowski was, well, a good Joe. Rick Aguilera waited at his locker while the media crew finished with manager Don Baylor. Randy Myers would face the music, but only after an extensive postgame weight-room session. In contrast, Antonio Alfonseca gestured reporters away with his six-fingered hand, grunting. His refusal to be accountable after blown saves angered both media and Cubs officials. The middleman and setup men have more time to cool down mentally after failures, but have the advantage of seldom having to meet the press afterward. That doesn't make them feel any better, though.

"I feel like crap," Eyre said. "I feel worse than crap. There's no Doc Brown, no DeLorean, you can't go back in time."

But all have to let go of failure quickly lest it consume them, their teammates, and families.

Six Innings of Lounging, Two Minutes of Terror

"I used to be pissed for a while and be mad at my wife," Eyre said. "That's childish."

"It's a matter of how you wake up the next morning," Ohman said. "How do I wake up? Tired! It's a cliché. To be a good reliever, you've got to have good stuff and a bad memory. You must not be willing to remember the times you failed. You need a good memory in terms of preparation. How do you grow out of it? You get older. I had some surgeries, and now I realize that every day is a gift out there. You don't take it for granted."

In the end, status as a reliever is well worth it, no matter if they experience postgame dejection or unmatched joy. The help that can be afforded others, saves or not, is appreciated as a big leaguer. Dempster reverted to his third side of his personality, after comedian and closer, as Father's Day 2006 approached. Along with wife Jenny, who had just given birth to their first child, Brady, Dempster hosted some 50 family members of servicemen in Iraq on the day before Father's Day at Wrigley Field.

"A lot of it was her idea," Dempster said. "She had an uncle who was shot down in Vietnam, a quite amazing story. One of her cousins just came back from Iraq in December. Just talking about it being my first Father's Day, having a baby, what a tough time it would be to be gone, how fortunate we are to be around our family. ... Here are people who miss holidays, birthdays, Father's Day, Mother's Day. What a neat opportunity, to have them out to the park and just kind of relax for a day to enjoy it. When Dad comes back, it would be kind of a neat story to tell him."

Jenny Dempster and Cubs official Mary Dosek worked on the idea together. The Dempsters arranged for the families to obtain tickets and "Cubs Dollars" to purchase food and drinks.

"We'd take care of all the ins and outs, loose ends, just enjoy the ballgame with family," Dempster said.

Interestingly, the fans can thank a man whose own country is not fighting in Iraq.

"My belief is I'm very, very proud to be where I'm from, to be Canadian," said Dempster. "I'm very patriotic about my country, but the United States of America has allowed me to have an opportunity that very few people in life experience, and I'm very grateful for that. In a way, even though I'm Canadian, I feel part-American, just because I've been here so long and been married to an American woman. I have a lot of respect for the country and what it's allowed me to attain and achieve.

"I don't believe in war," Dempster said, "but I believe in supporting anybody who's over there doing it. Those people are true heroes, and they put their life on the line every day to provide us a safe place to live, to be with our families. A lot of people don't realize when they join the Armed Forces, they don't know what's in their future. A lot of times, you could be sitting there and a war breaks out, and it's your duty to protect your country. It's really amazing to see these young men and women do it. It's even more amazing to see them come back and be with their families."

Dempster would become involved with various other community-service activities as a way to escape the vicious cycle of pressure, cheers, and boos that his job entails. On and off the field, the reliever's life features a wellspring of emotions that few other in sports dare handle. From quietly confident to uproarious slapstick, from churning stomach to exultation, the bullpen is, by necessity, a breed apart in sports' most unpredictable game. Add in a dose of the Cubs' crazy history and the eccentricities of Wrigley Field, and you have the perfect recipe for volatility.

eleven

PATIENCE IS PRUDENCE
AT THE PLATE

"WALKS score."

Cornered at a table in Wrigley Field's Stadium Club, Lou Piniella—his white dress shirt totally soaked with anxious perspiration, even on this cool October day—discussed his control-challenged pitching staff in his first official appearance as Cubs manager. Yet, as he talked about throwing strikes, Piniella inadvertently revealed the missing ingredient in the Cubs' attempted recipe for recent success—walks put pressure on the pitching and defense, directly aiding overall run production.

Minutes earlier, Piniella actually addressed the concept of on-base percentage, first tripping over the veil of political correctness. "Eight midgets up there that walk all the time," were the first words out of his mouth, as he attempted to liven up the press conference, no doubt recalling diminutive Eddie Gaedel's 1951 St. Louis Browns stunt at the behest of Bill Veeck. He would later apologize for any person offended.

Seriously, though, Piniella displayed recognition of the issue, vowing to address the most blatant Cubs shortcoming of the new century—too few base runners to provide reliable run production.

"You want hitters to hit in hitters' counts," he said. "Sometimes, certain pitchers—if they get ahead of you—they have a devastating pitch like the split finger, [so] you're defeating the purpose of being really selective. Obviously, if you swing at strikes, your chances of succeeding as a hitter are much greater. They've got some good hitters on this baseball team. I noticed they didn't walk all that much, but that's something we'll try to work at."

The proverbial journey of a thousand miles starts with one step. If Piniella could change the culture while recalibrating his Cubs away from their antiquated approach to favor a well-balanced offense, he'd merit a statue at Clark and Addison long before he'd guide the Cubs to a World Series title—if ever.

On-base percentage, which lacked emphasis in managerial outlooks, had dragged the Cubs down in so many different ways. The lineup underperformed in 2003, necessitating two Jim Hendry trades for offense in midseason—trades that perhaps distracted Hendry once again from acquiring sorely needed bullpen help. Lack of additional base runners most likely cost the Cubs the National League wild-card playoff berth in 2004. Their home-run-happy lineup could not score when the power faced periodic shutdowns that are normal during any long season.

Overall, impatient, undisciplined hitters cut down the efficiency of situational hitting. With a man on third and one out, the opposing pitcher obviously under stress, it did the Cubs no good for a statistically capable batsman to hack at the first pitch in a borderline hitting zone and pop up, stranding the runner. Wearing down the opposing starting pitcher—running up his pitch count to force him to be replaced by less effective middle relievers—was a nonexistent strategy. The Cubs could not fight fire with fire. All the while, Cubs foes were trying to make power pitchers Mark Prior, Kerry Wood, and Carlos Zambrano throw 100 or more pitches through five innings with the understanding, "If we can't beat 'em, try to tire 'em out and get them pulled from the game."

References to winning the World Series as the prime goal were scarce, and top-brass advocacy paid only superficial lip service to the concept of stressing on-base percentage. They continued to acquire players via free agency and trades who were high-strikeout, low-walk prototypes. With one exception (infielder Ryan Theriot), the handful of everyday players coming out of the farm system displayed little plate discipline—to outsiders, a very obvious trend.

"They don't have an offensive philosophy ... little attention is paid to on-base percentage," one veteran scout said in 2005.

The closest the Cubs have ever come to a new age hitting system were conversations between then-manager Jim Riggleman and confidant Dan

Patience is Prudence at the Plate

Radison in the late 1990s. In various coaching roles, Radison mentioned a favored author of his—baseball guru Bill James—whom he'd read since he began writing baseball analysis a generation ago.

"We would have conversations about it," Riggleman said. "Rad was in tune with that thinking, the value of bases on balls." But since Radison was not the Cubs' hitting coach at the time, James' ideas never went beyond the talking stage.

Much more recently, the Cubs have defined a hitting approach, but not a method that has netted positive results—an overly macho promotion of aggressive hitting, devaluing walks in comparison to scalding a pitch, which is human nature. Even as contending teams all over baseball found ways to balance aggressiveness and selectivity at the plate, the Cubs, under general manager Hendry and manager Dusty Baker, seemed stuck in some distant era, as the game and the upper reaches of the National League standings evolved away from them. More progressive teams were benefiting from the realization that walks plus hits equals victories.

Walks, which are nothing more than the byproduct of disciplined hitting, could be promoted by an identifiable organizational hitting philosophy. Yet, so many questions about walks directed to Baker were countered with comments about aggressive hitting. "Walks clog the bases," Baker even said on several occasions.

In a September 2006 interview lunch down the street from Wrigley Field, Hendry's true feelings about on-base percentage came forth as he claimed the Cubs did possess an organizational hitting philosophy.

"Certainly, you'd like to have high on-base percentage," Hendry said. Nomar [Garciaparra] had been a good hitter all his life—[Moises] Alou, too. They were not always considered patient, high on-base percentage guys. It's not like we ignore it. Juan Pierre's a pretty good leadoff hitter. There's a solid philosophy. We chart every pitch thrown to us and by us in the minor leagues; every count a ball is hit on. People put this on-base percentage phrase out and just defend it by the percentage.

"Try to be aggressive in certain hitters' counts, try to be patient in others. Everybody in this game has been a good hitter. Sometimes the best pitch you'll ever get in an at-bat is your first pitch. The philosophy the other way [pitchers] is trying to get ahead right away. We don't go up there and say, 'Boy, be aggressive, swing out of your ass.' I coach the same way. If it's the first pitch, [or other pitches later in count], I'm going to tell my guys to zone in, one spot, one pitch. I'm going to be real aggressive if I get a fastball, say, inner third of the plate and below the belly. Other than that, I'll take the pitch."

Hendry even related aggressive hitting to the foibles of his 2006 pitching staff.

"We gave up a ton of hits on 0-and-2 counts," he said. "Most of the 0-and-2 pitches in the world are out of the zone. Even Greg [Maddux] had a stretch. That guy who's swinging at a 0-and-2 pitch he's getting a hit on—that's not a bad at-bat, it's a good at-bat. But in some of the global theories of good counts or bad counts to hit, numbers don't always tell the truth."

Hendry became more specific in defining his logic. Here's where the adherence to the macho hitting style came forth again.

"The most important stat for me is knocking in runs and scoring runs," he said. "Obviously, the more times you're on base, the better chance you have.

"Matt Murton has been a tremendous player, a very high on-base percentage guy, very patient approach. Let's make up a game. We're playing the St. Louis Cardinals, and, first time up, he swings at a ball out of the zone, 3-and-1. It would have been ball four, but he popped up for an out. Next at-bat, man on third, one out, he hits a sacrifice fly to right field, knocks in a run. Next time up, man on third, he has a 2-and-0 pitch, with the infield back and the Cards winning 2-1. Matt reaches out—it's not great pitch to hit—hits the ball to the second baseman; the runner scores; it's 2-2. Matt comes up in the eighth, second and third, one out, a base open. Jacque Jones is on deck, a left-handed hitter who'd be facing a right-handed pitcher, it's 2-and-1, a hitters' count. Matt gets a hanging breaking ball a little up and away out of the zone—fly ball right center, run scores, Matt's out, but Cubs win 3-2. Matt went 0-for-4, swung at three questionable pitches in hitters' counts, but knocked in three runs. What's his on-base percentage that day? Didn't Matt have a great day? We beat the Cards 3-2.

"My point is this: there's a way to dissect every number," Hendry explained. "You can find guys who have very good or respectable on-base percentage globally. But maybe their on-base percentage in the seventh,

Patience is Prudence at the Plate

eighth, and ninth isn't that high. So there's all kind of stats that are just as meaningful."

The most meaningful stat, however, is runs scored. Although Hendry touted Murton's imaginary clutch performance, he didn't specify how the runners reached base to give the outfielder his RBI opportunities. The lack of those extra base runners has hurt the Cubs, and was never more pronounced than in the disastrous 2006 season.

Both the Cubs' .319 on-base percentage and 394 walks drawn qualified for last in the National League. Only the similarly underwhelming Pittsburgh Pirates saved the Cubs from a cellar ranking in runs scored, but even then, only by 25 runs. The Dodgers led the NL in on-base percentage with .348, and there was a definite correlation between walks and runs scored. The Philadelphia Phillies led the NL with 626 walks and 865 runs scored.

Only one Cub had a .400-plus on-base percentage—rookie second baseman Theriot in limited play (53 games). A regular over the final month, Theriot finished at .412 with 17 walks. Catcher Michael Barrett's .368 OBP paced the season-long regulars, just above left fielder Murton with .365. Leading run producer Aramis Ramirez had a .352 OBP and a team-leading 50 walks. Free-swinging right fielder Jacque Jones, acquired even though the Cubs already had OBP and strikeout problems, had just 35 walks along with 116 strikeouts in 149 games.

Those numbers are meager when compared to the NL's pacesetters. Barry Bonds had a .454 OBP along with 115 walks. Albert Pujols was .431 with 92 walks. Nick Johnson of the Nationals had a good eye with .428 and 110 walks. So did the Phillies' Bobby Abreu (before he was traded to the Yankees), who was .427 with 91 walks in 98 NL games.

Moving backward in times, the numbers are just as disconcerting for the Cubs.

In 2005, Derrek Lee had an all-time season, leading the majors in batting average with .335. He had 199 hits, of which 46 were homers and 50 were doubles. However respectable his RBI total (107) was though, his other offensive numbers openly indicate that total should have been 20 to 25 more than the result.

Why? Overall, the Cubs and Cardinals had similar team offensive numbers in most categories in 2005. Both had .270 team averages, and the Cubs actually collected 12 more hits. With 194 homers, the Cubs had

24 more than the Cardinals, but 119 of the Cubs' blasts were solo shots. The big difference was total walks. St. Louis had 534; the Cubs had an NL-low 419. The Cardinals' on-base percentage was .339 compared to the Cubs' .324. Thus, the Cardinals scored 805 runs to the Cubs' 703.

Lee had a team-leading 85 walks. Right fielder Jeromy Burnitz racked up 57 bases on balls. No other Cub had more than 40 walks, and the team's opponents drew 576 walks.

The hasty swings merely continued a trend from 2004, when the Cubs wasted their best raw power production in history. They slugged a team-record 235 homers, pacing the NL by 21 over runner-up St. Louis. However, the '04 Cubs ranked only seventh in runs and RBIs for a good reason—they were 11th in on-base percentage (.328) and a miserable 14th in walks (489). The Cubs had 141 solo homers, and their opponents drew 545 walks. In their fatal 1-7 final-week stretch, which knocked them out of contention for a previously near-certain wild-card berth, the Cubs scored four or fewer runs five times. Back-to-back 12-inning losses to the Reds at Wrigley Field, in which the Cubs scored just four runs, were particularly excruciating. A combination of poor offensive output and a shaky bullpen led to a 19-30 record in one-run games.

Despite his 39 homers and 36 doubles, left fielder Moises Alou drove in just 106 runs, mimicking Lee's output the following season. Alou did not have extra base runners to drive in, and he became overanxious in clutch situations, such as a man on third with one out. Meanwhile, a declining Sammy Sosa drove in just 80 runs on his 35 homers. Ramirez submitted the best clutch performance—with a .373 on-base percentage and .318 batting average, he had 103 RBIs in 145 games. He ranked sixth in the NL in batting average (.336) with runners in scoring position.

After Hendry failed to retain 2003 sparkplug and leadoff man Kenny Lofton because he could not offer him a regular outfield slot, the Cubs suffered during the '04 season, especially when management forced a reluctant Corey Patterson into the leadoff job. Although Patterson batted .336 in August after being moved to No. 1 on an everyday basis, he hit just .261 overall at the leadoff spot. His season on-base percentage was just .320, and he walked just 45 times compared to an alarming 168 strikeouts.

Interestingly, Lofton had ably demonstrated the concept of a skilled leadoff man generating on-base percentage over the final two-plus months of the 2003 season. The Cubs ranked just 13th in on-base percentage (.323) and 14th in walks (492 compared to NL-leading Philadelphia with 651). Lofton's .381 on-base percentage over his 56 games in a Cubs uniform netted 39 runs scored.

"Guys can't get RBIs, if the one-two guys are not on base," said Lofton in 2006, still an effective lineup igniter at 39 for the Los Angeles Dodgers. "Some people don't think that's important. It's more important than what people claim to think. They say guys get RBIs; but how would they get RBIs if guys are not on base?"

Add speed to the equation, and the table setters are even more effective.

"It's not so much the on-base percentage," Lofton said. "You can have a guy like Juan Pierre hit a ball to the shortstop. If [the infielder] is rushed, [Pierre's] on base. It won't show in the box score as on-base percentage. A lot of the time, with on-base percentage, the leadoff man has .350, but he's actually on base .370, .380. With guys rushing, his speed will cause at least a 30-point higher on-base percentage. There are other times, when they have the chance to double him up, that he's on base, and guys knock him in. It's not shown that he beat out a double-play ball so the next guy could hit him in. His speed helps him get on base. That's not talked about as much as it should be."

The mind-set of the top-of-the-lineup hitter is "get on base by any means," Lofton said. "If you're a contact hitter, you hit with two strikes. If you're not a good contact hitter, you have to hit the ball before two strikes. Just put it in play, let your legs work for you, not against you. You swing at strikes, that's the bottom line. If you swing at strikes, you have a good chance [to hit] strikes. If you're just swinging at balls, it's not a good thing. The leadoff hitter's job is tough—you have to have a fine line between swinging at a strike and swinging at [a pitch] that they've called a strike, but is not a strike. That's tough."

Hendry conducted an interview with writer Darrell Horwitz after the 2003 season. When asked about retaining Lofton, the GM said he had greater priorities—such as the bullpen and catcher—than the leadoff position. Two years later, Hendry admitted that he did not help out Dusty Baker's cause with the instability at leadoff. After failing to land free agent Rafael Furcal when the Dodgers grossly overpaid for the shortstop, Hendry traded several top pitching prospects to the Marlins for Juan Pierre, who had to hit his way on to be an effective leadoff man.

Even though repeated failures in on-base percentage failed to provoke epiphanies for the Cubs' top brass, slumping production did promote several studies on how to best assemble lineups. Thus, for the honchos to fail to notice a correlation between production and on-base percentage, they'd have to be wearing blinders.

On September 16, 2006, two weeks before he officially tendered his resignation as team president, Andy MacPhail revealed the Cubs had just begun a new-age baseball analysis.

"We haven't done the mathematical modeling for lineups that teams such as the Red Sox got into a few years ago," MacPhail said. "You've got some knowns like [Aramis] Ramirez, [Derrek] Lee, [Cesar] Izturis, and [Michael] Barrett. Start inserting names in and out [at other positions], and how many runs would this lineup generate over the course of the year? For example: if we took [Juan] Pierre out and put this guy in. … We haven't done that, but we'll start doing it."

The Cubs also looked at postseason teams from 1998 to 2005 for common trends to success. "We evaluated where they finished in every category," MacPhail said. "The categories included ERA of starting pitchers, quality starts, innings pitched per starter, relievers' ERA, on-base percentage, runs scored, runs allowed, and fielding percentage. We looked at all those stats; saw where they ranked in the league, and went to find the common denominator of what it takes to win, particularly in the National League. Where does your team have to rank?"

Problem is, the Cubs didn't have to bother with the research. They had to look no further than their own alumni, who provided, albeit sparsely, successful examples of what kind of team works at Wrigley Field. Pitching and high on-base percentage are the common denominators. Yet, the brass—especially heading into the homestretch of the 2006 season—had no institutional memory upon which to draw. None were Chicago-area residents or Cubs employees during those model years. New team president John McDonough, who has worked for the Cubs since 1983, may possess more of a personal timeline. The ideal lineup for Wrigley Field was assembled in 1984. Dusty Baker had little awareness of the NL East-winning team's nuances. MacPhail momentarily confused

Patience is Prudence at the Plate

the '84 Cubs with the NL East titlists of 1989, asking if Jerome Walton and Dwight Smith were on the '84 squad.

In 1984, the Cubs led the NL in runs scored with 762. They had speed and power, hitting 136 homers while stealing 154 bases. More interestingly, they are the last Cubs team to lead the NL in walks (567). They amassed the highest on-base percentage (.331) of any Cubs team between 1978 and 1998.

"The Daily Double" of leadoff man Bobby Dernier and No. 2 hitter Ryne Sandberg set the table deftly, stealing a combined 77 bases to complement Sandberg's all-around MVP season. No. 3 hitter Gary Matthews was the last Cub to lead the NL in walks with 103; strangely, he never was able to impart the knowledge of such patience to the Cubs or Brewers, for whom he served as hitting coach. Three other Cubs— Dernier, Leon Durham, and Ron Cey—had at least 60 walks. Dernier's good eye in taking a close 3-and-2 pitch from Bruce Sutter set up the second of Sandberg's two homers off the split-finger specialist in the hallowed June 23, 1984, "Sandberg Game" at Wrigley Field.

No 1984 Cub had more than 25 homers, but six players had 80 or more RBIs. Of course, pitching also carried the way, with Rick Sutcliffe's 16-1 Cy Young Award-netting record over the final three-plus months a key. The Cubs had the NL's most effective pitching in the second half of '84 and won 96 games overall—highest since the last pennant season in 1945.

In many ways, history repeated itself in 1989. The surprising "Boys of Zimmer" Cubs won the NL East again by leading the league in runs scored with 702. In a down offensive season for the NL, they were second in OBP with .319, on the strength of a trio of .300 hitters: Mark Grace (.405 OBP, 80 walks), NL rookie of the year Jerome Walton, and top-rookie runner-up Dwight Smith. Balance was achieved again with 124 homers and 136 steals. Pitching wasn't as deep as in '84, but with Sutcliffe, Greg Maddux (19 wins in his second full big-league season), and Mike Bielecki's (18-7) career year, the Cubs could trot out three solid starters every five turns through the rotation.

Nine years later, the Cubs' 1998 wild-card playoff berth is often degraded since the Braves swept them unceremoniously in three straight games. Yet, those Cubs won one more game in the regular season than the 2003 NL Central titlists and added one more in the wild-card tiebreaker against the Giants at Wrigley Field. Sammy Sosa's 66-homer season gets a lot of credit, but overall the Cubs benefited from efficient OBP. They were third in the NL in runs scored with 831, second in homers with 212, fifth in RBIs, sixth in walks, and tied for sixth in on-base percentage with .337. Grace, still going strong at first, led with a .401 OBP and 93 walks. Sosa learned some patience with 73 walks, netting a .377 OBP; and second baseman Mickey Morandini's 72 walks helped him amass a .380 OBP.

Even a forgotten, bedraggled Cubs team in the Gerald Ford presidency showed how patience paid off. The 75-87 Cubs in 1975 had baseball's worst pitching, wasting decent offense as a result. Despite slugging only 95 homers (team leader Andre Thornton had 18), the Cubs finished tied with Pittsburgh's noted "Lumber Company" for third in runs scored (out of a 12-team league). The Cubs had 650 walks, a franchise season high, along with a .338 OBP—highest since the 1945 pennant winner. Thornton (88 walks in just 120 games), leadoff man Rick Monday (83 walks), and No. 2 hitter Jose Cardenal (77 walks, .317) practiced patience. Bill Madlock's first NL batting-title campaign of .354—highest post-1930 average for a Cubs right-handed hitter—did not hurt either. The extra base runners permitted .270 hitter Jerry Morales, with just 33 extra-base hits (21 doubles, 12 homers) to drive in 91 runs, while .248 hitter Manny Trillo drove in 70 runs on just seven homers.

The 1945 Cubs, performing in a war year with a "mush" baseball, were hardly an offensive juggernaut. The pennant winners belted just 57 homers—one more than the fewest team total in the NL. Yet, they were able to plate enough runs due to a .349 OBP, which remains the highest season mark since 1937.

On the negative side, the year that most resembles the get-on-base pratfalls of 2003-06 was 1987, showing how non-patience and poor clutch hitting can sabotage a team. The '87 Cubs led the NL with 209 homers, but placed eighth (out of 12 teams) in runs scored, seventh in RBIs, 10th in walks, and ninth in OBP.

All these numbers would seem to back up the *Moneyball* patience-at-the-plate theory, first espoused by former Oakland Athletics general manager Sandy Alderson, then adopted and now identified with his successor, Billy Beane. The A's hitting system draws both praise and criticism throughout the game. Traditionalists don't like informal quotas or timeframes put on pitches taken. However, White Sox manager Ozzie Guillen praised the A's hitters for their patience when they swept his team at U.S. Cellular Field in the series before the 2005 All-Star Game. Others note that the A's are a good regular-season team, but one not built for playoff competition. Dusty Baker was one such critic—and he wouldn't have minded a call from Beane for the A's open managerial job after the 2006 season.

Hendry was more moderate in his view, having made deals with Beane. But it's clear he's no adherent of a Beane-style, one-size-fits-all hitting system, citing numbers that counter the A's advocacy of patience.

"We have a good relationship with Billy Beane," Hendry said in September 2006. "I respect him. He's a very smart guy. They are considered the on-base percentage [experts]. At the [2006 trade] deadline, they were in first, but they also were 25th or 28th in offensive category summation. They were in the bottom five or six. They're having the kind of year where they pitched their ass off, they caught it well, and they survived the injuries until they got healthier to the point where they were running away with it."

In the same manner of stereotyping the Cubs as "lovable losers," whose management only cared about filling Wrigley Field, the *Moneyball* philosophy was in reality different from its image. Beane's players never produced a bevy of bases-loaded walks and one-base-at-a-time advances. The logic of the philosophy produced more concentration on hitting's fine points, promoting the multiplicity of results created by taking first-pitch balls.

Far down the Athletics' chain, in the low-A level Midwest League, Kane County Cougars manager Aaron Nieckula defined *Moneyball* in a way different than its public image—and as outsiders at Wrigley Field may perceive it. At Kane County, Nieckula, his coaches, and roving instructors imprint the A's hitting standard. They've obviously had success, since Oakland has produced a decent flow of its own everyday players who have consistently contended in the American League West since 2000.

"You can have the best swing in the world," Nieckula said. "But if you're not swinging at good pitches, it does no good. We teach strike-zone discipline, selectivity to your hitting zone. Basically, everyone's different. What works for player X doesn't work for player Y. [Improvement] comes by repetition; it comes by getting professional at-bats. Knowing what zone is hot, knowing what zone is cold, being disciplined enough to focus on the zones. It does you no good to cover 17 inches of the plate early in the count. I've got to zone in on either the middle half, a middle, or a middle away—eight inches, eight inches, or eight inches. Get to two strikes, expand your zone.

"We're not taking away aggressiveness," Nieckula continued. "It's the exact opposite. We want guys to be aggressive—to their hitting zone, not the pitcher's hitting zone. It's the biggest misconception of our philosophy that we look for the walk. That could be the furthest from the truth. We look to swing. The walk is a byproduct. Get guys on base, and you have a chance to knock them in. If you don't get anybody on base, the only way to knock in runs is by a [solo] home run."

Nieckula insisted there is "no dictum to take the first pitch [automatically]." And another byproduct results from disciplined, patient hitters—more stress on the opposing pitcher as his pitch count mounts and eventually forces him out of the game.

"Your percentages of winning increase," Nieckula said. "If their pitch count increases, the percentage of the team on the offensive end has a higher chance of winning. Most of the time, your best six arms are the rotation plus the closer."

If a traditionalist believed the Athletics were alone in focusing on knocking out the opposing starter this way, he would be wrong. Detroit Tigers manager Jim Leyland said the New York Yankees and Boston Red Sox are tough to pitch to because their lineups are patient. The testimony of three prominent players from the Eastern axis of power backs up that stream of consciousness.

"You can't be afraid to hit with two strikes," said Yankees centerfielder Johnny Damon, who also played for the Red Sox and Athletics. "You can't be afraid of maybe taking that best pitch down the middle just so you can kind of wear the pitcher down. The starting pitchers are the best pitchers out there for the most part. If you can wear down the bullpen, they don't have the longevity to go 30 to 40 pitches, especially back-to-back days. The philosophy with the A's was: go in, get the starting pitcher out in the third inning, and the bullpen would be shot for the rest of the series."

Patience is Prudence at the Plate

Outfielder Bernie Williams, the most senior of Yankees, offers up a similar take.

"In my experience, all the teams that we have that were successful [Yankees] teams in the past 10 years, we have been able to work counts and take the starting pitcher out of the game early in the game. If you can knock him out in the first five innings, then you face not the closers or setup men, but the long men. Usually, that's not your best pitching. That's been in part the strategy we've been working on."

The Red Sox's philosophy on patience has been influenced by the presence of Bill James, an official team consultant. The most enthusiastic proponent of patience was first baseman Kevin Youkilis, whom Beane nicknamed the "Greek God of Walks" (even though the Greek-sounding surname actually belongs to a Jewish native of Cincinnati). On July 9, 2006, at U.S. Cellular Field, Youkilis demonstrated how a batter could wear down a pitcher simply through patience. He burned up 15 pitches in drawing two walks against White Sox starter Jose Contreras. The Cuban right-hander threw an alarming 95 pitches in just four innings. Contreras settled down over the next two innings, but was spent and had to leave after six.

"The pitcher's trying to make great pitches; and if they are just a little bit off the plate and you're not swinging at them, that's the biggest thing," said Youkilis, who finished 2006 with 91 walks and a .381 OBP. "That's to your team's advantage, making that guy throw the extra pitch instead of getting out and beating yourself with one of the pitches the pitcher likes to throw in a certain spot, which could be a ball or even a strike called. That pitch may not be exactly in the hitting zone you're looking for in that count.

"Until you get to two strikes, it's still in your favor. It's your at-bat, and you don't have to give in to the pitcher. You don't have to swing at pitches that are a little off the plate, a little high, a little down. For us, we have a lot of guys who know that, who understand the strike zone, and who are very good at being selective and aggressive at the same time."

Youkilis obviously had set out to practice patience at the plate from the start of his pro career. It's a mind-set and a strict discipline. Even if Cubs management adopted a *Moneyball* approach, a hefty number of players might revert to swinging over-aggressively when they reach the majors.

Entangled In Ivy

A good example is Mark Grace. The most patient Cub of his era, Grace lost out on a couple of chances to finally crack the 100-RBI mark by becoming overanxious, forsaking his disciplines in clutch-hitting situations. I repeatedly witnessed Grace suddenly lunge and swing at the first pitch, Moises Alou-style, with a man on second or third, or both. He'd pop up or hit a lazy short fly ball, stranding the runner(s).

Of course, Corey Patterson became the poster kid for undisciplined swinging. Patterson exasperated Dusty Baker and his coaches by refusing to listen to advice on how to tone down his undisciplined swing. A combination of stubbornness and pride prevented Patterson from fully utilizing his five-tool talents and bottling the good mechanics that had him flirting with .300 in the first half of 2003, before he injured his knee running out a grounder.

"Some of it is not putting a low emphasis on on-base percentage," said Jim Hendry. "You can teach a guy like that in the minor leagues; but when he comes up here, in front of 40,000 people, he doesn't have the same approach. He presses or panics."

That's why Hendry and farm director Oneri Fleita could have an uncommonly patient product in second baseman Ryan Theriot. Unheralded since he was drafted out of Louisiana State in 2001, the David Ecskstein-mimicking Theriot fell off track when he was persuaded to switch hit from his early minor-league days. When he finally began hitting right-handed exclusively, he perked up offensively. Dusty Baker ignored Theriot in several previous call-ups in 2005 and 2006. But after Cesar Izturis was injured and Ronny Cedeno spiraled into a deep slump in the waning days of the '06 season, Theriot seized the second-base job and would not let go.

Unfortunately, the arrival of free-agent infielder Mark DeRosa from the Texas Rangers would forcibly loosen Theriot's grip on the starter's job. Even after he displayed uncommon plate discipline, the Cubs weren't going to entrust a starting job to a virtually first-year player when they were under a self-mandate to improve dramatically and quickly. But Theriot was still projected as a spare infielder, and it was hoped his attitude would rub off on teammates.

"I want to be .400 [in on-base percentage]," said Theriot. "Not too many are there. If you have two or three guys at the top of the order doing that, you're going to be winning some ballgames. If they can run a little bit, they can score on doubles. That's what you can hope for, but realistically that won't happen. If I don't get on at .350 [OBP] or more, I'm not going to be in the lineup. If I'm not scoring 100 runs, I'm not valuable to a team. Players *do* have to buy into it. It's the players' responsibility. How do you win games? You either save runs or score them."

Theriot's theory?

"Play hard pepper," he said. "Put the barrel on the ball. Don't try to force the pitch somewhere. It's not easily definable. Wherever that pitch shows up, put the barrel on it. If you do that on a consistent basis, more times than not, you're going to have a positive outcome."

Theriot believes the key to getting on base is not standing around with the bat on your shoulder until you draw ball four. That's too simplistic. Walk, if necessary, but also hit your pitch—and do not be afraid to hit deep in the count.

"You hit the nail on the head," Theriot continued. "Hit with two strikes. If a hitter has confidence to do that, if you simplify it with me, the pitch shows up that you're going to hit, put the barrel on it. If the guy's pitch count is up, take a few pitches. If he's got dominating stuff and you know he can strike you out, hit the first straight one you see. It's real easy, but as a hitter you have to think along with a little bit and buy into it. If you don't buy into it, it's not going to work.

"It's not like *Moneyball*; it's not take till you get a strike. If there's a dominating pitcher on the mound—and I feel he can strike me out—if there's a ball up there I can hit and it's the first pitch, I'm going to hit it. I don't want to fall behind in the count against Roger Clemens or against Greg Maddux."

Theriot could adjust and take pitches if necessary. In the ninth inning of a September 2, 2006, game against the Giants, he took a close 2-and-2 pitch from closer Armando Benitez for ball three. Eventually, he used up 10 pitches, drawing a walk and forcing Benitez from the game. Theriot showed similar patience at other junctures as well.

If Kevin Youkilis' style is ever to creep into the Cubs' game plan, it likely will have to be through Theriot.

"I played with him in the Cape Cod league," Theriot said. "He has had that same approach since Cape Cod. He's a winner. He puts his personal goals aside for the team. In turn, every team he plays on wins, and that's the type of player I try to be. If I hit .250 and walk 150 times, I'm on base all year; and I'm fine with that because we're winning. Let's score runs; let's save runs.

"No doubt you can [be selective and aggressive at the same time, which is Youkilis' mantra]. That's possible [to run pitch counts up]. It's the confidence the hitter must have. If you're starting, work the count. If you're coming off the bench, hit the first straight strike you see. It's philosophies that have been proven to work.

"It starts in your development," he said. "You need quality at-bats; you can't give at-bats away. If I go up there and hit the first pitch hard at somebody, did I give the at-bat away? No, because I hit the ball hard. If I had a 10-pitch at-bat and I made an out, is that a quality at-bat? Of course, because he threw 10 pitches."

Theriot doesn't believe a standardized hitting system would work well for most minor-league players. "I think certain players respond to certain coaches. I don't think it can be a robotic thing to teach. Hitting is so circumstantial. Everyone is different. You going to tell Aramis [Ramirez] to take pitches? It's the player's responsibility to recognize what kind of player he is and pursue it. High on-base percentage wins games, if you have guys who buy into that philosophy."

Theriot has a couple of like-minded minor leaguers who share his ideas. A visit to watch the Cubs' Midwest League affiliate Peoria Chiefs play in June 2006 at Elfstrom Stadium, the Kane County Cougars' home field, netted the sight of catcher-turned-outfielder Yusuf Carter, nephew of original Cub and World Series hero Joe Carter. The younger Carter clubbed a three-run homer in the Chiefs' victory, during which the Cubs farmhands actually appeared more patient than their Athletics counterparts. The personable Carter, who looked absolutely thrilled to visit Wrigley Field a day later, struggled statistically in 2006, but the organization was high on his future.

"I think I hit the best when I work the count," said Carter, a 12th-round draft pick in 2005. "I have to battle a little bit; it makes me focus a little more. I'll focus on my strengths versus getting me to go on my weaknesses. I want to figure out his [the pitcher's] game plan."

The Chiefs also fielded catcher Mark Reed, a third-round pick from 2004, who was compared to Craig Biggio in style and temperament.

Patience is Prudence at the Plate

While not addressing OBP specially, Reed knew the kind of mold he'd try to achieve.

"I probably won't be a guy who will hit 20 homers," said Reed, brother of original White Sox product and Mariners outfielder Jeremy Reed. "I eventually could be a line-drive, doubles-type hitter. I think I've always been able to bunt, move runners. I've got to get better at strike-zone judgment, cut down on strikeouts, and have more walks."

That, however, is easier said than done for players just starting out in pro baseball, according to first baseman Ryan Norwood, a ninth-round pick in 2004 and the Chiefs' leading power threat.

"It's tough because you want to do your best to get up there and drive the ball, especially in the middle of the lineup," Norwood said. "There's a fine line of getting a pitch and taking it. I look at every pitch, trying to be patient. I look for my pitch and try to lay off a ball that might be on the outer black, which I might normally swing at instead of waiting for one to cross more of the plate."

The eagerness of youngsters to hit is a dilemma for all player development officials. They don't want to discourage aggressiveness. After all, they're practically teaching kids how to hit again after weaning them from aluminum bats. At the same time, they also have to teach pitch recognition and situational hitting.

"The players we drafted in 2005, we got those guys together to kind of let them know we were not Oakland, not Toronto. We would not put hard and fast numbers on how many walks you have to have to advance in the system," said Jim Riggleman, now the St. Louis Cardinals' director of instruction. "But we are taking a closer look at how many walks and on-base percentage, as far as how good a player is. It is frustrating for player-development people to see players continually have three times the number of strikeouts as walks. How can you better learn the strike zone? We're trying to stress to players to recognize the fact you have struck out two, three, four times as much as they've walked.

"To Billy Beane's credit, he said, 'We don't kid ourselves and think we can teach this. We try to identify players who play that way.' They value that. The only way you can really teach that is while they're in diapers. If you have a kid at a young age and his father introduced him to baseball, he'd keep pounding into that kid, 'That pitch is not a strike.'"

Entangled In Ivy

Oneri Fleita claims pitch identification is at the core of the instruction he supervises as Cubs farm director. A former Creighton player under Hendry, Fleita now is part of the Hendry inner circle. The pair sometimes drives together to Wrigley Field from their suburban Park Ridge homes.

"I don't think you have one way of hitting for each player," Fleita said. "It's not like [Walt] Hriniak [with the Red Sox and White Sox two decades ago]. We spend a lot of time individually with the players. Each player is brought in, and we run a computer program, offering to educate him. One involves how many pitches Eric Patterson [Corey Patterson's younger brother] saw this year, how many he had per at-bat. Each hitter is given the facts—here is where you need to do better on an individual basis. You treat each differently. The problem with kids today is it's not like 10, 15 years ago. Every kid has an agent—some are rising agents in the business—and that agent tells him, 'You haven't hit enough homers or driven in enough runs.'"

The Cubs' system appears similar to that of the rival Houston Astros, which also stress individual instruction.

"We try to look at each individual hitter, see what their strengths and weaknesses are," said Astros GM Tim Purpura. "Make their strengths stronger, even out their game. What kind of hitter are they—middle of the order, top of the order? Cater the program to them. Certainly, we emphasize guys going deep into counts. We have an approach called 'catch-up.' If you're down by a run or two in the late part of game, if you see a first-pitch fastball and it's your fastball to hit, have at it. Otherwise, take until you get a strike. We have our own system of statistical measurement. We take into consideration whether he's a contact guy or power guy."

Fleita has dramatically improved the Latin-American development program, which was almost moribund in the mid-1990s, badly trailing the Astros and other teams that had long tapped the rich talent source south of the border. A Cuban-American, Fleita is fluent in Spanish, helping with his young prospects. However, he sees his greatest challenge is teaching plate discipline to kids from the Caribbean. It goes beyond the old admonition that the young Dominican prospect has to swing the bat to get off the island.

Patience is Prudence at the Plate

"We've tried a lot of different ways," Fleita said. "I have machines that throw curveballs. They'll hit from sunup to sundown. You try to apply the approach of being selective. I've talked to Cleveland and Boston [development people], and they pull their hair out. You have to be delicate. What's changed in the Dominican is, years ago, plenty of kids were playing all day; it was always a street game. You'd get exposed to everything about baseball. Now you have a lot of agents grabbing kids as young as 12 or 13, preparing them to do a couple of things: run the 60, hit the ball over the fence, or throw the living shit out of the baseball. They end up with no feel for the game."

In the end, the Cubs will be as patient at the plate as top management wants them to be.

"It's always a byproduct of your major-league staff," Fleita explained. "We all work with the hitting coach at the major-league level. We've had a lot of change over time."

Sounds like the ball is in former Tampa prep basketball star Lou Piniella's court. Yet, Piniella has a boss, who in turn answers to another boss. Patience for winning has apparently worn thin at the very top of the management food chain. Problem is, to achieve their stated goal of winning it all, they're going to need far more patience at the plate than they've been practicing.

twelve

CARE AND FEEDING IN CRAMPED CONFINES

ON THE MORNING of August 23, 2006, the Cubs' weight room turned into an Animal House, even by the boys-club standards of big-league locker rooms. Doom and gloom pervaded the Cubs' season-to-nowhere after another three losses in a row. Yet, the decibel level emitted from the weight room was proof that one day's defeat does not linger into the next in daily big-league life.

Two Cubs had besieged the cozy facility, which is presided over by Tim Buss—the team's strength-conditioning coordinator. The pair was yelling orders to leave at those unworthy of their presence. "All left-handers," said catcher Michael Barrett, peering into the room. Within a minute, they were identified as Scott Eyre and Glendon Rusch.

The southpaw duo's shouts chased away traveling secretary Jimmy Bank. Then clubhouse man Gary Stark had to make a hasty retreat. Barrett entered but quickly made a U-turn—a broomstick was thrust out the door for emphasis. Seconds later, Eyre burst through the doorway holding a volleyball. "Where's Barrett?" he shouted. Seconds later Barrett, donning a catcher's mask, walked near the doorway.

"The boys are wound up today," said clubhouse man Rich Rupp as he attempted to enter the weight room. "It's getaway day."

"Get out!" the lefties barked.

Entangled In Ivy

Amid the tumult, card games continued uninterrupted at nearby tables. Reliever Michael Wuertz and first baseman Phil Nevin, soon to be traded to Minnesota, sat quietly by their lockers.

Buss arrived. "Want to come in?" he asked me, stirring up mock trouble. Then he asked the weight room masters if I could enter. "NOOOOO!" was the resolute answer. Pitcher Angel Guzman came out of the room smiling. Shouts of "Go away!" followed. Finally, reliever Bobby Howry entered, greeted by applause and cheers, and the mood changed. All relievers stick together.

Then Mark Prior walked in. "Gee-sus!" was his greeting.

The sights and sounds, considering the Cubs' place in the standings, were amazing. However, they weren't as amazing as the cramped, uncomfortable digs in which they had to both prepare and cool down before and after each game. The Wrigley Field home clubhouse, nearly state-of-the-art when it was built before the 1984 season, is the smallest in the National League. The 93-year-old ballpark has no room for expansion, though, making the cramped confines less than friendly to those who use them, and could arguably be another factor in the Cubs' inability to win consistently.

The clubhouse replaced a much smaller, airless area down in the left-field corner, now used as the groundskeepers' room. Players in the 1960s and 1970s claimed the old locker room was even warmer than the sultry Chicago summer weather. The Cubs had to shower in shifts, while rookie call-ups in September were consigned to a dungeon-like equipment room to commingle with mice.

How a 45-man NFL team in the form of the Bears, with their bigger bodies and bulkier equipment, could fit into that cubbyhole has yet to be fully explained. One day, Dick Butkus complained to linebacker mate Doug Buffone about a bad smell around his wire-mesh cubicle. After Buffone dutifully washed his sneakers and other gear, the odor persisted. On a hunch, Buffone tapped the false ceiling with a broom handle. Out dropped a dead rat.

The accommodations weren't quite that bad in the early 21st Century. Yet, the tiny area became an issue with no need of another problem as they tried to overcome myriad obstacles and shake sports' most perplexing championship drought.

Care and Feeding in Cramped Confines

The locker room is located a flight of stairs below the main concourse; it runs north-south behind the home dugout, which is connected by a tunnel that angles 90 degrees. The rectangular layout boasts cubicles on either side, leaving just enough room for card tables in the middle and a single-file passage along each side. More hip fakes are witnessed here when media are present than in any NFL game. Boxes are stacked two or three atop each locker, and an engineer could easily confuse the quarters with a submarine.

Media first tend to congregate at the bottom of the stairs, but then fan out throughout the clubhouse. Carlos Zambrano's locker is closest to the stairs, so the strapping ace has less room to maneuver than smaller teammates when the press assembles. Kerry Wood used that same locker when he broke in as a rookie—and, after he struck out 20 Houston Astros, he was pinned in there. As his seniority grew, and after the departure of buddy Mark Grace after the 2000 season, Wood eventually shifted his locker to the other end of the room, near the off-limits-to-media areas of the food room and showers.

The weight room, a low-ceilinged space with workout machines, faces the clubhouse at the bottom of the stairs. The training room, which leads to the showers, is through a northbound corridor off the tunnel to the dugout. Closer to the field are the storage areas for the team's equipment, located in another northbound corridor. Further down the corridor, amid stark cinder-block walls, is an informal players' lounge—just chairs and chilling players, the ultimate getaway from prying media eyes and ears. Beyond this area, the equipment room corridor leads to a back door to the main concourse closest to the players' wives room and the parking lot. Many Cubs use this exit to evade the potential postgame gauntlet of autograph seekers and hangers-on.

Wash-up sinks and mirrors flank the right end of the clubhouse and food room at the north end. Large-screen television sets hang from the walls above the food room and weight room. Make a left turn at the north end, and head up a flight of stairs to find the manager's office, coaches' room, and a shower. These areas have largely been off-limits to reporters since media-aloof Don Baylor took over as manager in 2000. However, in the previous decade, many stimulating conversations about baseball and life occurred in these areas. It was almost like sitting around the cracker barrel in the old, old days. One pregame conversation took place while the icy Ed Lynch, then general manager, popped his head in the coaches' room. No order to evacuate was issued by Lynch or relayed to his media-relations staff.

The coziness promoted media-players-coaches-manager contact and relationships when properly applied. But tensions were exacerbated as the Cubs started to win in 2003, and in the aftermath of the near-miss of the World Series that October. Five lounge chairs were set up in the north end of the clubhouse before the 2004 season, further cramping the too-small area. Media were told they could not stand at the north end of the clubhouse unless they were doing a specific interview. Television cameras, with the exception of a pool operator from Comcast SportsNet, were banned pregame to reduce the number of bodies present.

Before the restrictions look hold in 2004, I sensed growing player unease with their accommodations, which paled in square footage compared to spacious combinations of clubhouses, player lounges, trainers' rooms, weight rooms, and indoor batting cages available at the slew of new ballparks that have opened in the last decade.

"It's like you're driving a Honda Civic and then you're driving a Mercedes for a week," 2003 first baseman Eric Karros said. "Are you going to look forward to going back to driving that Honda Civic?"

Traditionalists will laugh at millionaires complaining about their dressing quarters. However, if they took a minute to think, the Cubs' space crunch is just another factor affecting their ability to compete consistently. Along with the heavy day-game home schedule, the understaffed baseball operations department, and the team's dismissal of on-base percentage when conceptualizing a productive lineup, the list of preexisting maladies continues to mount for the Cubs.

One day at midseason, 2003, while watching how the mass of people jammed up to Sammy Sosa's locker, I asked stand-up guy Mark Grudzielanek—then the second baseman—about being squeezed for breathing room as the mob swirled around Sosa a few feet away.

"It's hard to relax by my locker," Grudzielanek said. "You should have private areas, no guests. You can get maybe five guys in the lunchroom. When you go on the road, you can go in these private rooms, kick back and relax, talk the way you want to talk, voice your opinion on things. It's something where you have to be careful what you say, what you talk about."

Care and Feeding in Cramped Confines

Then-closer Joe Borowski seconded those thoughts.

"It's not having the sanctuary to get away from everybody," he said then. "You're married, and sometimes you have to get away for a while. You can't see the same person every single day and not [have it] get on your nerves."

A year later Greg Maddux, starting his second tour of duty with the Cubs, echoed the opinion about a getting-away-from-it-all area. Having played in spacious Turner Field in Atlanta, in which two Wrigley Fields could seemingly fit, Maddux did not complain vocally about the tight surroundings that had not changed since he made his big-league debut in September 1986. However, he recalled how Turner Field featured a spacious lounge area where players could get away from outside distractions as they prepped for games.

With the lack of a private area, Wood and others set up the informal lounge in the equipment corridor.

"You can get 10 people back there," reliever Will Ohman said in 2006. "You [media] have your job, and we have ours. It's an area. It's the bowels of the stadium. If you can't get to your locker, you want some time. You don't want to feel eyes burning in the back of your skull. I go stand over there, and I'm talking to my buddy—there's 17 people staring at me waiting for an interview. Why do I want to make myself feel rushed, or be quiet because I'm talking to my friend about something that's not for public dissemination?"

I always wondered how an entire roster of Cubs could disappear after a game in such tight quarters. Eventually, players would filter back to their lockers. Yet, if the space was at a premium, where were all the bodies piling up?

"After any game, most guys will do exactly what they do after any game," said Ohman. "They'll get food, go to the bathroom, talk in the trainer's room and ice down, lift weights. If you feel you were the guy who caused the team a bad day, you sit in silence by your locker. Some guys immediately shower; others go to the food room. Five can fit in the food room, five in the trainer's room, five guys in the weight room. It's not really one location. You go where you need to go to deal with thoughts. Then you come back and deal with questions."

Carving out more space seemed in the offing in 2005. Once expanded bleachers were completed for the following season, the next phase called for a "Wrigley campus"—the construction of a new building on the parking lot immediately west of the ballpark. The building would house restaurants, shops, offices, and possibly a Cubs Hall of Fame as well as additional parking. Beneath that "campus" would be expanded batting cages and weight-training facilities. However, the actual locker room would remain as is. The expansion became a moot point in 2006, when the new building was put on hold. Speculation abounded that owner Tribune Co.'s economic problems had a negative effect.

"It wasn't the right time to do it," said one Cubs official.

Even if the building project had proceeded, the players would not have been the first priority. Their discomfort fell on the deaf ears of then-Cubs president Andy MacPhail. The team's chief traditionalist did not advocate heavy tinkering with Wrigley Field, especially if those changes did not improve the bottom line dramatically.

I remember asking MacPhail in 1995 if he could build an elevator to the upper deck for easier press-box access. "Go to Comiskey Park," he responded. A year later, an elevator down the left-field line was constructed; rumors swirled that the Cubs installed the lift to forestall legal problems involving access for the disabled to upper-deck seats previously reached only by steep ramps. Room for the elevator shaft seemingly had been available the entire time, but Cubs business chief Mark McGuire said he and other team officials had overlooked the space somehow.

In 2003, MacPhail responded to the players' desires for more room.

"Players get exposed to extraordinarily lavish facilities at these new ballparks," he said, "where they don't spare much expense for accoutrements for the locker rooms, unlimited space for family waiting rooms, and weight rooms that were unheard of in 1914. Most of the [Wrigley Field] space is devoted to servicing our fans, the paid admissions that keep the game going. Absent a building that is separate from Wrigley Field, there is no solution. Frankly, there are other things that need attention ahead of that. We don't have enough washroom facilities for women—that needs to be expanded. We need to pay attention to their needs first."

MacPhail said he would never use the facilities as an excuse for not winning. Neither would general manager Jim Hendry.

Care and Feeding in Cramped Confines

"To me, we're going down a path that I refuse to be a part of, and that's excuses," Hendry said. "I don't want any excuses that it's tougher to win because of the day games. Facilities—that's not an excuse for me. We can turn this place into a positive. We were 20 games over .500 in 1998, with a team that probably overachieved to get to the wild card—God bless Rod Beck for saving 51 games. We were five outs away from eliminating every excuse here [in 2003]. Those last five outs we didn't get had nothing to do with the day games."

Perhaps some warmer hitters, though, might have amassed more than three runs in Game 6 of the National League Championship Series in 2003. The facilities do have an effect—lack of an accessible in-game batting cage to better prepare players. The effect of the cramped clubhouse can be debated, but the Wrigley Field indoor cage—underneath the right-field bleachers—cannot be used during games. In contrast, U.S. Cellular Field's cage is right behind the White Sox dugout. Designated hitter Jim Thome said he can take 100 swings in the cage during the game from a live batting-practice pitcher. An extra man, such as infielder Alex Cintron, can swing up to 200 times, guaranteeing he's warmed and ready if called upon late in the game. Meanwhile, Cubs opponents talk about how players loosening up in the on-deck circle at Wrigley Field have to hunch their shoulders and take half-swings in the modest foul territory.

Inside, the three men in charge of the care and feeding of the Cubs in the clubhouse make do as best they can. Clubhouse manager Tom Hellmann's main goal is keeping the area tidy.

"We have so much stuff on top of each other," he said. "We try to make it stay nice and neat. That is the biggest challenge. Cleanup is better because it's not so big. In spring training in Mesa, we're vacuuming [more space] for an hour. We try to do as much as we can with the space we have now; and if they give us more, we'll fill that up in no time. We'd like a bigger lounge so they don't have to sit in the back on boxes. We can fit in only six to eight. We have three [card] tables out here. This was state of the art in 1984—remember? Like everything else, everything changes."

Meanwhile, head trainer Mark O'Neal said "we get by" with his space, which he claims is adequate to provide proper treatment for ailing Cubs.

"It's smaller than in the newer—and some of the older—ballparks," O'Neal said. "We have an office for Ed [Halbur, assistant trainer] and myself. We also have a doctor's exam room, about ten-feet-by-eight-feet, with a table in there. There's a medicine cabinet, a work station for the doctors, and a fax machine."

The actual trainer's room has three tables: two for treatment and the other for therapeutic activities. One table can be raised to make it easier to tape ankles. The space includes a room with three whirlpools and an ice machine. Electric stimulating and ultrasound equipment, along with therapeutic strength exercise machine, are on site.

"At any point of time, we can put five to six guys in here, sitting on chairs or in the office with heat packs," O'Neal said. "When we're not running crazy with treatments, they do hang out. They sit on tables or chairs, use it as a kind of lounge to get away from the media."

The training area lacks the space for an underwater treadmill, a therapeutic device placed in a huge tank of water that relieves stress on joints. New ballparks possess the water tank. The Cubs have relationships with clinics to send their players to do the water therapy off-site.

Ideally, O'Neal could use more training tables, as did his predecessors. Most new ballparks have up to six tables. He said he's never been turned down when he's made requests for new equipment. There simply is a finite amount of space.

"I can't tell you how many people call me monthly trying to sell me a piece of equipment," O'Neal said. "We want it, but there is nowhere to put it. Guys in new ballparks complain they don't have enough. Could our facilities be better? Absolutely. Are they functional? Absolutely. We have 15 players living in Arizona in the off-season, and have equipment in there [at Fitch Park]. We've got the space to do what needs to be done."

Completing his sixth season as strength and conditioning coordinator in 2006, Tim Buss also makes do with his modest-sized weight room.

"I'm saying yes, it works, because I've done it for six years with these guys," he said. "It would be nicer to have a little more space. I think we've been able to get some very good workouts with the space we have. Guys just come in and get their stuff done. The problems I have arise when the other team comes over [before the game]—that's the biggest problem."

Care and Feeding in Cramped Confines

The weight room features a treadmill, an elliptical machine, a Stairmaster, two exercise bikes, a stretching board, weights, and other equipment. Buss' wish list includes adding another treadmill, an elliptical, and a Stairmaster to protect against breakdowns of the cardio equipment.

"We have eight to nine guys in here after each game," he said. "There are no issues. They do a good job. These guys work so hard. I don't think space and equipment is a bar. We get good work in. Injuries are not caused because we don't have enough space."

O'Neal and Buss were flummoxed by the mounting—and freaky—epidemic of injuries that hammered the Cubs in 2006. The three-season trend was so bad that the young pitchers who were called up to replace injured hurlers became injured themselves. The season ended in September for both Michael Barrett and Glendon Rusch. Barrett suffered internal scrotal bleeding due to a foul tip while catching, requiring emergency surgery. Diligent workout guy Rusch was hit with a blood clot in the lung that came out of nowhere. He was hospitalized for a week and was prescribed blood-thinning medication for at least six months.

"This is probably the most frustrating year I've ever been a part of," O'Neal said late in the 2006 season. "Do people report things more than they used to? Absolutely. Pitching through things is not the answer either. Back then, if you went down, someone took your job. You were back working on the farm. The demands of the game are incredibly difficult. These guys condition themselves so much that it's like putting a Porsche engine in a Volkswagen frame sometimes. You kind of overload the circuit."

"Look at [rookie left-hander] Ryan O'Malley. He never had a problem in his career. He goes out here, throws once, then feels a twinge in the muscular groups in his elbow. Do you ask why? One thing—and it's not an excuse—but throwing is not a natural motion. If it were, we'd all be born with our arms above our head. You can do everything you can to control the strength, control the motion, to give them the best advantage to prevent injury as best you can. If you don't want injuries, put the balls away and say you played the games. It's going to happen. There's not a sporting event where this doesn't happen. Our goal is to minimize damage done. Have they happened too much here? Absolutely."

Entangled In Ivy

The recurring nature of the injuries provoked some cynics to suggest that players such as Mark Prior weren't tough enough to work through some pain; but O'Neal said such opinions are off base.

"That's not to say one person is tougher than another," he said. "What one person is capable of pitching through, another person is not. That does not mean he's not as tough as the other guy. It just means he's just not capable with the same pain as someone else is. You can't treat one hamstring strain [the same as] another. They're all different. You can talk all you want to until you go through it and you have individual needs. There's not a cookie-cutter approach to any of this."

Similarly, Buss improves and enhances conditioning and stretching programs as more knowledge becomes available each year. Yet, he feels his best planning can be thrown to the winds through events beyond his control.

"You can do one thing one year and have no injuries; the same thing next year, a bunch of injuries," he said. "If we knew the answer to the question [of why some Cubs get hurt frequently], we wouldn't have two [key] guys on the shelf. As Woody aged, he got more mature, worked out so much harder. I've been with Woody since 1998. I see how he's evolved. I was with him every other day [in Arizona] in the off-season—and to have this go down? It's frustration for me with my job, and as a friend, to see a guy like him work so hard and get hurt. I think he'll be all right."

Wood and his fellow pitchers go through a prescribed off-season workout routine. A typical circuit involves an upper-body workout Monday, lower-body workout Tuesday, and an abdominal workout Wednesday. Another round of upper body (Thursday) and lower-body (Friday) close out the week.

"I'm not a big fan of pitchers lifting for their upper body," Buss said. "They make their money from the waist down. The legs are the most important."

Under his watch, Buss rated Joe Girardi (still cut in his postplaying career), Eric Karros, Bobby Howry, and Rusch as his best weight room workers.

"[Carlos] Zambrano is pretty good," Buss said. "Sometimes you got to pick your spots with him. He is flexible. This guy is an athlete. He could be a linebacker. He's one of the top five guys on the bases, and he might be one of the top five fastest guys on the team."

Care and Feeding in Cramped Confines

Injured or not, the Cubs have to feel as comfortable as possible in their confines. That job falls to Tom Hellmann and his clubhouse crew, who succeeded the legendary Yosh Kawano, now assisting—in his 64th season in baseball—in the visitors' locker room. Gary Stark is his full-time assistant. Brother Tim Hellmann, Rich Rupp, and Jonathan Veremis are seasonal helpers.

Tom Hellmann usually arrives for day games at 6:30 or 6:45 a.m. at the latest. The rest of the crew reports by 7 a.m. At least the game days offer short workday than night games, when the clubhouse men are on the job between 11 a.m. and noon. First orders of business are getting clothes distributed, finishing the towel-washing from the previous day, and getting breakfast started.

What qualifies Hellmann to be a chef to the stars?

"I got a Boy Scout cooking badge," he said. "I give them bacon every day, everyone likes bacon—also two different kinds of meats, bacon and sausage and ham, or corned beef hash. We go through anywhere from three to five dozen eggs every day, six pounds of bacon, 35 sausages, and four big ham steaks. We also make grits, waffles, cereal, and coffee cake."

In contrast to Kawano's prime as locker-room lord, when the players were responsible for their own meals, Hellmann and Co. provide three squares for day games. They serve a post-batting practice lunch.

"We try to get them something that's not too heavy on the stomach before the game," he said, "like lunch meat, pasta, salad, soup. We cut out the soup when it gets hot in the summer."

Hellmann's postgame spread "is nicer for night games and getaway day, they don't have a chance to go out. We have lighter fare for after day games, most go out to restaurants or eat at home."

Daily laundry duty starts out with uniforms. Two 50-pound washers and driers each handle more than 20 loads a day.

Getaway day is the most fast-paced. As players arrive pregame, they give their luggage to the clubhouse crew. Road uniforms are packed. The real rush comes when bats, duffle bags, and some of the medical supplies have to be packed after the game and then loaded on the equipment truck to be shipped to the Cubs' chartered flight.

"We can't even start loading until 45 minutes after the game because of people in the concourse, and they have to move concession stands so the truck can back in," Hellmann said.

Entangled In Ivy

He makes all the road trips, and Gary Stark joins him on several, during which they practically exult over the spacious accommodations of all the new ballparks.

Would the Cubs be too spoiled if they possessed "lavish" clubhouse facilities at home?

Short of a new ballpark, no one will ever know.

thirteen

AN INCREDIBLE ON-THE-AIR BALANCING ACT

THE SIGHT—more than the sound—of Len Kasper gliding through the Cubs clubhouse three hours before day games at Wrigley Field quietly amazed. The Cubs' television announcer worked the locker room earlier than most media. Kasper moved from player to player to a stray coach or two, picking up tidbits of information. In 2006, his second year in the Chicago booth, Kasper came downstairs at the same time as the traveling beat writers, who descended the ramp in a group and then set up in a clump of humanity, standing and waiting for business around the area at the bottom of the stairs while the television guy wandered the clubhouse. Then he'd follow the crowd into the Wrigley Field version of the Black Hole of Calcutta—the interview room off the tunnel leading to the clubhouse—to monitor manager Dusty Baker's pregame media briefing.

Why should the presence of a broadcaster, arriving early and prepping even better than the typical beat writer, be so unusual? One simple answer: Kasper is an utter rarity on his rounds in Cubs annals. His predecessors usually treated the locker room like a leper colony, preferring instead a kind of celebrity-among-celebrities role behind the batting cage more than an hour later than Kasper's typical arrival.

"It's the way I've always done it," Kasper said of his clubhouse beat. "I need to be informed. I feel like, if there are things that come up on the air regarding certain players and situations, I'd like to know beforehand what the manager had to say about it, what a particular player had to say about it. I read a lot about what a particular player had to say about it.

"I do a lot of research and a lot of reading about players. That will bring up questions in my mind about the thing I've read. I like to get it from that person directly if I possibly can. It's important to me to be down here as quickly as I can. I also like to have plenty of time to get ready for a game. I don't like to be rushed—I don't like to feel like I'm scrambling to get ready."

Making the rounds is simply an extension of Kasper's personality.

"Not only is it important for me as part of my job to do it," he said, "it's fun to talk major-league baseball with major-league players, managers, GMs, coaches, scouts, and front-office people. I get a kick out of doing that. I like to learn something every day, and I feel like I'm doing that when I'm down on the field or in the clubhouse."

Bob Brenly, Kasper's glib broadcast analyst partner, entered the home clubhouse less frequently for day games, arriving later than early-bird Kasper. But Brenly is no stranger.

"Just so the players see you," said Brenly, who has easily moved back and forth between the broadcast booth and the managerial and coaching ranks. "They see that you're doing your work. The players take batting practice, take ground balls. That's part of my preparation, asking them, 'How do you feel?' Once they get on the field, they're open game to writers and every fan. They don't open up. You don't have time to sit and talk to them. When you go into the clubhouse and catch a guy in the lunchroom or around his locker, it gives him an opportunity to explain what's going on with his body and mind, which gives you a better background when you go on the air. It may explain why certain things happen on the field."

The combination of Kasper and Brenly enjoying face time with players and other Cubs folks seemed like a fail-safe against the blowups between players and broadcasters that first simmered beneath the surface before tearing a hole in the fabric of the franchise near the conclusion of the 2004 season.

Kasper and Brenly would perform an incredible balancing act during the lost 2006 campaign. They'd promote the sagging Cubs as best as possible, but were also critical and honest about the on-field foibles. They displayed Jacque Jones repeatedly spiking the ball into the outfield turf

An Incredible On-The-Air Balancing Act

on throws and did not ignore Aramis Ramirez when he loped out of the batter's box, then having to turn on the jets to run out an extra-base hit.

For once, the rabbit-ear clubhouse did not turn on the guys in the booth as they first did with Chip Caray, then Steve Stone, whose mutual departures after the '04 season opened the jobs for Kasper and Brenly.

Caray uncommonly strode into the clubhouse and Stone never. "If a player has a problem, I'm always out here," Stone said in 2006—otherwise declining to comment on his Cubs broadcast days—while he stood behind the batting cage before a game at U.S. Cellular Field. But out in the open with scores of nosey witnesses is hardly the time and place to settle disputes over broadcast criticism, real or imagined.

"The last thing you want to do is cause problems and make a scene in front of other players, teams, other personnel, the high brass, the GM," said 2003-04 Cubs second baseman Mark Grudzielanek.

The Caray-Stone duo made the same mistake as hordes of sports columnists and radio sports talk show hosts. Facing the players at the ballpark after a critical commentary is considered the courageous, but proper, course of action. But even more important—and somehow less well-rated—were the relationships forged and the information gleaned from one-on-one clubhouse talks with the rank and file. Familiarity does not breed contempt here. Players have repeatedly said they could handle criticism if their side of the story was told in the commentary.

"They were very distant from the team," Grudzielanek said of Caray and Stone. "I don't understand it. I don't get it. Something was going on before I was there in '03."

Something indeed went seriously awry in the Cubs clubhouse as the 21st Century opened. Chip Caray was no clone of the vintage form of his grandfather, Harry Caray. The elder Caray in the booth threw barbs at Cardinals, Athletics, and White Sox, nearly coming to blows with Bill Melton at the Pfister Hotel in Milwaukee. The very mention of Caray's name caused Tony La Russa to purse his lips—even after his death.

Chip Caray did nothing out of the ordinary in broadcast criticism. Yet, for some strange reason, Sammy Sosa—with the assistance of then-manager Don Baylor—summoned Caray into a meeting with the entire team a few years back regarding his broadcasting style.

"Not one of those players had the balls to come up to me one on one to talk about this," Caray recalled.

Entangled In Ivy

"That wouldn't happen with me, because I wouldn't stand for it," Cincinnati Reds announcer Marty Brennaman said. "If I had to go justify my position I take on the air, and had to stand up in front of the whole baseball team and justify it, the hell with that. I'm not doing that."

Brennaman headed off such trouble by walking into the Reds clubhouse before games every day. If a Ken Griffey, Jr. had to hash out some Brennaman commentary from the previous day, the announcer was in his face.

The mounting trouble was yet another perfect storm in Cubs history. One end featured announcers who didn't have one-on-one relationships with players and didn't venture into the locker room. Those announcers clashed with players who took advantage of a clubhouse atmosphere that traditionally lacked the tight discipline of the Atlanta Braves or Minnesota Twins—a discipline that prohibited such distractions.

Stone was on a two-year sabbatical, prompted by health concerns, when Caray had his team meeting. Stone—despite decent doses of arrogance and politics in his personal portfolio—was one of the game's best broadcast analysts, and he'd seemingly achieved the perfect balance in his previous Cubs tenure from 1983 to 2000.

"I learned so much about baseball from Steve," said Kristine Charboneau, their stage manager on Fox Sports Net telecasts. But when Stone came back to rejoin Chip Caray in 2003, their reputation in an otherwise positive, winning-oriented clubhouse took a nosedive.

Shawn Estes, the Cubs' fifth starter in 2003, said the broadcasters became *persona non grata* in the clubhouse. A report even spread that the players had voted to bar Caray and Stone from the postgame celebration in the clubhouse after the Cubs had clinched the National League Central after a doubleheader sweep of the Pirates at Wrigley Field on September 27, 2003. But closer Joe Borowski said no such balloting had ever taken place. It was difficult enough to get 25 players on board on any issue, let alone to take such a vote, Borowski reasoned. The main complaint, according to multiple players interviewed, centered around Caray, especially, giving more credit to Cubs' opponents than to the Cubs themselves.

Interestingly, Charboneau said she heard of some viewer complaints that Caray was giving the St. Louis Cardinals, his hometown team, more airplay than one might expect on a Cubs telecast.

An Incredible On-The-Air Balancing Act

Caray's confrontation with the entire team in the Don Baylor era and the mounting troubles during 2003 never reached the public. The broadcasters' conflicts with the Cubs came to the surface first in an off-hand manner, then in soap-opera fashion as a loaded-up team underperformed during much of the 2004 season. Outfielder Moises Alou uttered a throwaway postgame comment about the broadcasters giving more credit to the Cubs' much-hyped pitching at the expense of the lineup. Alou wasn't making it a big issue, but in a sound-bite-crazed world with sports talk radio chewing on every nugget, the comment was blown out of proportion.

Then, during the Astros' 15-7 victory over the Cubs on August 27 at Wrigley Field, Caray noted how Roy Oswalt had kept his team in the game in tough conditions of heat and hitter-friendly winds. The Cubs were seething about Oswalt anyway. Five days earlier, the right-hander had plunked Michael Barrett in the back after Aramis Ramirez slugged a three-run homer in Minute Maid Park. When Oswalt came to bat in the top of the second, Barrett got out of his catcher's crouch to confront the pitcher. He also exchanged words with Oswalt when he grounded out and Barrett backed up first. Later, leading off the sixth, lefty reliever Kent Mercker hit Oswalt.

When Mercker returned to the clubhouse, he heard Caray's play-by-play about Oswalt's ability to persevere under the adverse playing conditions. He interpreted the broadcaster as praising Public Enemy No. 1 at the time. Under normal conditions, Mercker was known as a good clubhouse guy. But on this day, Caray had angered him amid the inflamed situation with Oswalt. He called Cubs media relations director Sharon Pannozzo in the press box to pass a message of his displeasure along to Caray. Stone was not the object of his ire, but Stone heard about the call, a violation of baseball decorum, and leaked the story to the media. The next day, Mercker said he contacted Pannozzo to send a message of reconciliation with the broadcasters. Mercker claimed that Stone felt it was too late to put the genie back in the bottle. Stone refused to confirm his version of the story. "I'm not commenting on 2004," he said. Mercker later had confrontations with Stone—the severity of the incidents is in dispute—on the team plane and in a hotel elevator in Pittsburgh.

Entangled In Ivy

"I don't care what you say about me on TV," said Mercker, who moved on to the Reds. "If you're ragging on me, you have a pretty good reason to rag on me because I'm probably giving up runs and homers. If I stink, say, 'He stinks.' We're all grown men. If you want to be critical of someone, why can't they be critical of you? I like Stoney. I never had a problem with Stoney until, all of a sudden, I read in the paper I did a lot of stuff that never happened. I called Sharon to ask Chip a question after the game. Harry Caray really wanted the Cubs to win. Harry was rooting for the Cubs. If you have a problem [with the broadcaster], you shake hands in the clubhouse after a disagreement."

All the good minds in baseball claim either Cubs manager Dusty Baker or general manager Jim Hendry—or both—should have put out the fires right then and there. Baker claimed he told the players to ignore the broadcasters' comments, but the issue festered throughout the final month of the '04 season.

"I've often said that the stuff that went on with the ball club and Chip and Steve could have been stopped stone cold by the manager," Marty Brennaman said. "And if he wasn't willing to do it, the GM could have called a team meeting and said, 'Gentleman, we have more to be concerned about with our play on the field than what they say or don't say on the air.' That stuff could have been nipped in a bud. They're a lot of people in this organization who could have stood up and gotten their back, but they didn't do it. By allowing it to go on, it becomes something that's talked about day in and day out."

Brenly's own experience as a manager dictated that such broadcaster-team problems be settled privately, out of the gaze of the prying media.

"There were things said [on the air] during my time managing the Diamondbacks by one of my best friends, Thom Brennaman [Marty's son and fellow announcer], former Cub Mark Grace, and before that Jim Traber," he said. "There were some things said that I felt were unnecessary and not based on what was going on, but based on what they felt they were seeing from the booth. I never thought it was important enough to drag my team into it. We had enough problems to worry about on the field; we had our business to take care of; they had their job to do. There was nothing in my job description as a manager that said I had to monitor what the broadcasters said.

An Incredible On-The-Air Balancing Act

"Things can be handled in a much more private way in which they usually are," Brenly continued. "There are ways to handle it so that it doesn't become a story in and of itself. I sat in my office many a time with Thom Brennaman about things that were said. But it was nobody else's business. I respect the job he does. I think because I've seen the game from so many different angles, perhaps I'm a little more tolerant than some managers, because everyone has a job to do in this game. It's not my place to tell somebody else how to do their job. That being said, if I feel there's an explanation and I feel their criticism is unwarranted, I feel it's my place to pull them aside privately, talk about it, know all the facts before they become openly critical of me or a player or the team in general."

A manager has to deal with the media anyway. Putting out the fires before they engulf the entire team is part of the job description.

"As a manager, you have to step in and be the buffer, take a hit for your team," Brenly said. "Confront a writer if you feel he's been unfair. But I don't think it should become an issue where you should call team meetings, talk to the writers. I remember, growing up, we were lucky to see the Game of the Week, one game a week. Now you can see a game every day on your computer. For two hours before and two hours after, you have talking heads on the radio, criticizing and ripping and slashing. The entire environment of the game has changed considerably. Part of the job as manager is to keep your players on task. Make sure they understand what's important. Make sure they understand because some guy on talk radio is ripping them and calling them names—that really should affect the way they go about their business once they get to the ballpark.

But Cubs management in the late summer of '04 couldn't put a lid on the problem. Once the story broke out in the open, it developed legs. The broadcasters-players feud haunted the Cubs the entire final month of September 2004. A report surfaced that the players wanted to bar Caray and Stone from the team plane. Even Hall of Famer-to-be Ryne Sandberg chimed in, uncharacteristically criticizing Cubs players on his regular radio segment on all-sports WMVP-AM.

"I'm reflecting back as a player—being in the locker room and having those distractions was not part of my daily routine," Sandberg said from the hindsight of 2006. "I had a focus on the game, I knew what I had to do, I knew who was pitching that day. All the other outside interferences, whether it was announcers on TV or fans booing, that's something if you're a professional baseball player you have to block out; and you have to go out and be more prepared the next time, work at it a little harder, and do the things right and produce. Everything else will fall into place. But looking for excuses and blaming other people was never part of my game."

Caray became extremely disenchanted with selected Cubs down the stretch and confided his frustration with members of the team's traveling party. But the grand finale of the caper took place when Stone asked Baker several tough questions on a postgame interview following a 2-1, 12-inning loss to the Reds on September 30, 2004, that crippled the Cubs' postseason hopes. Stone had first-guessed that Baker should have intentionally walked Javier Valentin with a man on second and first base open in the 12th. Valentin doubled in the winning run off reliever Kyle Farnsworth. The apparent strategic blunder sparked the question that blew things up even further and prompted hushed meetings between Stone and top management.

Caray was low-balled in a contract renewal offer and left to join his father, Skip Caray, on Braves broadcasts. Stone was offered his job back, but declined and joined all-sports WSCR-Radio as an analyst. Mt. Pleasant, Michigan-native Kasper, the second or third choice to replace Stone, came from the Marlins. Brenly was already a Cubs radio announcer in 1990-91 and had distinguished himself as a Fox Sports analyst when he wasn't managing or coaching. So if Stone couldn't return, Brenly was seen as a great 1-A choice.

Replacing a prominent name, Kasper treaded lightly at first, and being teamed with a new color announcer created a natural tentative reaction.

"[In 2005] there was a caution from my perspective," Kasper said. "We tried to ease in. I'm from the Midwest, not from Chicago, but I think I understand the Midwestern mentality. It was very new, a completely different booth. I wanted to establish my credibility as a baseball broadcaster. That was very important to me. My personality, I think, has come through a lot more in Year Two. To overdo that in Year One would have been premature. I didn't want to force it. Now that people know me a little bit better, that's coming through a little bit more.

An Incredible On-The-Air Balancing Act

I want to be myself as much as I possibly can, but I don't want to miss the big stuff."

The ease that Kasper envelops himself in his on-air relationship with Brenly extends to their co-workers. Kristine Charboneau, who continued as stage manager as the telecasts shifted to Comcast SportsNet in 2005, said the present voices she helps cue are genuine in their positive nature.

"They're very easygoing," Charboneau said. "Whatever we want to do, they're so agreeable. If we come up with an idea for on-camera open, there's a good chance they're going to do it. With Chip and Steve, it was definitely a little harder to feel them out, to know what their mood was. But Chip was always very respectful toward me."

Kasper has specific tastes in rock: "power pop," a genre that began in the late 1970s with Cheap Trick, the Knack, and the Romantics. "They all hearken back to the 1960s with the Beatles, Kinks, the British Invasion—a lot of stuff I like is not well-known."

Occasionally, some power pop tunes would accompany "FanCam" shots from the stands on WGN games. Again, Kasper felt more at ease with musical references in his second year compared to his Cubs debut. With a year under his belt and credibility established, Kasper guested and talked about "power pop" with longtime Chicago broadcaster Bob Sirott on a WCKG-FM talk show.

That Kasper can even find the time for his musical passion is amazing. He prepares so thoroughly that he's in touch with his producer the night before a game via e-mail. Then he arrives early. He has a full workday off and on the air. Kasper has no relief play-by-play announcer. Management's mandate for Kasper and radio voice Pat Hughes is to stay on the air for every inning of each game. Hughes, at least, usually takes a quick breather in the bottom of the seventh while Andy Masur fills in. Kasper does not turn the mike over to Brenly; as far as the television voice is concerned, he's it.

"I've never seen an announcer get here as early as Len," said Bob Albrecht, who produces the Comcast SportsNet Cubs telecasts and mans a camera on WGN-TV games. "He's here at 9 a.m. for a 1:20 start. For a 7 p.m. game on the road, he's in the booth at 3 p.m."

"Len does a lot more research," Kristine Charboneau said of comparing Kasper and his predecessors. "Len has so much respect for the game. He comes down from Glencoe. He's still there extra early. Len, more than any other TV person, had an appreciation of where he is. He wants to be the best he can be."

The early bird gets the proverbial worm in baseball, so Albrecht is an advocate of his announcers working the clubhouse. "It's probably better to make yourself available on a daily basis if anybody has a gripe, and do research. Announcers work for the team. Our primary goal is to sell tickets. We have to keep our objectivity to keep our respect of the fans. We have smart fans. We've had great announcers since the 1950s who have been educating all the Chicago viewers, both sides of town. When somebody screws up, you can't sugar-coat it. You have to be objective in your reporting. If somebody doesn't hustle, if a player stands there and admires a ball going out, and it hits off the ivy, and he's tagged out at second because he didn't run, we're still going to show that. It's still our job."

Kasper apparently can continue his balancing act both in the booth and in the clubhouse. But his style all starts with one-on-one relationships with players—a style that very few of baseball's media personalities seem to possess.

"If I read something intriguing and want to know more about it, the best way to get the whole story is to ask that person," Kasper said. "Cubs fans want to know what the players are saying about their swing, about the way they're playing, about the way they're pitching. About what's going on with the team. It's important that they get that daily news, so to speak, from that broadcast. I don't think I'm there to replace the newspaper. That's not my job. It's important that I don't miss the big stuff that happens."

Kasper figures he is enough of a diplomat to handle any player-relations problems that may arise. "I never played this game at any level above high school," he said. "But working with Bob, who's managed and played this game, recognizing how hard this game is ... when you talk to players about it, it gives you a better perspective on what they go through on a daily basis. I really try to be very fair if I can. I like to always be available if there are things that are said. I absolutely would talk to players about it.

"Fortunately, I haven't really had a lot of situations where anybody's been anything other than inquisitive about what was said. Often it's not even on our broadcast or it's about something else. I have no problems talking to people about something like that."

Kasper could never be as voluble as a Marty Brennaman in defending himself to a clubhouse critic. He'd be all ears first.

"First thing is, I always want to listen," he said. "I always take feedback seriously. If I said something that was deemed or heard as unfair, I'd definitely be willing to say, 'You're right, it's live television. Sometimes things come out a certain way you don't intend them to.' I certainly understand my limitations—I'm far from perfect. On the other hand, if I think it was something that was fair, if it was not gratuitous or over the top, I would state my case and say we have the right to disagree, but I appreciate you bringing it up.

"I'm not one of those people who thinks I can say whatever I want, and, tough, that's the way it's going to be. I hope to get better every day as a broadcaster. I try to be the same all the time and be very consistent. In that sense, you don't get into trouble because nobody can come back and say, 'You said this one day, and you said that the next day.' I am who I am, and that's just how it is. It makes it much simpler."

This might have been a Cubs first, since Harry Caray's most rollicking days in the booth. At least a few of the players could laugh along with Kasper and Brenly, even through the gloom and doom of 2006. Chuckling the hardest was Scott Eyre, one of the most good-humored Cubs.

"After all the bad things that went on [with Caray and Stone], I made up a sign," Eyre recalled. "They made fun of me because I was on the DL. They figured I was talking in the dugout. Bob said, 'I bet his teammates can't wait to get him off the DL and back in the bullpen because he talks a lot. I made a sign that said, 'That wasn't very nice.' He just laughed. I made a joke of it because of all the stuff that went on before. I did the pregame show the next day. I said I don't have a face for TV, but neither does Brenly."

Despite their varied backgrounds, Kasper and Brenly are almost of the same mind-set about their broadcast styles of balancing fairness, honesty, and criticism. The pair has steadily improved their on-air chemistry since joining each other in the booth.

"He's one of the best I've ever been around," Kasper said. "You hear the term low-maintenance. He's no-maintenance. He shows up, does the job every day. He does his homework. He knows the players and pitchers. When he gets on the air, he's as comfortable a listen as I've ever been around. He sees things I don't see. I've learned so many nuances. He does that every night, every day."

Brenly's truthful analytical style is the byproduct of all his baseball experiences. Just as a non-star like himself gravitated toward the coaching and managerial ranks, the necessity of paying even closer attention to the little things in baseball helps him in the booth.

"I've seen this game from every angle you can see it from," Brenly said. "The one conclusion I can come up with is: it's a tough game to play, even for the best players. It's a game of failure. You have to understand that, when players fail, it doesn't mean they aren't trying. It doesn't mean they don't care; it doesn't mean they aren't prepared. It's just the nature of the game. In our society, with talk radio and reality TV, it seems to be popular to rip, slash, and attack.

"From my experiences in the game, I have a hard time attacking a guy unless I see a lack of effort and lack of preparation. Those are two things I didn't tolerate as a player and didn't tolerate as a coach, I didn't tolerate as manager, and I don't tolerate as a broadcaster."

Brenly thus was repeatedly able to show the eccentric throws of right-fielder Jacque Jones, particularly those he spiked into the ground, without making the broadcast a referendum on Jones the person.

"In Jacque Jones' case, it's not due to a lack of effort," he said. "I watch Jacque come out here early almost every day and work on this throws from the outfield. But the reality is, come game time, he's had some problems with his throws. It's not due to a lack of effort. It's not that he doesn't care. He has shortcomings as a player.

"That would be like criticizing John Mabry for not being fast. Every player has their strengths and weaknesses. Unfortunately for Jacque, he occasionally has his problems with throws from right field. We've documented it, we've shown it, but I don't feel it necessary to attack Jacque and make it sound like he's not a good player. I'll be very complimentary when he does make a good throw."

Thus, the Kasper-Brenly broadcast stays the middle ground, a more matter-of-fact presentation than the old-style guerilla theater practiced by Harry Caray and Jimmy Piersall with the White Sox in the late 1970s.

An Incredible On-The-Air Balancing Act

"You just do the game," Kasper said. "You point out what happens, and you move on. I don't try to overdo stats, but stats tell the story as well. If a guy is one-for-his-last-23, that kind of says how he's hitting. If a guy has lost five straight starts with a 7.34 ERA, that kind of says it. You don't have to go too far beyond other than saying he has struggled a lot. An objective, factual statement doesn't get into an area where some guys might take it personally.

"The other thing that's very important to realize is, fans are smart. Cubs fans are very smart. They watch and listen every day. They read the papers and know what's going on. I don't believe I have to form their opinions for them. What they see, they can make their own conclusions, form their own opinions. The world is not always this way, that way. It's somewhere in the middle. Where some guys struggle in some areas, they excel in other areas. Jacque Jones is an interesting example. Offensively, he was really good since a slow start in April [2006]. He's had some defensive problems in right. But overall, Jacque has had a very good season with what he brings to the table and his track record. At the end of the year, when we talk about the Cubs' problems, Jacque Jones won't be on the list."

Another glaring example was third baseman Aramis Ramirez's failure to run out extra-base hits from the get-go. He'd often need to sprint suddenly after realizing that the ball would fall into the outfield instead of clearing the fence. Ramirez's loping was also documented on television. Ramirez obviously had deficiencies with the concept of all-out hustle, but Brenly said, even here, the issue was not all black and white.

"To be fair with Aramis, there have been occasions when he's had nagging leg problems," he said. "I know for a fact, as a manager I had players with leg problems, and I would tell them to save it. If you don't need to go hard, if you hit a two-hopper right at the first baseman, and he's running to the bag, I don't care if you run 100 percent down to the first-base line. But if you're on second base representing the go-ahead run in the ballgame, I expect you to give everything you have coming around third base to try to score that winning run."

From his former catcher's viewpoint, Brenly noticed on August 10, 2006, that Mark Prior was nibbling too much for a pitcher of his ability. He proclaimed that Prior should be challenging hitters more. Turns out

Prior was suffering from tendinitis that knocked him out of the rotation the rest of the season.

To err is only human, Kasper believes. Players have faults like everyone else, but they are displayed on a bigger stage than the average individual.

"We're all human beings," he said. "To sit here and say it's not personal when a player is criticized [is wrong]. A lot of guys do take it personally, and I do understand why. It's their livelihood. They're major-league baseball players, and everything they do is being dissected ad nauseam. I understand that. It doesn't feel good to hear that on a daily basis.

"I try not to talk about negative things … like, 'This guy is not a good player.' That's not something that I think is appropriate in a broadcast setting," Kasper added. "You can say that play maybe should have been made or that was not a smart play. But just to use a blanket statement, that's when guys have problems with what we say or write. Making a blanket statement about his abilities as a player can be insulting to a lot of guys. I don't try to force anything on the air. There's a sense of decorum doing a baseball game. I like to say it's not a talk show. We're there to present the game. We do have opinions. But I do think there's a line that has to be drawn on occasion when things happen, when things are said. I really try to watch that fine line."

Brenly believes the analyst's first priority is to research his own team. While Stone held court by the batting cage, he'd sometimes make a quick right turn toward the visitors' dugout to hobnob with players and managers. That time would have been better spent one on one in the Cubs locker room.

"It's not really my place to say Stoney did the right thing or wrong thing," Brenly said. "He did what he thought he had to do. Just as players have their own batting styles, pitchers their own style, broadcasters have their own style. I always felt it's more important that the home team, the team I'm going to be with 155 games a year, that it was more important they see me down there talking to them. Certainly, you need to talk to the other team, get some background on their ball club, especially the first game of a series. I think the majority of your time should be spent with the guys you're covering on a daily basis."

An Incredible On-The-Air Balancing Act

All the while, Kasper and Brenly are supported by an experienced crew working for both Comcast and WGN-TV. There's continuity from the production values of the legendary Arne Harris, whose Emmy-winning video artistry helped build the Cubs' popularity. Bob Albrecht, doing double duty for both production companies, started as a combination pre- and postgame stage manager and in-game relief camera operator during White Sox telecasts with Harry Caray and Jimmy Piersall in 1978. He was in attendance at the infamous Disco Demolition Night at old Comiskey Park the following year. Albrecht began working as a camera operator on Harris' WGN crew in 1984.

On his Comcast games, Albrecht works with seven manned cameras and another in the booth. The telecast had to be built from the ground up—but with a handy guidebook—when the old Fox Sports Net began doing a chunk of the games in 1999, the year Albrecht sold himself as an experienced insider to snare the producer's gig.

"The biggest challenge, from Day One, was to come on air and look like WGN," he said. Sure enough, the old Harris style of hat and "boob" shots was duplicated.

"One of the successes is to not only show what's happening on the field, but show the stands, people having a good time," Albrecht said. "Show good-looking women in the bleachers. That makes people want to be a part of it. When they show a woman, they'll always follow it up with a kid shot."

Some of the more exhibitionist female fans know the camera operators are prowling for them through their viewfinders. That leads to some quick switching when too much skin or frisky acts are about to be aired.

"Sometimes you just observe the situation first. If you suspect something rated more than 'R' will occur, then stay away from it," Albrecht said. "We've seen a little bit of it. That's what alcohol will do to you. We also will not show if someone runs on the field or a fight in the stands. But with [Dodgers catcher Chad] Kreuter [in 2000], it's instant news. You got a player strangling a fan in the stands, you have to show it. You walk a fine line."

In the end, all the bread, circuses, and ribald fan shots don't matter if the boys in the booth don't call it right and don't call it fairly.

Entangled In Ivy

"It's okay to be frustrated with what goes on down on the field," Kasper said. "It's okay to be excited with what goes on down on the field. But the No. 1 job of a broadcaster is to be fair. If a call goes against the Cubs, you don't have to like it. But if it's the right call, you owe it to your viewers to say it's the right call or it's a good call. I don't ever want to lose that. Sometimes, as a fan, you want to hope he was safe, but pictures don't lie. If it was too close to call, you say, 'It was too close to call.' They want you to call the game. They don't want you to miss the important plays. They want to know what's going on with the team, that's why it's important for me to be down in the clubhouse listening to Dusty with his news conferences. They want you to have fun. They want you to care and to have passion for the Cubs and what happens on the field.

"They also want you to be yourself. Being genuine and not robotic is important," Kasper explained. "I think I'm a pretty even-keel person. I try to bring that to the table. I know emotions can run high on a daily basis with this team up and down and all over the place. If, somehow, Bob and I can be the steady [presence], every day we're here, we're going to call the game whether it's a 10-game losing streak or a 12-game winning streak, you can count on us being there every day."

fourteen

THE CUBS' SUPERCHARGED BATTERY

UNLIKE MANY PITCHERS, Carlos Zambrano does not slip into a zombie-like trance in the hours before his first pitch. In fact, a casual observer might believe Zambrano, more commonly known as "Big Z" these days around Wrigley Field, might be the loosest guy in the locer room with the first pitch looming. He bounces around the clubhouse like an overgrown child—his 6-foot-5, 255-pound frame seemingly lighter than air.

Before one 2006 start, infielder Ronny Cedeno was trying to wrassle Zambrano, putting him into a headlock on the stairs leading into the clubhouse. Since he was spotting Zambrano probably 60 pounds, Cedeno wasn't too successful. Before another start, Big Z casually walked up to clubhouse manager Tom Hellmann and rubbed his bald head. But he insisted the action wasn't a traditional move to promote good luck.

A large television is festooned to the wall above Zambrano's cubicle. Three hours before a night-game start in 2006, Zambrano looked up to witness a larger-than-life *Chicago Sun-Times* columnist Jay Mariotti gesture, Big Brother-like, in another *Around the Horn* rant on ESPN. Mariotti usually doesn't enter a home-team baseball clubhouse in Chicago, but he was as close as possible to transporting himself into the Cubs' lair via hologram. Mariotti's hair was short, slick, and spiky on this late afternoon, and Zambrano noticed. "What did he do with his hair?" he asked.

Entangled In Ivy

A few feet away from Zambrano is catcher and batterymate Michael Barrett's locker. In a slightly quieter manner, Atlanta-native Barrett is just as loose before a game. He'll have animated conversations with teammates and media. Sometimes he puts on a game face and tries to emulate a stern manner, but it's a few minutes before the Barrett visitor realizes he's being had.

Like most humans, Zambrano and Barrett can present multiple faces in the same day or even hour. They're as fun-loving as any Cubs off the field. Between the lines, Zambrano and Barrett—entering their fourth season as a battery in 2007—can be something entirely different. They're hyper-intense, supercharged in their emotions. The majority of the time, the revved-up personas help them in the respective games they strive to improve, Zambrano as the Cubs' ace and Barrett as their best-hitting catcher in two decades, since Jody Davis' days.

"That's one of the things I learned from my dad [David Barrett], who was a football coach my entire life, one of the best youth coaches around," the younger Barrett said. "I grew up in a mentality where preparation means opportunity for success. I'm pretty passionate about how I prepare for a game. People say, 'Mike, you're different.' I'm competitive—always been competitive in everything I do. We could be playing board games, pickup games; I'm the same. My competitive nature makes me who I am."

Occasionally, though, the competitiveness and intensity boil over to detract from their talents—Zambrano in gestures toward opponents or teammates, Barrett in confrontations with opponents that crescendoed with his right cross to A.J. Pierzynski's jaw at U.S. Cellular Field on May 20, 2006.

"I'm a competitive person, and I'm always one step away from being on edge," Barrett said, defining himself. "A lot of people say, 'Michael you're always living on the edge.' I don't have a strong sense of fear. It's been a good thing, and, in some cases, a bad thing."

Zambrano's on-the-mound histrionics, propelling him to throw at the Cardinals' Jim Edmonds in a 2004 game and show up teammates after errors the same season, became so outlandish that then-manager Dusty Baker had to pull him into the clubhouse during spring training 2005 to admonish him. Pitching coach Larry Rothschild had been

The Cubs' Supercharged Battery

spotted following Zambrano into the tunnel leading from the Cubs dugout at Wrigley Field for a similar tongue-lashing.

"I'm in the process of learning [to be calm]," said Zambrano, a Venezuelan whose English is excellent for his second language. "I appreciated Dusty every time he called me in the office, showed me how to be a leader. I'm still learning how to take care of some situations—like if someone makes an error, don't show him up."

His improved sense of faith coincides with Zambrano's hoped-for maturation process. He makes no secret of his obligations to greater powers, pointing to the sky every time he finishes an inning, giving his thanks for another few minutes on the greatest stage of his game.

"Back in those days, I was younger. I make mistakes like any other player," he said. "I try to do too much. My relationship with the Lord wasn't that good. The Lord likes the way I've been playing. It's a process. I was talking to Woody [Kerry Wood] about how Brandon Phillips showed me up with a home run. I told them, 'Thank God, I'm a new man—I have Jesus Christ in my heart.' [In the past year] I would have hit him. Now, I strike him out the next two at-bats. I'm happy because I have Jesus in my heart."

Both Zambrano and Barrett have always realized right from wrong on the field. Maintaining focus so they don't veer into the latter category is their challenge. The biggest leap forward is recognizing the wrongs immediately.

"The biggest thing is, I don't want a play at the plate to happen in 12-year-old baseball," Barrett said not long after the Pierzynski incident, "and some kid just turns around and jacks a guy because he saw me do it on TV, because he thought it was cool and it gives him the right to do it. I'm learning. The way I look at it is there are times we react in situations because of emotional stress. Sometimes, it overrides what is practical and what is just.

"I'm not perfect. And probably done things on the field that have irritated them. But I don't showboat, and I play the game the way it's supposed to be played. I hit a long home run, I don't sit there and watch it. I put my head down and run. I bust my tail to run to first base on an intentional walk. It makes me who I am—on and off the field, I'm the same."

Entangled In Ivy

Full of motivation, talent, and just enough off-center stuff to make observers wonder about full potential ever being realized, Zambrano and Barrett won't ever raise questions about whether they're dogging it. In fact, their biggest challenge is dialing it down several degrees. Both have tremendous baseball intellect, some of it as yet untapped. They'll be among the best at their craft when they can maximize their diamond knowledgeability while controlling their sometimes white-hot emotions.

Both must learn as they go along.

Wandering around the infield in search of a position to play with the old Montreal Expos, Barrett desired to catch full time. He's still learning the nuances about the mentally challenging position, leading some critics to suggest he'd be better off back at third base or another position. Yet, Barrett is his own toughest critic.

Zambrano signed with the Cubs at 16 as part of the first concerted push to boost the team's sagging Latin-American talent flow. Looking back at the mid-1990s, general manager Jim Hendry said the Cubs were "last in Latin America" in scouting before aide Oneri Fleita began an active effort to turn around the problem.

"As soon as I signed with the Cubs in 1997, when you love baseball and play baseball with your heart, you expect many things," Zambrano said in 2003. "You do well for the fans, your family, and yourself. I prepared for a big season, big career."

I did not pay close notice to Zambrano the first time I saw him pitch at Class-A Lansing (Michigan) on a hot Sunday night, July 25, 1999. My focus was on a group of well-hyped young Cubs everyday-player prospects led by center fielder Corey Patterson and first baseman Hee Seop Choi. Also on my radar were third baseman David Kelton and catcher Jeff Goldbach. Zambrano was some 18-year-old kid who had welling promise, but who knew? He muscled the ball past the Ft. Wayne hitters at Oldsmobile Park that night, giving up three runs in a victory, yet I was paying more attention to Patterson's speed, Choi's power swing, and some local guy selling giant turkey legs down the right-field line.

All of those players—except Goldbach—made the Cubs at some point. But only Zambrano achieved stardom in Chicago, and even he took some detours along the way.

After impressing at Lansing with a 13-7 record, Zambrano quickly became the farm system's top starting prospect. But with the aging and

The Cubs' Supercharged Battery

decline of closer Rick Aguilera in 2000, the Cubs had an urgent need for relief pitching. Zambrano was converted, reluctantly, to the bullpen when he was promoted to Triple-A Iowa in the early summer of 2000. Meanwhile, Dominican Juan Cruz surpassed him as the Cubs' top homegrown starting prospect, and entered the rotation in August 2001.

Although Zambrano's first big-league appearance was as a starter on August 20, 2001—soon after Cruz's debut—he spent the rest of that season and the first half of 2002 miscast in the bullpen. Former Cubs president Andy MacPhail wondered why the '02 season went so badly with Zambrano and Prior already on the roster. The answer: Zambrano wasn't allowed to contribute as a starter until it was too late. Although he was 4-8 as a starter on a team with a bad bullpen, Zambrano was never again on the negative side of .500. He was 13-11 with a 3.11 ERA in 2003, but tired in the postseason at just the wrong time. Big Z's numbers kept improving the next three years, though, as he went a composite 46-21.

Early on, Zambrano realized he had a pitching gift—a hard, sinking fastball that could be bumped up past 95 mph. The action on the pitch and the toughness of its hurler resembled vintage Kevin Brown, who was, interestingly, Zambrano's favorite pitcher breaking into the game.

"I like how he throws the ball," he said in 2003. "I enjoy every time Kevin Brown throws the ball. I like his reaction, how the ball moves. I want to pitch like him when I'm older. Right now, I have my own style. I try to be Carlos Zambrano."

At times, Zambrano is Brown, or even better. On other occasions, he's as wild and unpredictable as the worst control-challenged pitchers of legend. He simply has thrown too many pitches and issued too many walks to jump to the pitching elite level just yet. Zambrano had a career-worst 115 walks in 214 innings in 2006.

Zambrano knew what he had to do coming into the season. During spring training, just before he departed for World Baseball Classic play for Venezuela, he stated a goal of throwing just 100 pitches in eight innings rather than the 120 or more in six or seven he typically amassed.

"With left-handers, he has to be able to throw inside," said Larry Rothschild. "He's got a very good cut fastball, but he doesn't use it a lot. He had a lot of problems with left-handed hitters. He had something like 75 walks to left-handed hitters. This year [2006] was worse than last year.

The trick will be to use his sinker to get quick first-pitch outs. He's got to trust his stuff more."

Again, Zambrano's realization of what's right for him is still ahead of his ability to execute the plan.

"I know now that there's nothing I can't do in the game," he said. "In a situation where I have a runner at first, I have to get a ground ball, I know what to do."

Rothschild hopes the two and a half seasons Zambrano spent with certified pitching genius Greg Maddux somehow sink in for the long run.

"The most important thing I learned from Maddux is the calm he has on the mound," Zambrano said. "He was sure what to do. He was so focused on the game. He learned how to get out of the situation. Even if you give up one or two runs, you have to trust your team to come back and win the game."

Amazingly, Zambrano's personal control jumped ahead of his pitching accuracy in 2006.

"Overall, he kept himself in check a little bit," Rothschild said. "What you don't to do is bottle him up in his competitiveness. We talked about leadership, and he's aware of it. He's still a young guy, and to hand him that mantle, that's asking a lot."

Even though he's the same age as many pitching teammates, Zambrano has a huge advantage in big-league experience.

"I try to be nice with my teammates and show them respect," he said. "If they consider me a leader, whatever they say. I consider D-Lee the leader of this team. We all have respect for D-Lee. That's how the leader is. D-Lee doesn't show up anybody. D-Lee doesn't embarrass anybody. That's when you deserve to be the leader.

"It's funny, I call them, 'Hey, kid' and I don't realize that I'm 25 and the same age as them. To Ryan Theriot, I was about to say, 'What's up, kid?' He's older than me. I have more experience in the big leagues. That's why I come early and do my job and talk to everybody in the clubhouse."

By necessity, Zambrano must grow up quickly. He's now the senior Latin American player on the roster. He looked up to others when he first came to the majors. Now his Spanish-speaking teammates look to him.

"There's nothing like Chicago," he said. "Anything that I can do for them, I'll do it. I'll always be here for them like [Greg] Maddux was for

The Cubs' Supercharged Battery

me, like Moises [Alou] and Sammy [Sosa] was there for me anytime I needed something."

But a legitimate leader can't go off on wild tangents, as he did so often in past years. Zambrano developed a bad reputation as a hothead.

"Many people say I'm cocky," he said in 2003. "The first time in rookie ball, I pitched like that. My style is to pitch like that. If I'm mad, I'm not mad at the hitter. I'm mad at myself because I don't throw a strike. I don't try to be cocky with anybody. I respect the hitters, everybody, because they have a bat. They can hit a home run against me."

Zambrano's emotionalism did not help him at all. When he struck out Barry Bonds with the bases loaded in San Francisco in one 2003 game, he practically did a dance on the mound, angering the bloated slugger.

Rotation mate Mark Prior defended Zambrano at the time.

"People can say whatever they want, that he's trying to show people up," he said. "I would never look at it that way. You got guys hitting home runs and standing there watching them 'til it drops. That's showing up people more than getting excited when you strike out a guy in a bases-loaded situation."

But Zambrano crossed the line when he reacted negatively to teammates' foibles in the field. A Todd Walker fielding miscue in a 2004 game in Houston netted a mini-tantrum near the mound from Big Z. Other incidents were so egregious that Baker—always giving his players the benefit of the doubt publicly—could not hide the fact that he took the pitcher to the woodshed in spring training 2005.

Zambrano simply hurt his team with his temper, and never more so than on July 19, 2004, before 40,033 at Wrigley Field.

The Cardinals' Jim Edmonds belted a two-run homer off Zambrano in the fourth. As Edmonds rounded the bases, the pitcher hollered at him. "He didn't say nothing," Zambrano said afterward. "I just told him to run the bases, don't be cocky." But the Cubs field staff thought Zambrano was the instigator in this instance. Rothschild grabbed Zambrano and lectured him on proper behavior in the dugout tunnel, out of sight of the crowd—but not of television cameras, which showed pitcher and coach disappearing into the corridor.

Zambrano did not take Rothschild's talk to heart. He appeared to shake his finger at Edmonds when he struck him out in the sixth. Two innings later, after Scott Rolen had belted a tie-breaking two-run homer off Zambrano, Edmonds was the next hitter due up. Zambrano plunked Edmonds on the hip. He and Baker were automatically ejected since the umpiring crew had already issued warnings to both benches.

Zambrano had periodic outbursts over the next one and a half seasons. He seemed to calm a bit in 2006, as he passed his 25th birthday, but Rothschild said there were still a "couple of incidents" that were unacceptable.

In contrast, Barrett's career was relatively uneventful in both Montreal and in his first four and a half months as a Cub. Then, on August 22, 2004, he was hit by the Astros' Roy Oswalt after Aramis Ramirez homered at Minute Maid Park. Five days later, while catching at Wrigley Field, Barrett began jawing at Oswalt as the pitcher came to the plate in his first at-bat. Barrett did most of the talking as Oswalt stared warily at him. The incident touched off the infamous Kent Mercker call to the press box to complain about broadcaster Chip Caray's apparent praise of Oswalt for hanging in during a tough game.

Barrett was peeved by Padre Dave Roberts' base-running as well in a May 12, 2006, game at Wrigley Field. Roberts stole third while San Diego was up by three runs. Barrett uncharacteristically clammed up after the game when mobbed by reporters. That could have been a key that something wasn't quite right for the '06 season, beyond normal disgust with the Cubs' overall play.

Then came the Pierzynski incident, which wasn't totally unprovoked. Pierzynski seemed to make a point of brushing by Barrett after scoring on a close play at the plate. The Sox's agent provocateur excused his own actions by claiming he had veered toward Barrett to reclaim his batting helmet.

But the two catchers had a reconciliation a month later when the Sox visited Wrigley Field. They talked, shook hands, and put the melee behind them—adhering to Barrett's own code.

"One thing people have to understand is, I have a mutual respect for people," he said. "I was raised to treat others the way you want to be treated. When I play the game, I have respect for the game. I have respect for my peers. I don't fear any one person or be intimidated by one person. You just have to be respected by them. What I did was out of a reaction to the whole situation. That situation is unique, something I've never

The Cubs' Supercharged Battery

experienced before, and that's why I reacted the way I did. I didn't know how to take it. Certainly, hindsight is 20-20. I'm a competitive person, and I'm always one step away from being on edge.

"Looking back on it, I don't think A.J. was doing anything, or Oswalt was doing anything, or Roberts doing anything personally to provoke me. At the same time, they have to understand, if I feel disrespected or I feel I've been wronged, I'll tell them myself or deal with it myself. I'm not going to leave things undone."

The melee and subsequent 10-day banishment from the game was a tough lesson for Barrett, but one he had to learn.

"The way I look at it is: there are times we react in situations because of emotional stress," he said. "A lot of times, it overrides what is practical and what is just. Certain cases in my career involve finding something to respect about others. As I said, I understand that I'm not perfect."

Barrett had to bust his tail to become a big-league regular and shake the tag as a utility player best suited to move around the infield. He always had the confidence that he could hit if he could stabilize his defensive position. Even so, he felt he underperformed at the plate after breaking in with a .293 average with Montreal in 1998. Then he began to scuffle, eventually dropping to .208 in 2003.

"I still feel I'm a potential .300 hitter," Barrett said upon being acquired via a trade from Oakland, to which he had been dealt the day previously, late in 2003.

After hitting .287 and .276 his first two Cubs seasons, even batting leadoff one game in 2004, he finally realized his goal with a .307 mark in a suspension- and injury-marred 2006, in which, by necessity, he sometimes batted in the middle of a depleted Cubs batting order. But Barrett also achieved an amazing statistical even keel—he slugged 16 homers for three consecutive seasons. In 2005, he also won a Silver Slugger Award for catchers.

Barrett and Zambrano could talk hitting on the former's trips to the mound. Zambrano displayed the heart of a batsman. A rare switch-hitting pitcher, he's a frustrated regular player. Zambrano helped himself with several clutch homers in past seasons. He outdid himself in 2006, tying Fergie Jenkins' 35-year-old Cubs season record for pitchers with six homers. Zambrano was used as a pinch hitter on several occasions.

Entangled In Ivy

Zambrano's also considered by team insiders as a "plus" base-runner who can move his huge frame quickly around the basepaths. In this respect, he is practically the second coming of Rick Reuschel, another large, agile Cubs sinkerball pitcher who was used as a pinch runner and helped himself at the plate.

"When I was little, I was always thinking to become a first baseman or left fielder," Zambrano recalled. "I like those two positions. When I was 15, the man who was training me told me that it's faster to get to the big leagues as a pitcher."

There's more old school than not in both Zambrano and Barrett—and there's a lot about 21st Century baseball that sometimes puts them out of their time.

"The game has changed in so many ways," Barrett said. "Twenty years ago, if someone had a problem with somebody else, they talked it out. They settled it as men. Now, sometimes I feel the game doesn't allow it to happen—suspensions, fines, the DH, a lot of things have changed the game to where things are unsettled at times. That's just the way it is. I was brought up from a guy [a cousin, former Cub Scott Fletcher] who played during that time period. You played with passion, no fear, respect. As we've seen, a lot of that has changed.

"It's not about respecting anybody across the field. Guys hit home runs, throw their bat across the field into the other team's dugout. The only thing they may get in return is a pitch in the back or a beanball. I don't like the beanball. Some of the guys throw today at 96 to 97 mph, so if they miss slightly, it can be detrimental. If you have a problem with somebody, talk to them face to face. Go to them. Do it. Get it out of the way. Why hold back? Wait to hit them two years later in the back for something they did? No!"

The Cubs' supercharged battery certainly doesn't wait two years to make their feelings known. They definitely know how to vent.

fifteen

BLEACHER FANS-TURNED-CUBS SOUTHPAWS

RICH HILL AND RYAN O'MALLEY share more in common than just tossing the pelota with their left arms. Both are earnest young men who are one month apart in age, turning 27 as the 2007 season began. Both grew up watching their favorite teams from the bleachers, paying as little as $3 to occupy Hill's vantage point in Boston's Fenway Park and O'Malley's at Wrigley Field. Both came to the Cubs organization in 2002 and were teammates in each of the five successive seasons in the minors, steadily rising together.

To put the exclamation point on their friendship, Hill's appearance as the last man in the bullpen in the final two innings of the Cubs' 18-inning, August 15, 2006, road win over the Astros scratched his scheduled start the next afternoon—and forced the emergency call-up of O'Malley to work in his stead. The unheralded southpaw, who loved the Cubs growing up in Springfield, Illinois, ended up shutting out the Astros on five hits over eight innings before a sore elbow interrupted the fairytale story.

Yet, O'Malley's pain could not diminish the pleasure of coming to the Cubs, rejoining Hill at baseball's highest level, and pitching with his parents having hurriedly hitched a ride on a private plane that morning to dash from Springfield to Houston. O'Malley's was a rare feel-good tale of the moribund 2006 Cubs, while Hill's story was a breather in an unbroken line of disaster, providing promise of a brighter future. Off-track in so many ways, the Cubs would be in great shape if they could bottle the passion and motivation wrapping up O'Malley and the renewed good feelings of Hill.

"I used to go see my grandma over at her house, and she'd be sitting there watching the team, and she'd say, 'One day, Ryan, you got to go up there and help the Cubbies,'" O'Malley recalled. "Unfortunately, she didn't make it to see my debut. All the time, I'd go there, she'd have the Cubs game on and say, 'These Cubs need help; go help them.'"

That he did, and Hill followed suit in an even bigger way, proving the proverbial third time—the last of his three call-ups from Iowa—was the charm.

"I'm fortunate, they stuck with me to turn the corner," Hill said. "They could have sent me back to Triple-A or traded me. Things happen for a reason, I believe. Something's going on here that's going to happen pretty soon. It's going to be really special."

If O'Malley could somehow join Hill as a long-term Cub, life would be doubly special for the pair of left-handers. Hill, a former University of Michigan star, got all the publicity as a strikeout king of Triple-A while O'Malley flew under the radar, an undrafted free agent without that blazing, standout fastball. But if there's any justice in the world—and the baseball fates owe an excess of justice to the Cubs—O'Malley will make it and employ some uncommon institutional memory of team history to his personal game.

Like Hall of Fame pitcher Robin Roberts, O'Malley grew up a Cubs fan in Illinois' state capital city, which tilts toward the Cardinals with it being just 90 miles northeast of St. Louis. In that location, O'Malley got his Cubs fix wherever he could find it.

"I probably saw more [Cubs games] at Busch Stadium, because it was closer," he said. "Still, coming to Wrigley Field was unreal. We used to sit in the bleachers because that was the cheap seat at the time. I remember my first game. I came with my other grandma on Dad's side. They took us on a bus trip up. I got a Starter jacket, and I was six—it was 1986. I still have the jacket. They were playing the Cards, and Ozzie Smith was playing. Ryne Sandberg was my guy because we shared 'Ryno' [nickname]. I wanted to be like him. I think they lost 1-0, and the Cards scored in the first inning.

Bleacher Fans-Turned-Cubs Southpaws

"I've always battled with Cards fans in Springfield. It was a great thing. My uncle and I bet 10 cents each on the games. He was a diehard Cards fan. He was about the only one in the family. He's from Nokomis, closer to St. Louis. It's a great rivalry for baseball. When I go home to Springfield, they ask me when I'll be traded to the Cards. I tell them I'm right where I ought to be."

O'Malley got to Wrigley Field in spirit long before he did so in uniform. A first baseman and outfielder before he pitched full-time, he took to the field in his youthful mind.

"We had a big back yard, a sandlot deal," he said. "I'd come running out of the garage, onto home plate. I thought that was Wrigley Field. I got to visualize the stuff."

O'Malley was a junior college All-America hitter at Lincoln Land Community College in Springfield. Transferring to the University of Memphis, he played outfield and pitched.

"Scouts came to me and said, 'You've got to keep pitching, put your bat down,'" O'Malley said. "I was a right-handed hitter with average speed, average power. I threw upper 80s [mph] in college. I put up some decent numbers in Memphis."

Cubs scout Pat Portugal watched O'Malley pitch against Tulane in 2002. O'Malley thought the White Sox and Cleveland Indians might draft him that June.

"Through the whole draft, [the Memphis] coach called a couple of times, said I was going between 20th and 25th," O'Malley said. "When there was two rounds left, I was giving up. I was laying in bed crying. I thought it was over.

"My mom then brought the phone to me. I didn't want to talk to anyone. I was devastated. She said, 'Talk to this gentleman.' It was Portugal. He said, 'Ryan, we didn't draft you, but we'd like to give you an opportunity to sign as a free agent.' I said, 'I'm ready to go.' He said, 'Leave in three days for Arizona mini-camp, then go to [short-season A-level] Boise.' He gave me a little money to sign. I went to Boise and had a nice season [3-1 in 23 games as a reliever]. At that time, I was over it [not being drafted]. I wasn't going to dwell on why it didn't happen. I got the same amount of money as a lower-round guy."

Entangled In Ivy

Unlike many other pitching prospects, the overlooked O'Malley did not stall out at a lower minor-league level. He kept advancing through the Cubs system.

"If you get another opportunity to get out there, that's saying they still like you," he said. "I kept pitching pretty well. Every year, I've gone up. I take that as proof that they like my progress. I always thought I had a chance. I was pitching with guys they were calling big prospects. I was getting the same guys out, pretty close numbers. I was staying under the radar. I just came to the field every day, gave it everything I had."

The majority of O'Malley's minor-league work came out of the bullpen. That's where he started the 2006 season at Iowa. He got an opportunity to spot start and threw five shutout innings. Several other starts were just as spectacular. Yet, as the Cubs' staff was thrown into chaos by injuries and ineffectiveness, O'Malley did not get a call to Chicago. Hill, Angel Guzman, Carlos Marmol, and Juan Mateo were summoned to go into the rotation.

"I always have that thought in my mind that I'd get an opportunity," O'Malley said. "I'd work as hard as I can, go out there, and take care of what I could take care of. I stayed in the rotation. I can't get mad, can't get frustrated. After his first time in Chicago, Rich came back down, told me how it is. He'd talk about pitching, talk about hitters. I didn't write it off. It's a crazy game—you don't know day to day what will happen."

O'Malley was prepping for his next start August 16 in Round Rock, Texas. He went to bed the previous night realizing the Cubs won an 18-inning game with Hill having to pitch, but with no inkling his call would come only hours later.

At 6 a.m. on August 16, Iowa trainer Bob Grimes woke up O'Malley.

"He said I was going to pitch in Houston," O'Malley said. "They had a limo for me to drive over at 6:45 [to make the three-hour drive]."

The lefty rubbed the sleep out of his eyes quickly and worked his cell phone frantically in the limo.

"I was calling everyone, telling everyone that I'd be on WGN, to watch," he said. "People were calling me. About an hour and a half later, I turned the phone off and locked in on what I had to do that day."

One of the calls was to his parents in Springfield. There were no flights from St. Louis that would get them to Houston in time to see his 1 p.m. start. Fortunately, a family friend had access to a private plane. The O'Malleys were airborne as their son arrived at Minute Maid Park. He could not be concerned with whether his parents made the game, even though he had left tickets for them. O'Malley had the chance of a lifetime. Even with his early-morning wakeup, he still had more energy than most of the regular players on the field after the previous night's marathon.

"In the game, it's kind of like a no-hitter," he said. "You know it, but you don't think about it. I just went pitch to pitch, hitter to hitter, inning to inning. I gave it everything I had, every single pitch. Michael Barrett was outstanding behind the plate, coming out, calming me down, 'Get this pitch here down.' He could not have been any more helpful."

The innings mounted and the Astros did not score. When he finally was pulled after eight innings, O'Malley had allowed just five hits. The Cubs scratched out a run and made it stand up for their rookie's victory.

"I'm still pinching myself every day," O'Malley said. "The eight-inning shutout was a great thing, but at the same time, I was just pumped that I was there. If I had given up five in the first, I still would have been on a high."

After O'Malley came out of the game, he finally realized his parents were in the house. "After the eighth inning, I stood up on the dugout step and looked up, and they were all waving and yelling at me," he said.

The O'Malleys celebrated, but it was short-lived. There would be no encore at Wrigley Field before an even bigger contingent of family and friends. A few days later at home, O'Malley—who had never had an arm injury—reported soreness around his elbow. He would not pitch again in 2006.

"It was unfortunate I got hurt," he said. "It's not going to keep me down. I hope to have many more eight-inning shutouts."

O'Malley has the same amount of confidence in Hill. While on the shelf, he was able to root on his longtime minor-league roommate, who finished strong in 2006 and put behind the nightmare of two previous disastrous call-ups.

"I thought something was up, the way Rich was mowing through Triple-A," O'Malley said. "I've always said, out of all the pitchers I've played with in the minors, he's got the best stuff—fastball, curve, live arm. If he can just put it all together, he'll be dynamite."

The combo baffled minor-league hitters starting in 2003 in Boise. Hill struck out 136 in 109 1/3 innings at high-A Daytona in 2004, 90 in

57 2/3 innings at Double-A West Tenn in 2005, and 92 in 65 innings at Iowa later in '05. However, the majors were entirely different. In Hill's first call-up in June 2005, he was 0-2 with a 9.13 ERA in 10 games (four starts). He had poor control with 17 walks and 25 hits allowed in 23 2/3 innings.

"Coming up there, trying to stick to the same thing you're doing in Triple-A is the hardest thing," Hill said. "It is a big gap, a huge gap. You can prepare yourself for big leagues or Triple-A, but when you get up here, you can't prepare yourself for the travel, the crowds. Those take a little time getting used to. You get to the park a little bit earlier, go over hitters—there's a massive amount of information on each hitter. It's abundant. You don't have that in Triple-A."

Hill hit rock bottom in the spring of 2006. After another fast strikeout start at Iowa, he was recalled as the wheels came off the Cubs in May. But his big-league performance was even worse than in 2005. He had the worst of two worlds—a batting practice pitcher with no control.

Hill was 0-4 in May, giving up 20 earned runs in 19 1/3 innings, walking 15 while striking out only 11. In the May 20 start at U.S. Cellular Field—in which Barrett punched A.J. Pierzynski—Hill said his catcher was justified in his actions. That comment drew White Sox manager Ozzie Guillen's ire. He called Hill a Triple-A pitcher who was trying to get Cubs manager Dusty Baker fired with his horrid work on the mound. Some loud-mouthed Cubs fans agreed. One day, Hill stood steaming in the players' parking lot outside Wrigley Field, upset about fans who harangued him from beyond a mesh fence. It seemed whatever momentum he had built moving up in the Cubs organization had quickly reversed direction.

Another demotion to Iowa seemed like a one-way ticket. But the Cubs simply ran out of healthy, effective starters. They had no choice but to recall Hill again in late July. This time, he clicked. He was 6-3 with a 2.93 ERA in 13 games, including 12 starts. He walked only 24 while fanning 79 in 80 innings. Hill racked up the only two complete games for the staff, saving the Cubs the ignominious record of going an entire season without a route-going start.

"I struggled a lot in high-A in Florida," Hill recalled. "I struggled in my freshman year at Michigan. My first year in Chicago, I struggled. You get used to surroundings, get used to the environment. Same thing with pro ball—I'm way more relaxed coming to the ballpark. It's a big puzzle. If you don't have success, you keep getting beat, keep walking guys, it hurts your confidence. I got my stuff together in Triple-A with [pitching coach] Alan Dunn. It's been a 180 since I last came up.

"It's something that doesn't phase me anymore. I find myself being more of a predator. You want them to fear you. You're the one with the ball in your hand. I'm looking forward to having a great year next year."

If anything, Hill had good training growing up in the curse-minded Red Sox environment in Milton, Massachusetts.

"It's a huge media market in Boston, along with here, New York, and L.A.," he said. "It's tough to have patience here. We have a lot of young guys. I don't think about losing. Nobody has a losing attitude. That comes from the farm system. Every team we've been on, from A ball to Double-A, we've won. It might take a little time here. But keep going, keep rolling. They instill that in the minor leagues—it's about getting it done. Winning is the bottom line."

The Red Sox purged their "curse," which was a media creation anyway. Babe Ruth never put any hex on his old team. And the supposed curse on the Cubs was a nice tall tale written by columnist patrons of the Billy Goat Tavern. Winning and losing is a state of mind, supplemented by moves—right or wrong—made by team management.

"I grew up as a Red Sox fan," Hill said. "I thought the Red Sox were never going to win. They always had great teams the majority of the time, but they always had the Yankees in front of them. It's the Cardinals here. If you believe you're going to lose, you're going to lose, If you believe you're going to win, you're going to win. That's why I think we're looking forward to a bright future here. Nobody thinks about not winning, that it's almost 100 years [since the last Cubs World Series championship]. It doesn't go through your head. Just win the game that day. You get seasoning. Get guys more comfortable up here, and I believe this group can play together.

"Who's to stay we can be stopped?"

sixteen

THE ARTICULATOR IN THE PRESIDENT'S CHAIR

THE POWER CENTER of Cubs management is not on the 23rd floor of Tribune Tower as popularly envisioned, but appropriately located amidst a string of offices along a corridor below the famed red Wrigley Field marquee that faces Clark and Addison.

Turn right and a double set of offices is spotted. To the right is general manager Jim Hendry's private redoubt. At the left is the team president's office. In between, the executives' assistants work, Gayle Finney to the left and all-time Cubs front-office staffer Arlene Gill to the right.

On this autumn morning, just more than one month after Andy MacPhail's resignation as team president, there was hardly a hint the blue-blooded baseball patrician had toiled in the left-side office. MacPhail's successor had hurriedly transferred some special photos from his former digs at the far north end of the corridor. Festooned on one wall were some of the most off-key singers of the seventh-inning "Take Me Out to the Ballgame", including Ozzy Osbourne and Mike Ditka. On another wall were photos of the new president greeting a couple of American presidents—Ronald Reagan and Bill Clinton—at Wrigley Field. The office was not particularly large, just room for a desk, a small round table for mini-meetings, and a two-piece blue-colored couch.

Entangled In Ivy

Hearing my verbal accounting of the photos, John McDonough announced from Finney's workstation next door that the "marketing photos"—ostensibly the singers—will come down soon. No doubt they'd be replaced by more appropriate baseball images.

That was the transition enveloping McDonough's entire life following the 2006 season. He had to morph from a skilled, even slick, salesperson marketing the sizzle of the Cubs and Wrigley Field experience to an owner-by-proxy who had to ensure he could also sell the steak, the true centerpiece of the operation.

However, one all-important factor of McDonough's being would not waver. For nearly two decades, he had been the glib spokesman in charge of selling the Cubs, be it the ballpark, ticket prices, innovative promotions, Harry Caray, or other broadcasters.

All along, though—and prompted by no one—he cautioned that, for all the unique attractions of Wrigley Field, the best marketing tool was winning the World Series. Interestingly, McDonough the slick salesman, an ad-libber who could have held his own with Johnny Carson, seemed to be the only Cubs official who spoke consistently of baseball's ultimate prize as a firm destination for his franchise.

MacPhail and Co. had often talked about being "competitive," contending, but without a sense of urgency. MacPhail's first motto for improvement in 1994 had been the aforementioned "slow, steady, unspectacular," which soon evolved into, "We're working on it." Not until two weeks prior to his October 1, 2006, resignation did MacPhail admit that a Cubs World Series victory would be good for all of baseball. Yet, no matter what came out of his mouth, MacPhail preferred a much lower profile, dodging sports talk programs, funneling his message through malleable newspaper beat writers, and pushing other executives to the front to speak for the Cubs. He would not be the one rallying the troops or reassuring the multimillions of frustrated fans.

When he returned to his new office and began his own stream of measured consciousness, McDonough refused to comment on the verbal leadership style of his predecessor. But adding one and one together, he was asked if his own success in articulating his message was a major motivating factor in Tribune Co. CEO Dennis FitzSimons' decision to anoint him president. Using United States history as an analogy, Franklin Roosevelt tried but failed to end the Great Depression with his New Deal programs. But FDR was able to lift the national mood off the bottom with a sense of hope, resolve, and promised action through his "fireside chats" on radio in a way predecessor Herbert Hoover could not.

"I would certainly hope that it helped," McDonough said of his communication skills. "I think Dennis knows, I think the Tribune people know that I'm very competitive, very energetic, and very passionate. For 15-plus years, on many issues regarding the marketing and, in some cases, the business operation, I have been the spokesperson. This is a completely different role, overseeing the entire operation, including the baseball team."

Now McDonough speaks for the entire Cubs operation.

"I feel very comfortable doing that," he said. "What I wanted to articulate—and it was by design when we had the press conference following the season's final game—was, the mission is to win. What I said specifically was, 'Our goal is to win the World Series.' I didn't say we are going to win [in 2007]. We need to reward these fans. I feel that, with my previous position, I was in the epicenter of the heartbeat of what the fans were feeling and thinking. I was observing and listening—that was my job. Now I'm in a much different position, but one where I recognize that I've got to do a lot of listening and observing to learn what I don't know. There are areas that I think are my strengths. I can address things that I think need to be addressed.

"It's important for the organization to think that way, to articulate what that mission is," McDonough continued. "When you have a franchise as steeped in history and tradition—as impactive and meaningful to millions of people as the Cubs are—we've waited 98 years and the fans have waited 98 years. We have to get in the winning business. Winning has to be part of the vocabulary here. It will be, I'm very confident of it. Our goal as an organization—and it's not a guarantee, it's not a promise—is to win the World Series. There's nothing wrong with stating that if there's a plan to do that. And I think we're on course to have a plan to do that."

If FitzSimons wanted to pick the one executive with the ability to stand out front and assure the paying customers that the Cubs indeed wanted to win, not just fill Wrigley Field, he got the best available man in McDonough.

Entangled In Ivy

Self-described as "very strongly" possessing a "Ph.D. in people," the tall, salt-and-pepper-turning-white-haired marketing guru hails from the Chicago Northwest Side neighborhood of Edison Park. He graduated from Notre Dame of Niles High School, the same alma mater as the brothers in the Chicago Bears' ruling McCaskey family, former White Sox slugger Greg Luzinski, and Bradley University basketball coach Jim Les. McDonough grew up a White Sox fan, but cut his teeth in sports as sales director of the Chicago Sting pro soccer club. Yet, he quickly adapted to all things Cubs when he was hired at Wrigley Field in the fall of 1983. In the ensuing generation as a Cubs marketing executive, first as No. 2 man to Jeff Odenwald and then running the operation himself, he had alternated faces as a tough boss and the ultimate back-slapping, hand-shaking super-salesman.

Although a slew of other factors had given the Cubs a historically huge advantage in baseball-consumer appeal over the cross-town White Sox—with only the team's 2005 World Series title closing the gap—McDonough's own personal style seemed to personify the North Siders' popularity edge.

In 1994, I invited McDonough and Sox counterpart Rob Gallas to appear together on my weekly baseball radio program in its first season, then called *Chicago Baseball Review*, at the Arlington Heights, Illinois, studios of WCBR-FM. After the show ended, the station employees and several other hangers-on gathered around McDonough and Gallas to talk. Afterward, they remarked how much more personable McDonough appeared compared to Gallas. Then, in 2001, I had helped assemble an interactive Jack Brickhouse exhibit for the Museum of Broadcast Communications in downtown Chicago. I made sure a White Sox section for Brickhouse was included, even though scant tape existed of the legendary Chicago broadcaster's 20 seasons of Sox telecasts from 1948 to 1967. Gallas was on the board of directors of the museum. Yet, neither he nor any other Sox representative showed for the opening ceremonies. It ended up an unintended Cubs-centric affair with a slew of team officials, headed by McDonough, present. He deftly offered a tribute to Brickhouse and introduced longtime broadcast-booth partner Vince Lloyd.

McDonough also had his firm management side. Running Cubs marketing and broadcasting, he could be a taskmaster. He mandated that radio voice Pat Hughes stay on the air for every inning of every game instead of the typical baseball broadcast rotation of six innings on, three off; or other similar combinations. Hughes had taken the bottom of the seventh off while Andy Masur filled in. McDonough's modest-sized, youngish marketing staff—smaller than that of the Sox—was worked hard. Annual turnover yielded achievers moving on to bigger jobs and better salaries.

Those who recognized the McDonough style knew to take care to approach him at specific times. The wrong occasion was when he had a laser focus during interaction with a ball-club employee, sponsor, or celebrity guest, or was officiating at a team event. Somehow, he balanced his welcoming and tough sides to build up far more friends than enemies while developing a positive image in the media.

McDonough was also the chief team salesman for corporate sponsors. He never had a 100-percent success rate, telling of seemingly sure thing, high six-figure deals slipping away at the last minute. Yet, the same verbal skills that enabled him to be the top team executive interviewee helped reel in millions of dollars of revenue. Such talents evidently appeared the second factor in his hiring as Cubs president.

His marketing department started to experience difficulty securing sponsors in the winter of 2005-06, after the Sox championship eclipsed a 79-83 Cubs season. More trouble could be forecast in 2006-07, after the 66-96 disaster that left the sourest taste among fans and media since 1980-81 and the end of the Wrigley family ownership decades. Empty seats mushroomed around Wrigley Field throughout September 2006, the majority no-shows who already had bought tickets. Most startling were huge swaths of empty bleacher seats, normally the most popular in all of baseball. Tickets purchased meant money had long been in the bank, but the no-shows cost the team considerable revenue in unsold concessions and parking. The empty seats threatened to spook some advertisers.

Now the man with whom sponsors dealt for years was in charge of the entire operation, holder of the purse strings. That had to signal the corporate crowd not to jump ship, and McDonough believed his own sponsor relations "played a role in [his promotion], sure. ... They're familiar with my style. They know I'm very confident, aggressive, and passionate. They know I'll carry that into this position.

Entangled In Ivy

"Every one of these corporate partners, every one of these sponsors, every one of these season-ticket holders—needs to be viewed as an investor in our team," McDonough proclaimed. "No matter if it's someone who owns one season ticket or our largest sponsor, everybody by human nature wants to be associated with winning. They love the aura; they love the unique mystique, the phenomenon, and everything that goes with the Chicago Cubs and Wrigley Field and coming to the park with three million fans three years in a row. They like that. If you provide them with three million fans year after year, they're in the impressions business, and we're in the impression business. The more people that walk through these turnstiles, the more people will hear their corporate message. That's great.

"But everybody likes to be associated with a winner, that's the direction we want to go. We want to increase that fan base, that wonderful fan base that I really believe is tens of millions throughout the country. The ultimate payoff, the reward for this allegiance, is to win the World Series. That's what we have to start talking about. I don't think we can hide from that. We have to look at it and say, 'We've been deficient. We haven't done this in almost a century. How do we get there? Let's go about it the right way, but let's not be afraid to articulate this mission.'"

McDonough followed up his own hiring with a flurry of quick big-ticket signings before Thanksgiving 2006 to offer another message of confidence to the sponsors and fans. He put his money where his mouth was by approving a $73-million payout to re-up third baseman Aramis Ramirez, then signed a $13-million deal with infielder Mark DeRosa. The coup was a $136-million deal to 40-40 man Alfonso Soriano that MacPhail likely would have never okayed. Jim Hendry would have insisted there was no coincidence, but the quick signings early in the fall corporate sales season went a long way to wipe out the negative vibes of the 2006 season.

The moves were a good start. Yet, McDonough will have to do far more than talk a good game if the Cubs are to achieve his oft-stated Fall Classic goal. He'll need to be as proactive and creative in re-tooling an underperforming baseball operation as he was in conceiving the Cubs Convention—the granddaddy of all off-season fan fests, founded in 1986—along with the seventh-inning sing-along and Beanie Babies giveaways.

The Articulator in the President's Chair

The marketing program maximized dollars, drawing fans into Cubs-controlled venues like Wrigley Field and the Cubs Convention, which kept the profits from being shared with outsiders. With the exception of some Cubs Care charity events and sponsorship of the venerable Thillens Stadium youth baseball field on the North Side, the Cubs hardly felt the need to go the White Sox route in promoting themselves via events away from the ballpark. Rarely did Cubs players appear outside the ballpark or at a formal gathering in the Chicago area or surrounding states other than the Convention-connected winter caravan. The idea of an "alumni club" of former players was briefly contemplated in the early 1990s, then dropped. Former players appear at the Convention and sing during the seventh-inning stretch, but not in events in Arlington Heights, Rockford, or Bloomington. Although Cubs fans permeated all corners of the Midwest and beyond, team emblems and other symbols weren't all that common on front doors of homes or on cars. If you wanted a part of the Cubs experience, you had to go to the ballpark or Convention—and bring a wide-open wallet, too.

The coffers were full as a result, and McDonough had complete access to the cash machine as the ball-club chief executive. A minor barrier left to overcome was the word "interim" attached to his president's title. Crane Kenney, Tribune Company's top attorney and the Cubs' corporate overseer, said McDonough would have the full powers and budget-setting latitude of a president unburdened by the "interim" tag. Either the boys in the Tower wanted to see how McDonough would perform early on, or they were hedging their bets if the Cubs suddenly were put up for sale in any kind of Tribune Company asset-shedding frenzy.

"I would hope so," McDonough said of having "interim" struck. "I'm doing everything I possibly can. I have a job to do. I know what that job is. In order to do that, I'm not concerned about titles or labels. My role is to be proactive in the Cubs organization. If I do my job well, and I'm very confident that I will, the rest will take care of itself.

"It's difficult to put a timetable on this. There are things that I've already observed. I want to make sure that any decisions or changes I make in the Cubs organization are well thought through. I value other people's input. If there's one common refrain in the marketing and business operations, we're in the people business. We just so happen to be

Entangled In Ivy

affiliated with a baseball team. Trying to have a pretty good understanding, this is not my first day on campus, which is going to help me make some important decisions here."

So, before the Cubs can be in a position to win it all, shouldn't they field the No. 1 baseball organization in the game, to scout, evaluate, and develop talent better than anyone else? Falling short in this ranking has condemned the Cubs to consistent also-ran status. The shortfall was so bad that the only time the Cubs had produced their own position players consistently was one six-year period of amateur drafts—1982 to 1987—under GM Dallas Green and the late player-development guru Gordon Goldsberry, who is still held in reverence within Wrigley Field. Goldsberry's final draft in 1988 and many of the ones to follow over 15-plus years yielded average to poor results.

McDonough is in hearty agreement with this second goal, to make the Cubs "the gold standard of both business and baseball" in the game. All the while, he wants to unite them into one cohesive unit and not have one regarded as so much better than the other, like so many past Chicago Bears' defensive groups versus pitch-and-putt, quarterback-poor offensive units.

"One area that you can take a look at—and my goal as president of the Cubs—we should strive to be the blueprint organization," he said. "I understand that [the team has a long way to go to achieve that status]. One of the things that I've observed in five weeks of the position is, the business operation of Cubs may be perceived as the best in the game. They see the team has not had a consistent history of winning, yet you're playing to almost a capacity crowd every day, [generating] strong revenues while playing primarily in the day. ... Play day games in April against the Pirates and whomever else, and you're playing to 90-percent capacity. Give some credit to [business operations chief] Mark McGuire. It's important we diminish and completely minimize what is known as the baseball side and the business side. My goal is to have one Chicago Cubs."

Those inside and outside the organization already compared the Wrigley Field fishbowl atmosphere for players to the New York Yankees and Boston Red Sox, the two highest profile franchises in baseball. In the meantime, smaller market teams like the Minnesota Twins and Atlanta

The Articulator in the President's Chair

Braves have developed consistent pipelines of fresh talent through their minor-league systems.

McDonough believed the Cubs start from the strongest possible base, but still must catch up with the legendary East Coast teams in the won-lost column.

"Commensurate to winning, our brand may be the strongest in sports history—commensurate to winning," he said. "The Yankees have won 27 world championships. That's a Herculean international symbol of excellence. The Red Sox just recently won. We do have an elite brand, but it's not tethered to the golden ring. In order for us to get into that elite category, we have to win the World Series.

"It's great for visibility, we're on a super-station, it's a lovable franchise. When they say it's 'the lovable losers,' I want us to be lovable without us being losers. I want winning to be a major component of what makes this franchise in that elite category with the Red Sox and Yankees. Although the Red Sox have won just one World Series in the last 80-some years, if you take a look at their history the last 25 to 30 years, they're generally getting 87-to-97 wins per year in a very tough division. That's the era we need to get. We need to get consistent in winning—this can't be a once-in-a-while thing. This has to be an all-the-time thing.

"There's some preposterous number over the last [35] years, we've only been over .500 in back-to-back years twice. That has to change," McDonough persisted. "Consistent excellence is what we're going to strive for. That's the idea. I can tell you, the message we're trying to send internally to our organization and to our fan base and everything is: we're going to be in the winning business, without a timetable. I think that would be a little bit disingenuous to slap a label on it and say, 'Right now.' We hired a manager [Lou Piniella] who was the perfect fit for this franchise today. The more time I get to spend with him and the more we speak, the more positive I feel—if that's possible—that we made a great decision on the next manager of the Cubs."

If McDonough is truly a people person, then he privately has to realize the Cubs were short in the manpower department. Even before that organization became flush with cash by winning the World Series, the White Sox had more front-office employees than the far more affluent Cubs. The lack of an assistant general manager and possibly another senior advisor for GM Hendry—along with farm director Oneri Fleita stating he was the only such executive in baseball doubling as Latin American director—could have a negative effect on player acquisition and development. And McDonough himself, in his introductory press conference on October 1, 2006, said the Cubs may have not been as "judicious" as possible in spending on some players.

As a slew of American industries are in a panic, then, slashing employment to keep profits at stockholder-mandated ridiculous levels, will McDonough go against the trend and boost the Cubs front-office staff? Will he move baseball operations staffing to the levels of other big-market teams?

"Some of those issues are in the process of being addressed—putting additional people in the right spots," McDonough said. "If you were to poll any professional organization in sports or if you were going to corporate America, everyone would say they're understaffed, regardless of the size of their staff. We're going to try to give Jim [Hendry] and the baseball people all the resources they need. We're reviewing staffing, among other things. If you were to talk to any other franchise, go in there and even if they were double the size of the Chicago Cubs, they'd say, 'We could use three more people in player development. We could use three more people in scouting. We don't have enough people covering the Pacific Rim. We don't have enough people covering Latin America.' That's also true on the business side. That's a different perspective to me. I can assure you, Jim's going to have the people and resources that he needs."

Parallel to the staffing-level issue is the cramped space for players. Wrigley Field is a great place to watch a game, but a lousy facility in which to work for baseball people, front-office types, and media. Complicating matters in the search for more breathing room has been the postponement of construction of a multipurpose building on the west side of Wrigley Field.

"I think you have to do everything you can to maximize space you have," McDonough said. "This was our 93rd year at Wrigley Field. Since 1984 [when the present Cubs clubhouse was built], well into double-figures new stadiums have been built in the majors. The clubhouse size is what it is.

"Can we transform certain areas? Can we provide more space for lockers? Can we provide more space for fitness? Conditioning and trainers' rooms are very, very important to me, and it's something we're going to take a look at—maximizing that finite space you're talking about. Not knowing what the future of that triangle building is or when it might be erected, we need to look at that space we have. How can we best utilize every inch of the square footage we have?"

That space may be the only thing limiting John McDonough if he uses his executive power to the fullest. Even back to the first day that William Wrigley, Jr. assumed ownership—around World War I—the Cubs potentially have had more financial resources available to them than any other team in baseball. Due to built-in conservatism and a lack of baseball savvy and vision, though, that money spigot has never been fully tapped.

While keeping his own counsel for all those years as marketing and broadcasting chief under MacPhail and cold-blooded Tribune suits John Madigan, Don Grenesko, and Stanton Cook, McDonough no doubt had his own wish list and fantasy modus operandi of how he'd run the Cubs. Now he's liberated.

By how much will be determined by his ability to transform electric words into powered action.

seventeen

SUMMING UP WHAT SHOULD BE A DYNASTY

DO THOSE POWERS IN CHARGE of the Cubs really want to win rather than just fill Wrigley Field?

Of course. Always. Even the befuddled Phil Wrigley wanted to win. He just did not know how through classic baseball methodology. Ol' PK's many successors were of a like mind-set, yet practiced self-restraint due to a variety of reasons, namely philosophy, vision, passion, and a sense of absolute urgency.

A score of Cubs players and opponents, particularly in the 1950s and 1970s, got the feeling team honchos did not know how to win. Much more recently, the attitude has changed.

Former team president Andy MacPhail thought the Cubs had finally turned a corner permanently after an 88-victory 2001 season in which the team held first place for three months through mid-August. The following spring training, ace Kerry Wood concurred, backing MacPhail's leadership when he also doubled as general manager.

"I think it [team attitude] is changing," Wood said at the time. "They had a losing tradition, the worst streak in any sport. It's known. For a long time, people knew if you came to the Cubs, there's a pretty good chance you're not going to win. You saw some of the players the Cubs brought in. They did not go after the best available. Today, the front office has changed people's opinion on the will to win. That was the big question mark for a long time. I even had that, to be honest with you; but now there are no question marks. Without a doubt, there's a statement we are turning things around and are serious about winning.

"One year of winning is not going to change everything. In order to change a losing tradition into a winning tradition, you can't just win one year. You have to be the Yankees, Atlanta, the Mets. You have to prove you can make it there and deserve it every year."

Well, after a succession of injuries to himself and fellow fireballer Mark Prior, an aborted World Series berth in 2003, a fractious season that fell short of the wild card in 2004, and a startling decline in 2005-06, are the Cubs similarly committed to winning with MacPhail and Dusty Baker both departed?

"Absolutely," Wood said after the 2006 season. "I think they wanted to win the last few years. I look at '04 as we didn't get it done as players; '05 and '06, the team was there. We didn't have starting pitching."

Wood said point-blank that if "two of the three top starting pitchers are out, yes, we'll have problems. Two years running, say Boston loses David Ortiz. Then they lose [Curt] Schilling and [Josh] Beckett, it makes it tough. That's no excuse, but it's killed us. It's been extremely difficult. In '03 we do well; next year they invested in us. [But after the Wood-Prior injuries] we haven't been right since. I don't think we've been in rotation for three, four starts together since '04. And Mark doesn't break camp three years in a row."

Wood and Prior were caught up in a palpable curse within a media-created overall curse—the curse of injuries to key pitchers. The third time this has bedeviled the Cubs has definitely not been the charm.

In 1957-59, the Cubs thought they had a quartet of hard-throwing young pitchers—Dick Drott, Moe Drabowsky, Glen Hobbie, and Bob Anderson—who would form the nucleus of a contender. Drott set the franchise's single-game strikeout record of 15 in 1957, which was tied by Burt Hooton and Rick Sutcliffe, but not bested until Wood broke it in 1998 with his legendary 20-whiff outing. Hall of Famer Frank Robinson, who batted against the young Cubs quartet, believed they were good enough to propel the team to a World Series if they had stayed healthy. But Drott, Drabowsky, Hobbie, and Anderson all got hurt. Their injuries were compounded by the combination of near-witch-doctor-level sports medicine of the era and the prevailing macho credo of pitching until your arm fell off, to keep your turn in the rotation.

Summing Up What Should Be a Dynasty

In 1984, Dallas Green spent millions to keep a young rotation that had propelled the Cubs to a post-war high of 96 victories that season. But Sutcliffe, Dennis Eckersley, Steve Trout, and Scott Sanderson all were injured in 1985, the malady so bad that all four—plus fifth starter Dick Ruthven—were on the disabled list together in August that season. Their injuries and slow recovery doomed Green's regime and furthered a domino effect on Cubs history that is still felt today.

Still, in spite of the injury bug, Wood believed there's no turning back for the franchise after the near miss of 2003 and subsequent pratfalls.

"They don't have a choice anymore in Chicago after 2003," he said. "We all got a taste of it. They want to go further and win the World Series. Everybody wants to be a part of it. But if players don't play, they get good managers fired. Dusty [Baker] got more shit than he should have. Dusty never ripped on guys in the paper. I wish him luck. When players go out there and play like shit, this is what happens. Managers get fired and club presidents resign."

The best-laid plans can be sabotaged by injuries and poor on-field performance. Yet, the talent base has to be deep enough and the organization smart enough to overcome the inevitable roadblocks of the long season.

As committed as management appeared to be, the Cubs had shortfalls on the field in both 2003 and 2004. In '03, the lineup started out short several bats while the bullpen successively worsened, and no moves were made to rectify its decline. Even after general manager Jim Hendry had added bats like Kenny Lofton, Aramis Ramirez, and Randall Simon by mid-August, the Cubs, who had been under .500 at 51-52 a month earlier, still were just 69-66 at the end of that month. Only the second-hottest September in modern team annals propelled them to their date with destiny in the Bartman Game. In 2004, the lineup and rotation appeared loaded, and Hendry made the mashers even stronger when he deftly pulled off a three-way deal to land Nomar Garciaparra at the trade deadline. Problem was, Hendry had left the team without a legitimate leadoff man; and, when Joe Borowski was injured, no good alternative existed at closer other than the uptight LaTroy Hawkins.

The MacPhail style of player acquisition was to add on at midseason when the team contended, but divest of talent when the Cubs were out of it July 31. Hendry, groomed by MacPhail in his job, became a disciple.

Entangled In Ivy

A sub-angle was signing injury-rehabbing pitchers like Ryan Dempster and Wade Miller with the hope they might be able to recover by the end of the following season. Again, the philosophy is fraught with problems. Loading up at midseason supposes the Cubs play well, even overachieve, in the first four months. It's pennywise and pound-foolish. If the Cubs don't go into the season believing they have a full roster on hand, they're asking for trouble if they intend to play with several holes in the lineup and a pitching staff that can be patched later. The franchise can certainly afford to pay full price for players to have them available on Opening Day instead of shopping for discounts from non-contenders dumping salaries or pitchers on the comeback trail.

MacPhail failed to perform a dual task in the mid-1990s: spending at the big-league level to get the Cubs out of the doldrums in the short-term while fulfilling his goal of becoming a player-development-oriented organization. It's the walk-and-chew-gum-at-the-same-time syndrome. A team can do both at once. In addition to free agents, the Cubs at some point need several everyday-player prospects rising through the farm system to stake a claim to a big-league regular's job. Perhaps there might be an Albert Pujols or Ryan Howard in the group at some point. While MacPhail succeeded in his goal of producing a pipeline of homegrown pitching, the lack of everyday players has crimped the franchise.

Never having believed in a farm system in the first place, Phil Wrigley fell 20 years behind Branch Rickey's deft work in building up the chains of the St. Louis Cardinals and Brooklyn-Los Angeles Dodgers. The Cubs never truly caught up. Wrigley's only successful period of producing position players came in 1959-61, when Billy Williams, Ron Santo, Lou Brock, George Altman, Kenny Hubbs, and Lou Johnson made their big-league debuts. The only sustained success came between 1982 and 1986, when the sainted Gordon Goldsberry, Dallas Green's right-hand man, brought Mark Grace, Rafael Palmeiro, Shawon Dunston, Jerome Walton, Dwight Smith, Davey Martinez, Joe Girardi, and others into the system.

Hendry believes he's fixed the program by hiring old chum Tim Wilken, who ran a successful scouting operation with the Toronto Blue Jays in the 1990s, as scouting director. "You will see Tim Wilken be the best we've had since Gordy [Goldsberry]," Hendry said.

Better than Hendry's own days as scouting chief from 1996-2000?

Summing Up What Should Be a Dynasty

"Absolutely," he said. "Tim Wilken's been a proven scouting director above [the level of] Jim Hendry. Tim Wilken grew up and helped Pat Gillick. He helped run 10 drafts. Everyone he ever took in the first round is a big leaguer. I'd put Tim Wilken in the same breath as Mike Radcliffe of the Twins. After Paul [Snyder, all-time Atlanta Braves talent maven] and [scout] Gary [Hughes], you go to Mike and Tim. No doubt, Tim Wilken is a better scouting director than Jim Hendry."

Hendry said scouting the right kind of position-player prospects was more difficult due to the transition from the aluminum bats they use in high school and college. Even in an era of a supposed pitching shortage, Wilken said good hitters have been harder to find than moundsmen over the last 15 to 20 years of the amateur draft.

"Pitchers come from all walks of life," Wilken explained. "They can come from the lower rounds. Chuck Wasserstrom [the top Cubs stats analyzer] did a survey of the draft rounds below No. 30 and found how many [position players] went to the big leagues. There have been a few. Orlando Hudson was in the 43rd round. One common thing is, they were good baseball players who did not have the strength, and added to their body later. The conclusion is, you'll get a lot more pitchers in those [lower] rounds."

Even after Wilken concentrates his position-player selections up top in the draft, he and his scouts have the challenge of better identifying position players who are able to climb the ladder in the farm system. Hitters who rack up good numbers at Class A often fizzle out as they try to advance to the competitive Double-A level, from which some players make a direct jump to the majors. Pitchers can make it to Triple-A or even the majors on pure stuff, but if hitters end up with a "slider-speed" swing, they'll never cut it in The Show. Wilken said some talented prospects, like Ryan Howard, freeze up when they realize scouts are monitoring them.

"[Howard] was like the perennial bad-test person," he said. "Scouts went to see him [as a high school senior], and he was horrible. He had eight at-bats in a doubleheader and struck out seven times. After the draft, he went to play for the USA Juniors, and played well. Johnny Damon hit .285 in high school, but .300 in the Gulf Coast League. When Derek Bell hit three homers in one [high school] game, there was not one scout at the game. He was relaxed, so he hit three homers."

Entangled In Ivy

Under new president John McDonough, the Cubs must not fall even further behind in scouting new areas of talent. Derrek Lee's father, Leon Lee, was the Cubs' Pacific Rim coordinator, drawing upon his longtime relationships in the Far East, in the late 1990s. At one point, Lee wanted to scout Mainland China for raw talent, but MacPhail rejected the notion, taking the orthodox approach that Lee should stick to Japan and South Korea. Lee left the organization and was not replaced. Immediately afterward, Japanese, Korean and even Taiwanese players began showing up in large numbers on big-league rosters, but not the Cubs.' Just recently, after former Cubs manager Jim Lefebvre held baseball clinics in China, Major League Baseball announced plans to open an office in the world's most populous country.

The Cubs must be in the forefront of a changing baseball talent procurement landscape, not sitting in the background as they did for decades, allowing teams like the Pirates, Dodgers, Blue Jays, and Astros to establish firm beachheads to acquire Latin American players.

So the challenge will be for Wilken's scouts to project better while ranging much farther geographically for new signees; then for farm director Oneri Fleita to develop them better as young hitters. That will depend on the concurrent development of an abiding philosophy, a "Cubs Way," that the most successful franchises possess. No smart minds in the game could figure what the Cubs stood for other than fun in the sun at Wrigley Field and the "lovable losers" media stereotype.

Overall, the Cubs have to toss away the franchise's self-imposed shackles of conservatism that have stuck with them from Wrigley to MacPhail. Anything short of such a move condemns them to more of the same tiresome also-ran finishes and solidifies the negative image.

Then there's another barrier.

Even if management updates its practices and upgrades to a fully staffed baseball operation—and it's the most painful cut of all in their attempt to win—the Cubs need to explore a successor ballpark to Wrigley Field.

Heading toward its 100th birthday in 2014, the Friendly Confines are a living, breathing time machine to a more bucolic baseball era. For the occasional fan, the inconveniences of traversing the old girl are dismissed for all that history and the close-up view of the action. But Wrigley Field is a pit by the standards of the 21st Century version of the game. The clubhouses and training area are too small; the batting-

Summing Up What Should Be a Dynasty

practice facilities are inadequate; and, worst of all, the Cubs are locked into a maximum of only 30 night games. No Friday night games can be scheduled, either—an appeasement to Wrigleyville club owners, who don't want 40,000 baseball fans flooding the streets when they do their best band-and-dance business. That means the Cubs might as well go directly to Wrigley Field after playing a Thursday night game on the road, then flying in after midnight for a 1:20 p.m. Friday game.

Although the heavy day baseball schedule has had its supporters, the most recent being new manager Lou Piniella, the overall trend is that major leaguers do not like it. And the constant switching back and forth, with the majority of day games at home and night games on the road, over the six-month season plays havoc with the body clock, which includes sleeping patterns and meal schedules. Fatigue late in the season is a common factor.

Taking extra batting practice before day games is almost impossible, unless players desire to form the Dawn Patrol. The additional workout is a common sight at 2:30 p.m. for the night games beginning four and a half hours later at U.S. Cellular Field and all other big-league ballparks. Cubs players in 2006 reported they rarely took extra batting practice, even on the road. For a team notoriously impatient at the plate, the lack of extra work had a negative effect.

In the end, baseball at night is on an entertainment schedule. As much as those in the game desire a 9-to-5 life, the money trail demands night work. That's the standard, and any deviation from the norm invites trouble. Cincinnati strongman Adam Dunn spoke for a slew of big leaguers when he stated the Cubs will have trouble winning consistently with the present complement of day games at home.

"Spreading them out would make more sense to me," Dunn said of spacing night games more efficiently, "as long as they don't have six straight day games. ... It's still baseball, but day games are the big issue for me."

Former Cub reliever Mike Remlinger has strong feelings on day games.

"It's good, to be able to come off the road and play at night," he said. "For me, coming off the road and playing three day games, I'm tired. For a team to come here and play three day games, you get through it. It's a little bit better than the 18 they had before. There's definitely a factor in recovery time. If you're an early riser, you get up at 7:30 and play a one o'clock game, you've got five to six hours to wake your body up. If you're a late riser, you get up at noon for a seven o'clock game, you're still awake for seven hours. If you sleep till 10 a.m., you get up, have a nice lunch, go in and do early work, then go back to cool off; but overall you have a lot more time to work on your game, and that's part of it."

The common trends thus all add up to a winning deficit—conservative management, inconsistent player development, and a creaky old ballpark in an era of spanking-new, spacious facilities. They are tangible causes that often take a back seat to the strangely romantic concepts of curses and lovable losers. However, all that ails the Cubs can be cured, and there's more than enough money to do it.

All that's needed is willpower, passion, and vision—the human factor, as it's always been.

Index

Index

Index

Index

Index

Celebrate the Heroes of Chicago Sports
in These Other Releases from Sports Publishing!

Game of My Life: Chicago Cubs

In *Game of My Life: Chicago Cubs*, Cubs legends like Ernie Banks, Billy Williams, Ferguson Jenkins, Don Kessinger, Ron Santo, Ryne Sandberg, Mark Grace, and Ken Holtzman reflect on many special plays and special games. Available Spring 2007.

2007 Release • ISBN-10: 1-59670-173-0
ISBN-13: 978-1-59670-173-1
$24.95 hardcover

Ruling Over Monarchs, Giants & Stars: Umpiring in the Negro Leagues & Beyond

Former Negro League umpire Bob Motley talks about working with such baseball legends as Satchel Paige, Hank Aaron, Ernie Banks, and Willie Mays is his revealing, humorous, and one-of-a-kind memoir.

2007 release! • ISBN-10: 1-59670-236-2
ISBN-13: 978-1-59670-236-3$16.95 softcover

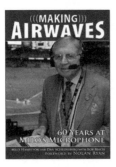

Making Airwaves: 60 Years at Milo's Microphone

Baseball Hall of Fame broadcaster Milo Hamilton takes fans through his lengthy career, pointing out highlights ranging from calling Hank Aaron's record-breaking 715th home run and partnering with the legendary Harry Caray.

2007 release • ISBN-10: 1-59670-218-4
ISBN-13: 978-1-59670-218-9
$16.95 softcover (first time in softcover)

Glory Days: Legends of Illinois High School Basketball

Among the many high school basketball legends covered in *Glory Days: Legends of Illinois High School Basketball* are Mannie Jackson, now the owner of the Harlem Globetrotters, and Quinn Buckner, now an executive with the Indiana Pacers.

ISBN-10: 1-58261-945-X
ISBN-13: 978-1-58261-945-3
$14.95 softcover

Dennis Rodman: I Should Be Dead by Now

Controversial and flamboyant former basketball star Dennis Rodman details his struggles since leaving the NBA, the breakup of his marriage to actress Carmen Electra, his problems with alcohol, and his life today.

ISBN-10: 1-59670-152-8
ISBN-13: 978-1-59670-152-6
$16.95 softcover

More Tales from the Cubs Dugout

This humorous and revealing title offers a huge chunk of tasty Cubs' fun, fantasy, heartbreak, and happiness during unforgettable afternoons in the Wrigley Field sun, rain, wind, and fog. *More Tales from the Cubs Dugout* is a must-have for any Cubs fan.

ISBN-10: 1-59670-033-5
ISBN-13: 978-1-59670-033-8
$14.95 softcover

All books are available in bookstores everywhere!
Order 24-hours-a-day by calling toll-free **1-877-424-BOOK (2665).**
Also order online at **www.SportsPublishingLLC.com.**